PERICLES

The RSC Shakespeare

Edited by Jonathan Bate and Eric Rasmussen

Chief Associate Editors: Jan Sewell and Will Sharpe

Associate Editors: Trey Jansen, Eleanor Lowe, Lucy Munro,
Dee Anna Phares, Héloïse Sénéchal

Pericles

Textual editing: Eric Rasmussen and Lucy Munro

Introduction and Shakespeare's Career in the Theater:
Jonathan Bate and Lucy Munro

Commentary: Lucy Munro and Héloïse Sénéchal

Scene-by-Scene Analysis: Will Sharpe

In Performance: Penelope Freedman (RSC stagings) and
Peter Kirwan (overview)

The Director's Cut (interviews by Will Sharpe and Kevin Wright):
Adrian Noble, Adrian Jackson, and Dominic Cooke

Playing Marina: Laura Rees

Editorial Advisory Board

The RSC Shakespeare

William Shakespeare

PERICLES

Edited by Jonathan Bate and Eric Rasmussen

Introduction by Jonathan Bate

The Modern Library
New York

2012 Modern Library Paperback Edition

Copyright © 2007, 2012 by The Royal Shakespeare Company

Published in the United States by Modern Library, an imprint of
The Random House Publishing Group, a division of
Random House, Inc., New York.

The version of *Pericles* and the corresponding footnotes that appear
in this volume were originally published in *William Shakespeare:
Complete Works*, edited by Jonathan Bate and Eric Rasmussen,
published in 2007 by Modern Library, an imprint of The Random
House Publishing Group, a division of Random House, Inc.

ISBN 978-0-8129-6943-6
eBook ISBN 978-1-58836-890-4

Printed in the United States of America

www.modernlibrary.com

2 4 6 8 9 7 5 3

CONTENTS

CONTENTS

INTRODUCTION

A lone figure, venerable and archaically dressed, steps onto the bare stage: "To sing a song that old was sung / From ashes ancient Gower is come." Probably begun by a hack dramatist in 1607 and completed by Shakespeare in 1608, *Pericles* marks a fresh departure for the master after his exclusive focus on tragedy in the previous few years (*Macbeth*, *King Lear*, *Timon of Athens*, *Antony and Cleopatra*, and the contemporaneous *Coriolanus*). In his next group of plays, Shakespeare worked in a much more mellow form. The sea, the voyage, the storm, the unlucky and lucky chances, the years of quest and grief, the child lost and found, the resurrection of the apparently dead: this is the matter of the enduring literary form of romance.

One of the most widely circulated and oft-repeated tales from ancient Greece was that of Apollonius of Tyre, who wandered around virtually the whole of the Mediterranean world before what he had lost was restored to him. Chaucer's friend John Gower included a version of it in his rambling poetic repository of old stories, *Confessio Amantis*. Just over two hundred years later, Gower was brought back to life on the boards of the Globe Theatre, with Apollonius renamed Pericles. The poet serves as chorus, guiding the audience through the story, asking us to hold in imagination the wanderer's ship, two great storms, and a series of landfalls at Antioch and Tarsus in the northeastern corner of the Mediterranean, way over at Pentapolis in North Africa, back at Tarsus and Tyre, and eventually at Ephesus and Mytilene on the Aegean.

Old songs are true in deep but simple ways. If we come to *Pericles* looking for the psychological complexities of Shakespearean tragedy, we will be disappointed. There are none of the subtle shades of moral gray which endlessly fascinate us in *Antony and Cleopatra*, another play which circles around the ancient Mediterranean world and which may have been written immediately before *Pericles*. Instead, we have to accept black and white, and, most disconcertingly, white becoming black (Dionyza is protectress one moment, murderess the next), then black becoming white (Lysimachus sets out to deflower Marina in a brothel, but ends up being deemed a fit husband for her).

The play proceeds by a series of tableaux and formal dumb shows, which offer stark contrasts: first Pericles woos a daughter whose relationship with her father is turned inward in incest, then he woos a daughter whose father banteringly pretends to play the oppressive patriarch when really he is delighted that she has fallen in love with the knight in rusty armor. The narrative begins with a daughter who is "an eater of her mother's flesh / By the defiling of her parents' bed." It ends with a daughter who regenerates her father. In Pericles' extraordinary line, "Thou that beget'st him that did thee beget," the daughter seems to father her father without any trace of illicit desire. Having converted the clientele of the brothel, and even the randy old Bolt, from lust to honesty, now Marina brings her father from unshaven sackclothed wandering to a new life. The fifth act's inversion of the first act's perversion suggests that, episodic though it may be, the play has its own unity. Though the first two acts were written by another dramatist, George Wilkins, and the last three by Shakespeare, the stitching together of the plot was effectively done.

The language is more variable. It begins to thrill with the hum of late Shakespearean verse only from the great storm speech onward: "O, still / Thy deaf'ning dreadful thunders, gently quench / Thy nimble sulphurous flashes!" From here to the end of the play, there are certain speeches of quite extraordinary beauty and power. Most revelatory of all is the reunion of father and daughter, which recapitulates yet somehow goes beyond the reunion of Lear and Cordelia. Shakespeare never wrote a more moving scene.

THE CRITICS DEBATE

Pericles' early reputation was as the epitome of theatrical success. The narrator of Pimlico or Run Red-Cap (1609) compares a crowd that he encounters to the hubbub at a theater presenting a successful new play such as Jane Shore (now lost) or Pericles:

> all the room
> Did swarm with gentles mixed with grooms,

So that I truly thought all these
Came to see *Shore* or *Pericles*.[1]

Similarly, the prologue of Robert Tailor's 1614 play *The Hog Hath Lost His Pearl* concludes by saying, "if it prove so happy as to please, / We'll say 'tis fortunate like *Pericles*."[2] Shakespeare's friend and rival Ben Jonson was forced to acknowledge that *Pericles* was successful, but he had serious reservations about its popular appeal:

No doubt some mouldy tale,
Like *Pericles*, and stale
As the shrieve's crusts, and nasty as his fish-
Scraps, out [of] every dish
Thrown forth and raked into the common tub,
May keep up the play-club.[3]

Jonson criticizes the romance mode in which *Pericles* is written, and—in contrast with *Pimlico*'s vision of happy upper- and lower-class spectators—he implies that it appeals only to the more menial and (he suggests) less discriminating part of the theater audience.

By the late seventeenth century, *Pericles* was falling into neglect both on the stage and in the study. John Dryden was typical of his age in criticizing Shakespeare's plays for not conforming to neoclassical requirements of unity and decorum in both plot and character:

Poetry was then, if not in its infancy among us, at least not arriv'd to its vigor and maturity: witness the lameness of their plots: many of which, especially those which they writ first, (for even that age refin'd itself in some measure,) were made up of some ridiculous, incoherent story, which, in one play many times took up the business of an age. I suppose I need not name *Pericles, Prince of Tyre*, nor the Historical Plays of *Shakespear*.[4]

Similarly, he argued that characters in a play "must be consistent with the manners which the *Poet* has given them distinctly" and that "He who enter'd in the first Act, a Young man like *Pericles, Prince of*

Tyre, must not be in danger in the fifth Act, of committing Incest with his Daughter."[5]

TEXT AND AUTHOR(S)

For Dryden, *Pericles'* failings suggested that it was an early work; comparing it with *Othello*, he writes that "*Shakespear's* own Muse her *Pericles* first bore, / The Prince of *Tyre* was elder than the *Moore*."[6] Others have sought different explanations. As one recent scholar summarizes:

> Theories put forward to account for the oddity of the first two acts are (a) that they are remnants of a very early Shakespeare script; (b) that Shakespeare deliberately wrote them, at the same time as Acts 3–5, in a style consonant with the medieval mode of his choric narrator, Gower; (c) that, as the 1609 quarto presents them, they are a reporter's fumbling paraphrase of a greatly superior original, which may have been wholly Shakespeare's; and (d) that they are the work of another dramatist.[7]

One of the earliest arguments for collaboration was put forward by Shakespeare editor Nicholas Rowe in 1709:

> Mr *Dryden* seems to think that *Pericles* is one of his first Plays; but there is no judgment to be form'd on that, since there is good Reason to believe that the greatest part of the Play was not written by him; tho' it is own'd some part of it certainly was, particularly the last Act.[8]

Rowe's eighteenth-century successors either omitted *Pericles* altogether, or treated it with condescension:

> This absurd Old Play ... was not entirely of our Author's penning; but he has honour'd it with a Number of Master-Touches so peculiar to himself that a knowing Reader may with Ease and Certainty distinguish the Traces of his Pencil.[9]

For many nineteenth-century critics, the textually and morally suspect went hand in hand. Much disapproval was focused on the opening scenes. Henry Tyrell wrote, sniffily, in 1860,

> The opening incident respecting the criminal association of King Antiochus and his daughter is not calculated to please the taste of a modern audience. Incest is a crime not to be recorded by the poet; it is, as it were, an unhallowed and unlawful subject: our literature should not be associated with an offence so repugnant to humanity.[10]

Such unease led to a desire to dissociate Shakespeare not only from the opening scenes but also from those set in the brothel; the textual scholar F. G. Fleay offered a radical solution:

> Shakespeare wrote the story of Marina, in the last three acts, minus the prose scenes and the Gower. This gives a perfect artistic and organic whole: and, in my opinion, ought to be printed as such in every edition of Shakespeare: the whole play, as it stands, might be printed in collections for the curious, and there only.[11]

Eighteenth- and nineteenth-century scholars put forward a number of candidates for co-authorship in *Pericles*, of which the more credible were William Rowley, Thomas Heywood, John Day, and George Wilkins. Modern scholarship has demonstrated that by far the most likely collaborator is Wilkins, although some critics continue to argue for Shakespeare's solo authorship.[12]

ROMANCE? LATE PLAY?

Despite Fleay's distaste for *Pericles*, the 1870s also saw the first hints of its critical rehabilitation. Although he agreed with Fleay about the play's authorship, in his influential account of Shakespeare's writing career Dowden grouped *Pericles* with *Cymbeline*, *The Tempest*, and *The Winter's Tale* in a final phase that he called "On the Heights." At this time Shakespeare "ascended out of the turmoil and trouble of action, out of the darkness and tragic mystery, the places haunted by terror and crime, and by love contending with these, to a pure and serene elevation." Dowden describes the plays of this period as having a particular set of characteristics:

> In all there is the same romantic incident of lost children recovered by those to whom they are dear—the daughters of Pericles and Leontes, the sons of Cymbeline and Alonso. In all there is a beautiful romantic background of sea or mountain. The dramas have a grave beauty, a sweet serenity, which seem to render the name "comedies" inappropriate; we may smile tenderly, but we never laugh loudly, as we read them. Let us, then, name this group consisting of four plays, Romances.[13]

Although he devotes little space to it, Dowden gives *Pericles* a special position and value as the first of the romances:

> Taken in this context, almost any critic who enjoyed the last three would have to at least appreciate the first one—the worst he might say of it was that it was a "study" for themes that would soon come to fruition . . . Under the heading of "romance," *Pericles* now had a new paradigm, one far more accommodating than neoclassicism or realism had ever been . . . In this genre, it was understood that such conventions as vast expanse of time and space, fairy-tale improbabilities and sketchy characterization were not necessarily signs of an inferior talent but were simply part of the generic terrain.[14]

The idea of the "late play"—a special phase at the end of a great artist's career, featuring works characterized by a newfound serenity and wonder—took forceful hold on mid-twentieth-century criticism of *Pericles*. G. Wilson Knight's account of the play is idiosyncratic yet in many respects typical:

> The depth and realism of tragedy are present within the structure of romance. The two extremes, happy and sad, of Shakespearian art coalesce to house a new, and seemingly impossible,

truth; as though the experiences behind or within the composition of *King Lear* and *Timon of Athens* were found not necessarily antithetical to the happy ending but rather reached therein their perfect fulfilment. Hence the sense of breathtaking surprise, of wonder and reverence, in the reunions, and the cogent presence of the miracle-worker, Cerimon . . . Shakespeare's drama is aspiring towards the eternal harmony and the eternal pattern.[15]

There have, however, been dissident voices. Lytton Strachey mischievously argued as early as 1904 that the "late plays," including "the miserable archaic fragment of *Pericles*," were the product not of benign serenity but boredom.[16] Moreover, Suzanne Gossett points out, to describe *Pericles* as a late play at all is to overlook some important facts:

the lateness paradigm is inadequate to describe a play which is not entirely by Shakespeare; on which Shakespeare worked when he was not yet forty-four years old; which reworks a plot that had already served as a frame for one of his earliest comedies; and which he may have been writing simultaneously with or shortly before *Coriolanus*, a play with ties to an entirely different section of Shakespeare's *oeuvre*.[17]

SEXUALITY AND GENDER

The attempts of Victorian critics to come to terms with the sexual material in *Pericles* foreshadow the trajectory taken in the twentieth and twenty-first centuries. For William Watkiss Lloyd,

[Pericles'] original difficulties spring from his suit to the daughter of Antiochus, a suit unblessed by any better passion than deceptive beauty stimulates, and the politic desire to furnish his realm with an heir. His error, for by the standards of Shakespeare's moral feeling so it must stand, is recognized soon, but not so soon as to evade all its consequences; hence his exile and wanderings and vicissitudes; prudence and noble sensibility, and patience when fortune admits no better, help and preserve him, and weariness and melancholy are roused at least to renewed enjoyment of affection and prosperity.[18]

In an important essay of 1969, C. L. Barber argues that "where regular comedy deals with freeing sexuality from the ties of family, these late romances deal with freeing family ties from the threat of sexual degradation."[19] This line of argument has been developed by feminist and psychoanalytic critics. For Coppélia Kahn, *Pericles* is one of a group of plays focusing on "the male passage from being a son to being a father," in which the hero

> struggle[s] to accept their difference from and dependence on women, and to take parenthood as the measure of their mortality. Shakespeare resolves this crisis through the father-daughter relationship, using the daughter's chaste sexuality and capacity to produce heirs as a bridge to the hero's new identity as father . . . [Marina's] purity banishes the shadow of oedipal sexuality, and brings the hero back to his wife and to the world.[20]

For Janet Adelman, the later acts of the play engage in "working and reworking" the threat posed in the first act:

> acts 3 through 5 are structured counter-phobically, as though all sexuality were tantamount to that initial act of incest and all families based in the sexual body were similarly contaminated . . . In the end Shakespeare will reestablish Pericles's masculine identity only by first detoxifying the contaminating female body and the family relations based on it, in effect undoing the initial trauma of the play and freeing the family from its sexual origin.[21]

Kahn and Adelman see the events of Act 5 as both resolution and containment of the threat posed in Act 1; others have been less certain:

Pericles and Marina are safe and the way is clear for rebirth and restoration . . . And yet there is an unresolved indeterminacy in the text which makes it possible to read the ending of *Pericles* not as a mandala closure but as a dizzying return to square one.[22]

In a striking recent reading, Margaret Healy views skeptically Pericles' decision to marry Marina to the apparently reformed brothelgoer Lysimachus. Describing *Pericles* as "a satirical play," she writes,

Through marriage, an innocent young woman will be placed at his disposal by the very person who should most seek to protect her—her father. Marina's response to the intended match is articulate silence . . . Pericles is a prince who is seldom in his own state . . . who flees from danger rather than confronting it; who readily commits his young daughter to the care of rather dubious others; whose wallowing in self-pity comes dangerously close to incurring a charge of effeminacy . . . and who, through betrothing Marina to a potentially diseased son-in-law, is putting both her health and his future princely heirs' at stake.[23]

TIME AND SPACE

Healy's interest in the specific social, medical, and educational contexts of *Pericles* is part of a wider challenge to older views of the play as primarily aesthetic or ahistorical. For some critics, the play represents a rejection of topicality which is in itself political. Steven Mullaney argues that *Pericles* is political in spite of itself, a "radical effort to dissociate the popular stage from its cultural contexts and theatrical grounds of possibility—an effort to imagine, in fact, that popular drama could be a purely aesthetic phenomenon, free from history and from historical determination."[24] For Amelia Zurcher, the play

rejects entirely the humanist notion of history's utility for the present, and with it any possibility for a dynamic relation between present and past . . . History is valuable in *Pericles* because it offers a vision of time when we too will be past interest, past all temptation to betray our integrity by extending and propagating ourselves through time, and instead fixed and hypostatized in a state in which time and integrity no longer need be at odds.[25]

Other scholars have instead argued, like Healy, that Shakespeare and Wilkins' play does engage with contemporary debates. Constance C. Relihan suggests that *Pericles'* eastern Mediterranean locations

amplif[y] the political implications of his text . . . Instead of sensing a merciful conclusion that unites the action of the play, the political ambiguities with which the play ends confound such a perception: the rulers who have been least willing to govern, Pericles and Thaisa, will control the best of the play's societies; Marina, an inexperienced ruler, and Lysimachus, a reformed "john" who encouraged moral profligacy in Mytilene, will rule Tyre, a country they have never seen; Tharsus and Antioch's governments are left undefined; Mytilene—the land of Pander, Boult, and Bawd—will be left without a ruler; and Ephesus will, apparently, continue to encourage the magic of Cerimon and the isolation possible within Diana's temple. That all of these locations are part of an ambiguously imagined Asia Minor which resonates with Turkish and "reprobate" cultures as well as with Christian and classical traditions makes the political resolution of *Pericles* less reassuring and idyllic than much criticism of the play suggests.[26]

Stuart M. Kurland looks closer to home. Pericles' "obliviousness" and "remoteness and general passivity" are contrasted with the "energetic conduct of the daughter who will inherit his authority," and he argues that

These political aspects of *Pericles* . . . are best appreciated in the context of early Jacobean politics, notably the problems associated with King James I's disinclination to stay in London to dispatch government business—that is, to govern and to be seen as governing.[27]

We must always be wary of attempts to map Shakespeare's life onto his work. He was the least autobiographical of great writers. But even he must sometimes have drawn upon his own experience. Consider his stage doctors. In his earlier works there are just two of them, both comical—Pinch in *The Comedy of Errors* and Caius in *The Merry Wives of Windsor*—whereas in the plays written after the arrival in Stratford-upon-Avon around the year 1600 of Dr. John Hall, Shakespeare's future son-in-law, there are several dignified and sympathetically portrayed medical men: the physician who has to deal with that difficult patient Lady Macbeth, the doctor who revives the exhausted King Lear in the Quarto version of that play, Dr. Cornelius in *Cymbeline* (who tricks the wicked stepmother, giving her a sleeping draught rather than the poison she desires). And, most suggestively, there is Cerimon in *Pericles*, a play about father and daughter, death and rebirth—a play written in the wake of the death of Shakespeare's brother Edmund and the marriage of his daughter Susanna to Dr. Hall.

Pericles was probably completed during the final months of Susanna's pregnancy or the early weeks of the life of Shakespeare's first grandchild, Elizabeth. At the point where Shakespeare took over the writing from George Wilkins, there is a dumb show in which Thaisa is shown pregnant. A baby girl is then born in a storm. The mother dies in childbirth, only to be revived in the following scene by the medical arts of the Lord Cerimon. He voices a doctor's credo:

> I hold it ever
> Virtue and cunning were endowments greater
> Than nobleness and riches. Careless heirs
> May the two latter darken and expend,
> But immortality attends the former,
> Making a man a god. 'Tis known, I ever
> Have studied physic, through which secret art,
> By turning o'er authorities, I have,
> Together with my practice, made familiar

To me and to my aid the blest infusions
That dwells in vegetives, in metals, stones,
And I can speak of the disturbances
That nature works and of her cures, which doth give me
A more content in course of true delight
Than to be thirsty after tottering honour,
Or tie my pleasure up in silken bags
To please the fool and death.

Given that John Hall had a formidable library of medical "authorities" as well as a thriving practice and an encyclopedic knowledge of herbal cures ("the blest infusions / That dwells in vegetives"), it seems at the very least felicitous that Shakespeare wrote these lines in this context at this time in his life.

This is not to say that Cerimon *is* Hall, that the pregnancy of Thaisa is that of Susanna, or that Marina is Elizabeth Shakespeare. But family circumstances, and in particular the stabilizing figure of Hall, could not have been far from Shakespeare's mind. At a deeper level, beyond the biographical, the speech establishes an opposition between the knowledge of nature on the one hand, and the pursuit of wealth and "tottering honour" on the other. For Shakespeare, London was the place associated with honor, status, wealth, and recognition at court. But it was also the place of plague and mass death. And of the commercialization of sex: the link between the theater industry and the sex trade was symbiotic. Not only did prostitutes work the playhouses for trade: George Wilkins, co-writer of *Pericles*, went on to a second career as proprietor of a string of brothels. Intriguingly, it was Shakespeare rather than Wilkins who wrote the play's brothel scene, which simultaneously offers a quasi-magical act of grace and a highly realistic glimpse into the language and attitudes of the early modern sex trade.

Stratford-upon-Avon, in contrast to London, was associated with stability, community, garden, field, and health. Whether or not Shakespeare ever did take the mercury-bath cure for syphilis, as his final two sonnets strongly imply, he regularly took the nature cure by returning to his hometown. Like the Lord Cerimon, Master Shakespeare speaks of the disturbances that nature works and of her cures.

ABOUT THE TEXT

Shakespeare endures through history. He illuminates later times as well as his own. He helps us to understand the human condition. But he cannot do this without a good text of the plays. Without editions there would be no Shakespeare. That is why every twenty years or so throughout the last three centuries there has been a major new edition of his complete works. One aspect of editing is the process of keeping the texts up to date—modernizing the spelling, punctuation, and typography (though not, of course, the actual words), providing explanatory notes in the light of changing educational practices (a generation ago, most of Shakespeare's classical and biblical allusions could be assumed to be generally understood, but now they can't).

Because Shakespeare did not personally oversee the publication of his plays, with some plays there are major editorial difficulties. Decisions have to be made as to the relative authority of the early printed editions, the pocket format "Quartos" published in Shakespeare's lifetime and the elaborately produced "First Folio" text of 1623, the original "Complete Works" prepared for the press after his death by Shakespeare's fellow actors, the people who knew the plays better than anyone else. *Pericles* was not included in the Folio but appeared in a poor Quarto text in 1609—reprinted again the same year and in 1611, 1619, 1630, and 1635—full of errors and incomprehensible passages, and far more badly printed than anything in the Folio. The fact, however, that the job of printing the First Quarto was divided between two printing shops seems strongly to suggest that the fault lay with the underlying manuscript rather than with the shoddiness of the printers' work. It is therefore largely assumed that the text of the First Quarto *Pericles* is a "memorial reconstruction": a pirated text put together from memory by actors or audience members or other nonauthorial agents. Shakespeare's collaborator on the play, George Wilkins, wrote a novella entitled *The Painful Adventures of Pericles*, which some editors have used to flesh out some of the

Quarto's more apparently incomplete passages, a practice not followed here due to the conjectural nature of the enterprise.

The following notes highlight various aspects of the editorial process and indicate conventions used in the text of this edition:

Lists of Parts is editorially supplied. Capitals indicate that part of the name used for speech headings in the script (thus "PERICLES, Prince of Tyre").

Locations Given that Shakespeare wrote for a bare stage and often an imprecise sense of place, we have relegated locations to the explanatory notes at the foot of the page, where they are given at the beginning of each scene where the imaginary location is different from the one before.

Act and Scene Divisions were provided in Folio in a much more thoroughgoing way than in the Quartos. Sometimes, however, they were erroneous or omitted; corrections and additions supplied by editorial tradition are indicated by square brackets. Five-act division is based on a classical model, and act breaks provided the opportunity to replace the candles in the indoor Blackfriars playhouse, which the King's Men used after 1608, but Shakespeare did not necessarily think in terms of a five-part structure of dramatic composition. The Folio convention is that a scene ends when the stage is empty. Nowadays, partly under the influence of film, we tend to consider a scene to be a dramatic unit that ends with either a change of imaginary location or a significant passage of time within the narrative. Shakespeare's fluidity of composition accords well with this convention, so in addition to act and scene numbers we provide a *running scene* count in the right margin at the beginning of each new scene, in the typeface used for editorial directions. Where there is a scene break caused by a momentary bare stage, but the location does not change and extra time does not pass, we use the convention *running scene continues*. There is inevitably a degree of editorial judgment in making such calls, but the system is very valuable in suggesting the pace of the plays.

Speakers' Names are often inconsistent in Folio, though are quite consistent in the Quarto text of *Pericles*. We have regularized speech headings but retained an element of deliberate inconsistency in entry directions, in order to give the flavor of Folio, and, in this case, the Quarto text. Thus SIMONIDES is always so-called in his speech headings but "the King" in his entry directions.

Verse is indicated by lines that do not run to the right margin and by capitalization of each line. The Folio printers sometimes set verse as prose, and vice versa (either out of misunderstanding or for reasons of space). We have silently corrected in such cases, although in some instances there is ambiguity, in which case we have leaned toward the preservation of Folio layout. Folio sometimes uses contraction ("turnd" rather than "turned") to indicate whether or not the final "-ed" of a past participle is sounded, an area where there is variation for the sake of the five-beat iambic pentameter rhythm. We use the convention of a grave accent to indicate sounding (thus "turnèd" would be two syllables) but would urge actors not to overstress. In cases where one speaker ends with a verse half line and the next begins with the other half of the pentameter, editors since the late eighteenth century have indented the second line. We have abandoned this convention, since Folio does not use it, and neither did actors' cues in the Shakespearean theater. An exception is made when the second speaker actively interrupts or completes the first speaker's sentence.

Spelling is modernized, but older forms are very occasionally maintained where necessary for rhythm or aural effect.

Punctuation in Shakespeare's time was as much rhetorical as grammatical. "Colon" was originally a term for a unit of thought in an argument. The semicolon was a new unit of punctuation (some of the Quartos lack them altogether). We have modernized punctuation throughout but have given more weight to Folio punctuation than many editors, since, though not Shakespearean, it reflects the usage of his period. In particular, we have used the colon far more than many editors: it is exceptionally useful as a way of indicating how many Shakespearean speeches unfold clause by clause in a developing argument that gives the illusion of enacting the process of thinking in the moment. We have also kept in mind the origin of punctuation in classical times as a way of assisting the actor and orator: the comma suggests the briefest of pauses for breath, the colon a middling one, and a full stop or period a longer pause. Semicolons, by contrast, belong to an era of punctuation that was only just coming in during Shakespeare's time and that is coming to an end now: we have accordingly used them only where they occur in our copy texts (and not always then). Dashes are sometimes used for parenthetical interjections where the Folio has brackets. They are also used for interruptions and changes in train of thought. Where a change of addressee occurs within a speech, we have used a dash preceded by a full stop (or occasionally another form of punctuation). Often the identity of the respective addressees is obvious from the context. When it is not, this has been indicated in a marginal stage direction.

Entrances and Exits are fairly thorough in Folio, which has accordingly been followed as faithfully as possible. Where characters are omitted or corrections are necessary, this is indicated by square brackets (e.g. "[*and Attendants*]"). *Exit* is sometimes silently normalized to *Exeunt* and *Manet* anglicized to "remains." We trust Folio positioning of entrances and exits to a greater degree than most editors.

Editorial Stage Directions such as stage business, asides, indications of addressee and of characters' position on the gallery stage are used only sparingly in Folio. Other editions mingle directions of this kind with original Folio and Quarto directions, sometimes marking them by means of square brackets. We have sought to distinguish what could be described as *directorial* interventions of this kind from Folio-style directions (either original or supplied) by placing them in the right margin in a different typeface. There is a degree of subjectivity about which directions are of which kind, but the procedure is intended as a reminder to the reader and the actor that

Shakespearean stage directions are often dependent upon editorial inference alone and are not set in stone. We also depart from editorial tradition in sometimes admitting uncertainty and thus printing permissive stage directions, such as an *Aside?* (often a line may be equally effective as an aside or a direct address—it is for each production or reading to make its own decision) or a *may exit* or a piece of business placed between arrows to indicate that it may occur at various different moments within a scene.

Line Numbers in the left margin are editorial, for reference and to key the explanatory and textual notes.

Explanatory Notes at the foot of each page explain allusions and gloss obsolete and difficult words, confusing phraseology, occasional major textual cruces, and so on. Particular attention is given to nonstandard usage, bawdy innuendo, and technical terms (e.g. legal and military language). Where more than one sense is given, commas indicate shades of related meaning, slashes alternative or double meanings.

Textual Notes take the following form: the reading of our text is given in bold and its source given after an equals sign. "Q" signifies a reading from the First Quarto of 1609, "Q2" a correction introduced in the Second Quarto text of 1609, "Q3" one from the Third Quarto text of 1611, "Q4" one from the Fourth Quarto text of 1619, "Q5" one from the Fifth Quarto text of 1630, "F3" a correction from the Third Folio text, second issue, of 1664, "F4" a correction from the Fourth Folio text of 1685, "PA" a reading in George Wilkins' novel *The Painfull Adventures of Pericles, Prince of Tyre* (1608), and "Ed" one introduced by a later editor. Thus, for example: **"1.1.25 boundless** = Ed. Q = bondlesse" indicates that at Act 1 Scene 1 line 25 we have accepted the editorial correction "boundless," which makes better contextual sense within the line, "To compass such a boundless happiness."

MAJOR PARTS: (*with percentage of lines/number of speeches/scenes onstage*) Pericles (25%/121/10), Gower (13%/8/8), Marina (8%/63/5), Simonides (6%/42/3), Helicanus (5%/37/5), Cleon (5%/19/3), Cerimon (4%/23/3), Lysimachus (4%/40/2), Bawd (4%/43/2), Dionyza (4%/19/4), Thaisa (3%/32/6), Bolt (3%/38/2), Antiochus (3%/12/1).

LINGUISTIC MEDIUM: 80% verse, 20% prose.

DATE: 1608. Registered for publication May 1608; Wilkins' novel *The Painfull Adventures of Pericles*, cashing in on the success of the play, published 1608; performance seen by Venetian and French ambassadors, probably between April and July 1608. Frequency of editions and subsequent allusions suggest that the play was a considerable popular success.

SOURCES: Based primarily on the story of Apollonius of Tyre (an ancient romance) in book 8 of John Gower's fourteenth-century poem *Confessio Amantis*; some use of Lawrence Twine's version of the same story in the 1607 novella *The Patterne of Painefull Aduentures*, which was also borrowed from extensively by Wilkins in his novelization of the play.

TEXT: Not in the First Folio, perhaps because the editors knew that Shakespeare contributed only the second half. Added to the second issue of the Third Folio (1664), together with a number of "apocryphal" plays. Though originally registered in 1608 by Edward Blount, who would eventually publish the Folio, *Pericles* appeared in Quarto in 1609 under the imprint of a different publisher, with the title *THE LATE, and much admired Play, called Pericles, Prince of Tyre. With the true Relation of the whole Historie, aduentures, and fortunes of* *the said Prince: As also, The no lesse strange, and worthy accidents, in the Birth and Life, of his Daughter MARIANA. As it hath been diuers and sundry times acted by his Maiesties Seruants, at the Globe on the Banck-side. By William Shakespeare.* The printing is of poor quality, with many corruptions and incomprehensible sequences, thus requiring more editorial intervention than is necessary in any Folio play. Wilkins' novelization assists in the interpretation of some passages, but since we do not know the exact status of his treatment in relation to Shakespeare's, it is unsafe to incorporate its readings into the text, as some editors have done. The Quarto went through six editions (two in 1609 alone), attesting to the play's popularity. The Sixth Quarto of 1635, together with the 1634 Quarto of *The Two Noble Kinsmen*, may have been intended to supplement the 1632 Second Folio.

PERICLES

LIST OF PARTS

GOWER, the Chorus

PERICLES, Prince of Tyre

MARINA, his daughter

Antioch

ANTIOCHUS, King of Antioch

Antiochus' DAUGHTER

THALIARD, a lord

MESSENGER

Tyre

FIRST LORD

SECOND LORD

HELICANUS, a grave and wise counselor

ESCANES, an old counselor

THIRD LORD

Tarsus

CLEON, governor of Tarsus

DIONYZA, Cleon's wife

LORD

OTHER TARSIANS

LEONINE

FIRST PIRATE

SECOND PIRATE

THIRD PIRATE

Pentapolis

FIRST FISHERMAN, the master

SECOND FISHERMAN

THIRD FISHERMAN

SIMONIDES, King of Pentapolis

THAISA, Simonides' daughter

FIRST KNIGHT, of Sparta

SECOND KNIGHT, of Macedon

THIRD KNIGHT, of Antioch

FOURTH KNIGHT

FIFTH KNIGHT

FIRST LORD

SECOND LORD

THIRD LORD

MARSHAL

On the ship

FIRST SAILOR, the ship's master

SECOND SAILOR

LYCHORIDA, Marina's nurse

Ephesus

Lord CERIMON

PHILEMON, his attendant

FIRST SERVANT

A survivor of the storm

FIRST GENTLEMAN

SECOND GENTLEMAN

CERIMON's SERVANT

DIANA, goddess of chastity

Mytilene

PANDER

BAWD, pander's wife

BOLT, pander and bawd's servant

FIRST GENTLEMAN

SECOND GENTLEMAN

LYSIMACHUS, governor of Mytilene

SAILOR OF TYRE

SAILOR OF MYTILENE

FIRST GENTLEMAN, of Tyre

LORD, of Mytilene

Marina's companion

Followers, Attendants, Gentlemen,
    Messengers, Lords, Servants,
    Priests of Diana

[Prologue]

Enter Gower

GOWER   To sing a song that old was sung
       From ashes ancient Gower is come,
       Assuming man's infirmities
       To glad your ear and please your eyes.
5   It hath been sung at festivals,
       On ember eves and holidays,
       And lords and ladies in their lives
       Have read it for restoratives.
       The purchase is to make men glorious,
10   *Et bonum quo antiquius eo melius.*
       If you — born in these latter times,
       When wit's more ripe — accept my rhymes,
       And that to hear an old man sing
       May to your wishes pleasure bring,
15   I life would wish, and that I might
       Waste it for you like taper light.
       This Antioch, then: Antiochus the great
       Built up this city for his chiefest seat —
       The fairest in all Syria.
20   I tell you what mine authors say:

Prologue   GOWER John Gower (?1330–1408), medieval poet whose *Confessio Amantis* is an
important source for *Pericles*   **1 old** long ago   **2 ancient** old/venerable   **3 man's infirmities**
human form   **6 ember eves** evenings before festival (**ember**) days   **holidays** religious
feasts   **8 restoratives** medicine   **9 purchase** profit   **glorious** eager for/worthy of glory
10 Et . . . melius "A good thing improves with age" (Latin)   **12 wit** wisdom/poetry   **ripe**
mature/sophisticated   **15 I . . . wish** I would hope to give it life   **16 Waste . . . light** i.e. like a
candle (**taper**) my story will consume (**waste**) itself in the telling   **17 Antioch** one of the
largest cities of the Roman Empire, capital of the province of Syria   **18 chiefest seat** capital
20 authors authorities/sources

This king unto him took a peer,
Who died and left a female heir,
So buxom, blithe and full of face
As heaven had lent her all his grace,
25   With whom the father liking took
And her to incest did provoke:
Bad child, worse father, to entice his own
To evil should be done by none.
But custom what they did begin
30   Was with long use account' no sin.
The beauty of this sinful dame
Made many princes thither frame
To seek her as a bedfellow,
In marriage pleasures, playfellow,
35   Which to prevent he made a law
To keep her still, and men in awe:
That whoso asked her for his wife,
His riddle told not, lost his life.
So for her many a wight did die,   *Points to the heads on display*
40   As yon grim looks do testify.   *above, or reveals them*
What now ensues, to the judgement of your eye
I give my cause, who best can justify.   *Exit*

[Act 1 Scene 1]   *running scene 1 continues*

Enter Antiochus, Prince Pericles and Followers

ANTIOCHUS   Young Prince of Tyre, you have at large received
The danger of the task you undertake?

21 **peer** mate/companion   23 **buxom** lively/pliant   **full of face** beautiful   **full** complete/
perfect   24 **As** as if   25 **liking** lustful affection   29 **But custom** but (through) habit
30 **use** usual practice (playing on **use**, i.e. "sexual intercourse")   **account'** an elision of
"accounted"   32 **frame** take themselves   36 **still** silent/motionless/always   **awe** reverence/
subjection   37 **whoso** whoever   **for** as   38 **His . . . not** and left (Antiochus') riddle unsolved
39 **wight** person   40 **yon** those   **grim looks** stern faces (i.e. the heads of former suitors)
41 **to . . . justify** I give my business (**cause**) to those discerning viewers (**judgement . . . eye**)
who are most able (**best**) to judge/confirm (**justify**) it   **1.1   *Location: Antioch   Pericles***
from Latin for "peril"   1 **Tyre** Phoenician trading city on the coast of Syria   **at large**
received fully comprehended/heard in detail

PERICLES   I have, Antiochus, and with a soul
            Emboldened with the glory of her praise

5   Think death no hazard in this enterprise.

ANTIOCHUS   Music!   *Music plays*

            Bring in our daughter, clothèd like a bride
            For embracements even of Jove himself,
            At whose conception, till Lucina reigned,

10   Nature this dowry gave: to glad her presence
            The senate house of planets all did sit,
            To knit in her their best perfections.

Enter Antiochus' Daughter

PERICLES   See where she comes, apparelled like the spring,
            Graces her subjects, and her thoughts the king

15   Of every virtue gives renown to men:
            Her face the book of praises, where is read
            Nothing but curious pleasures, as from thence
            Sorrow were ever razed, and testy wrath
            Could never be her mild companion.

20   You gods that made me man and sway in love,
            That have inflamed desire in my breast
            To taste the fruit of yon celestial tree
            Or die in the adventure, be my helps,
            As I am son and servant to your will,

25   To compass such a boundless happiness.

ANTIOCHUS   Prince Pericles—

PERICLES   That would be son to great Antiochus.

---

8 For embracements fit for the embraces   **Jove** Jupiter, king of the gods in Roman mythology
9 whose i.e. the Daughter's   **till Lucina reigned** until her birth   **Lucina** Roman goddess of
childbirth, associated with Diana and Juno   **10 glad her presence** make her presence
welcome   **11 senate house** council   **12 knit . . . perfections** unite all virtues in her
13 the spring Flora, Roman goddess of the spring   **14 Graces her subjects** the Graces
(personifications of beauty, grace, and artistic inspiration) are inferior to her   **15 gives** which
gives   **renown** reputation/honor   **16 book of praises** collection of everything praiseworthy
17 curious exquisite/rare (also unusual/peculiar)   **as** as if   **18 ever razed** forever erased
testy irritable   **19 mild companion** companion to someone as mild as she   **20 sway** rule
22 taste . . . tree enjoy Antiochus' daughter sexually; also refers to the apples stolen by
Hercules from the garden of Hesperus and the one eaten by Eve   **yon** that   **25 compass**
achieve/embrace   **27 son** son-in-law

ANTIOCHUS   Before thee stands this fair Hesperides,
With golden fruit, but dangerous to be touched,
30   For deathlike dragons here affright thee hard.
Her face, like heaven, enticeth thee to view
Her countless glory, which desert must gain,
And which without desert, because thine eye
Presumes to reach, all the whole heap must die.
35   Yon sometimes famous princes, like thyself   *Points to the heads*
Drawn by report, adventurous by desire,
Tell thee with speechless tongues and semblance pale
That without covering save yon field of stars
Here they stand, martyrs slain in Cupid's wars,
40   And with dead cheeks advise thee to desist
From going on death's net, whom none resist.
PERICLES   Antiochus, I thank thee, who hath taught
My frail mortality to know itself,
And by those fearful objects to prepare
45   This body, like to them, to what I must:
For death remembered should be like a mirror
Who tells us life's but breath, to trust it error.
I'll make my will, then, and as sick men do
Who know the world, see heaven, but feeling woe
50   Grip not at earthly joys as erst they did.
So I bequeath a happy peace to you
And all good men, as every prince should do,
My riches to the earth from whence they came,—
But my unspotted fire of love to you.—   *To Daughter*
55   Thus ready for the way of life or death,   *To Antiochus*
I wait the sharpest blow.

---

28 this . . . fruit i.e. Antiochus' daughter; Hesperus' garden was known as the Hesperides
30 deathlike deadly   **dragons** Antiochus' followers/the dragon that guarded Hesperus' apples
32 countless beyond value   **desert** worthiness   **34 reach** reach out for   **heap** company/
multitude (i.e. Pericles' body)   **35 Yon** those   **sometimes** once/formerly   **36 adventurous**
made bold   **37 semblance** appearance   **38 yon** that   **41 going . . . net** entering into death's
trap   **43 mortality** mortal nature/humanity   **44 those fearful objects** i.e. the heads of the
former suitors   **46 remembered** brought to mind   **47 life's but breath** life is ephemeral
48 as . . . did like terminally ill men who can see heaven and no longer cling to the earthly
pleasure that they once (**erst**) pursued   **54 unspotted** pure/free from lust

ANTIOCHUS   Scorning advice, read the conclusion   *Gives Pericles*
        then,   *the riddle*
    Which read and not expounded, 'tis decreed,
    As these before thee, thou thyself shalt bleed.

60 DAUGHTER   Of all 'ssayed yet, mayst thou prove   *To Pericles*
        prosperous,
    Of all 'ssayed yet, I wish thee happiness.

PERICLES   Like a bold champion I assume the lists,
    Nor ask advice of any other thought
    But faithfulness and courage.

The riddle   *Reads*

65 'I am no viper, yet I feed
    On mother's flesh which did me breed.
    I sought a husband, in which labour
    I found that kindness in a father.
    He's father, son and husband mild,
70 I mother, wife and yet his child:
    How they may be, and yet in two,
    As you will live resolve it you.'
    Sharp physic is the last!— But O, you powers   *Aside*
    That gives heaven countless eyes to view men's acts,
75 Why cloud they not their sights perpetually
    If this be true, which makes me pale to read it?—
    Fair glass of light, I loved you, and could still   *To Daughter*
    Were not this glorious casket stored with ill.
    But I must tell you, now my thoughts revolt,
80 For he's no man on whom perfections wait,
    That knowing sin within will touch the gate.

---

57 **conclusion** riddle   59 **these** the former suitors   60 **'ssayed** assayed/tried   62 **assume the lists** enter the combat/tournament area   63 **Nor** Nor do I   65 **viper . . . flesh** young vipers were supposed to eat their way out of their mother's womb   67 **labour** hard work/ sexual exertion   68 **kindness** affection/kinship/sexual acquiescence   71 **two** i.e. two people 73 **Sharp physic** harsh medicine   **the last** the final line of the riddle   74 **countless eyes** the stars   75 **cloud . . . sights** do they not shield their eyes   77 **glass of light** the Daughter is imagined as a lantern holding a candle or a shining glass vessel; **light** can mean lustful, and **glass** often represents a woman's (fragile) chastity   78 **casket** i.e. the Daughter's body 80 **on . . . wait** who is attended by heavenly virtues   81 **knowing . . . gate** will enter knowing that there is evil inside/will engage in sexual relations with a depraved person   **gate** vagina

You are a fair viol, and your sense the strings,
Who, fingered to make man his lawful music,
Would draw heaven down, and all the gods to hearken.

85 But being played upon before your time,
Hell only danceth at so harsh a chime.
Good sooth, I care not for you.   *Pericles gestures towards*

ANTIOCHUS   Prince Pericles, touch not, upon thy life,   *the Daughter*
For that's an article within our law

90 As dangerous as the rest. Your time's expired:
Either expound now or receive your sentence.

PERICLES   Great king,
Few love to hear the sins they love to act,
'Twould braid yourself too near for me to tell it.

95 Who has a book of all that monarchs do,
He's more secure to keep it shut than shown.
For vice repeated is like the wandering wind
Blows dust in others' eyes to spread itself.
And yet the end of all is bought thus dear,

100 The breath is gone and the sore eyes see clear
To stop the air would hurt them. The blind mole casts
Copped hills towards heaven, to tell the earth is thronged
By man's oppression, and the poor worm doth die for't.
Kings are earth's gods: in vice, their law's their will,

105 And if Jove stray, who dares say Jove doth ill?
It is enough you know, and it is fit,
What being more known grows worse, to smother it.

---

82 **viol** stringed instrument played between the legs   **sense** senses/reason   83 **fingered . . .
music** "played" by an appropriate sexual partner   85 **played upon** used sexually   86 **Hell . . .
chime** i.e. only the devil could approve   87 **Good sooth** in truth/truly   89 **article** stipulation/
requirement   94 **braid** reproach   **near** closely/intimately   95 **Who** whoever   97 **vice . . .
itself** to talk about evil deeds (of powerful people) is to behave like the wind, which blows dust
into eyes (of the offenders or of innocent people)   99 **And . . . them** but the painful lesson is
that the wind (**breath**), i.e. the rumor, runs its course and those people harmed by it (whose **sore
eyes** can now see) can take action to prevent further indiscretions   102 **Copped** heaped/
humped   **tell** tell that   **thronged** crushed/overwhelmed   103 **worm** creature (either the
person who dares to criticize or an innocent bystander)   107 **What . . . it** i.e. it is appropriate
(**fit**) to suppress something that would be made worse by its exaggerated repetition

All love the womb that their first being bred,
Then give my tongue like leave to love my head.

110 ANTIOCHUS   Heaven, that I had thy head! He has found   *Aside*
the meaning,
But I will gloze with him.— Young prince of Tyre,   *To Pericles*
Though by the tenor of your strict edict,
Your exposition misinterpreting,
We might proceed to cancel of your days,
115 Yet hope, succeeding from so fair a tree
As your fair self, doth tune us otherwise.
Forty days longer we do respite you,
If by which time our secret be undone,
This mercy shows we'll joy in such a son.
120 And until then your entertain shall be
As doth befit our honour and your worth.

[*Exeunt.*] *Pericles remains alone*

PERICLES   How courtesy would seem to cover sin,
When what is done is like an hypocrite,
The which is good in nothing but in sight.
125 If it be true that I interpret false,
Then were it certain you were not so bad
As with foul incest to abuse your soul:
Where now you're both a father and a son
By your untimely claspings with your child —
130 Which pleasures fits a husband, not a father —
And she an eater of her mother's flesh
By the defiling of her parents' bed.
And both like serpents are, who though they feed
On sweetest flowers, yet they poison breed.
135 Antioch farewell, for wisdom sees those men
Blush not in actions blacker than the night

---

109 like leave similar permission   **111 gloze with** speak plausibly to   **112 tenor** substance/
content/purpose   **edict** (royal) order   **113 exposition** explanation   **114 cancel of** put an
end to   **116 doth . . . otherwise** adjusts our mood/intention   **118 undone** solved   **119 joy**
rejoice   **120 entertain** entertainment   **122 would seem to** deceives in order to   **124 sight**
appearance   **129 untimely** premature   **133 though . . . breed** although they appear
beautiful, they only produce evil   **135 those men** that those men who

Will 'schew no course to keep them from the light.
One sin, I know, another doth provoke:
Murder's as near to lust as flame to smoke.
140   Poison and treason are the hands of sin —
Ay, and the targets to put off the shame.
Then lest my life be cropped, to keep you clear,
By flight, I'll shun the danger which I fear.   *Exit*

Enter Antiochus

ANTIOCHUS   He hath found the meaning,
145   For which we mean to have his head:
He must not live to trumpet forth my infamy,
Nor tell the world Antiochus doth sin
In such a loathèd manner.
And therefore instantly this prince must die,
150   For by his fall my honour must keep high.
Who attends us there?

Enter Thaliard

THALIARD   Doth your highness call?

ANTIOCHUS   Thaliard, you are of our chamber, Thaliard,
And our mind partakes her private actions
155   To your secrecy, and for your faithfulness
We will advance you, Thaliard.
Behold, here's poison and here's gold:
We hate the Prince of Tyre, and thou must kill him.
It fits thee not to ask the reason why:
160   Because we bid it. Say, is it done?

THALIARD   My lord, 'tis done.

Enter a Messenger   *Running*

ANTIOCHUS   Enough.—
Let your breath cool yourself, telling your haste.   *To Messenger*

MESSENGER   My lord, Prince Pericles is fled.   [*Exit*]

---

137 'schew eschew/avoid   **keep . . . light** i.e. keep their actions hidden   **141 targets** shields
put off deflect   **142 cropped** harvested/cut down   **clear** free from blame   **146 trumpet
forth** proclaim   **151 *Thaliard*** in the sources either a Privy Councillor or Antiochus' steward
153 of our chamber one of our most trusted attendants or advisers   **154 partakes** imparts/
communicates   **163 Let . . . haste** use your rapid breathing to cool yourself by telling me why
you are in such a hurry

165 ANTIOCHUS   As thou wilt live, fly after, and like an   *To Thaliard*
         arrow
      Shot from a well experienced archer hits
      The mark his eye doth level at,
      So thou never return unless thou say
      Prince Pericles is dead.

170 THALIARD   My lord, if I can get him within my pistol's length
      I'll make him sure enough, so farewell to your highness.

      ANTIOCHUS   Thaliard adieu.— Till Pericles   [*Exit Thaliard*]
         be dead,
      My heart can lend no succour to my head.   [*Exit*]

[Act 1 Scene 2]   *running scene 2*

Enter Pericles with his Lords

      PERICLES   Let none disturb us!   [*Exeunt the Lords*]
      Why should this change of thoughts,
      The sad companion, dull-eyed melancholy,
      Be my so used a guest as not an hour
5   In the day's glorious walk or peaceful night,
      The tomb where grief should sleep, can breed me quiet?
      Here pleasures court mine eyes and mine eyes shun them,
      And danger which I feared is at Antioch,
      Whose arm seems far too short to hit me here.
10   Yet neither pleasure's art can joy my spirits,
      Nor yet the other's distance comfort me.
      Then it is thus: the passions of the mind,
      That have their first conception by misdread,
      Have after-nourishment and life by care,
15   And what was first but fear what might be done,

---

167 level aim   **170 length** range   **171 sure** harmless (i.e. I'll kill him)   **173 My . . . head** i.e.
I will have no peace of mind   **1.2   *Location: Tyre*   2 change of thoughts** altered mental
state   **3 dull-eyed** sluggish/lacking insight   **4 used** familiar/regular   **as** that   **5 day's
glorious walk** daily movement of the sun   **6 breed me quiet** produce peace of mind for me
10 joy gladden/bring joy to   **spirits** emotions   **11 the other's** danger's   **12 passions . . .
mind** emotions/obsessions   **13 misdread** fear of evil   **14 Have . . . care** are fed and kept alive
by anxiety

Grows elder now, and cares it be not done.
And so with me. The great Antiochus,
Gainst whom I am too little to contend,
Since he's so great can make his will his act,
20 Will think me speaking though I swear to silence.
Nor boots it me to say 'I honour',
If he suspect I may dishonour him.
And what may make him blush in being known,
He'll stop the course by which it might be known.
25 With hostile forces he'll o'erspread the land,
And with th'ostent of war will look so huge,
Amazement shall drive courage from the state,
Our men be vanquished ere they do resist,
And subjects punished that ne'er thought offence.
30 Which care of them, not pity of myself,
Who am no more but as the tops of trees,
Which fence the roots they grow by and defend them,
Makes both my body pine and soul to languish,
And punish that before that he would punish.

Enter [Helicanus and] all the Lords to Pericles

35 FIRST LORD   Joy and all comfort in your sacred breast.

SECOND LORD   And keep your mind peaceful and comfortable.

HELICANUS   Peace, peace, and give experience tongue!
They do abuse the king that flatter him,
For flattery is the bellows blows up sin,
40 The thing the which is flattered, but a spark
To which that breath gives heat, and stronger
Glowing, whereas reproof, obedient and in order,
Fits kings as they are men, for they may err.

---

16 cares takes care   19 can that he can   make . . . act turn his thoughts into actions
21 boots it me is it any help to me   24 course flowing stream   26 th'ostent the display/
manifestation   27 Amazement (that) terror   28 ere before   29 ne'er thought offence
never offended even in their thoughts   31 as . . . them like the treetops (i.e. the monarch),
which protect and defend the roots (i.e. the people) that nourish them   32 fence protect
34 And . . . punish Pericles' own body punishes itself before it can be punished by Antiochus
37 give experience tongue let the wise/experienced speak   39 blows up that inflames
41 breath i.e. the air from the bellows (the flattering speech)   42 in order orderly/delivered in
the correct manner

When Signior Sooth here does proclaim 'peace',
45   He flatters you, makes war upon your life.
Prince, pardon me, or strike me if you please,
I cannot be much lower than my knees.   *Kneels*

PERICLES   All leave us else, but let your cares o'erlook   *To Lords*
What shipping, and what lading's in our haven,
50   And then return to us.— Helicanus,   [*Exeunt Lords*]
Thou hast moved us, what see'st thou in our looks?

HELICANUS   An angry brow, dread lord.

PERICLES   If there be such a dart in princes' frowns,
How durst thy tongue move anger to our face?

55   HELICANUS   How dares the plants look up to heaven,
From whence they have their nourishment?

PERICLES   Thou know'st I have power to take thy life from
thee.

HELICANUS   I have ground the axe myself,
Do but you strike the blow.

60   PERICLES   Rise, prithee rise! Sit down. Thou art   *Helicanus rises*
no flatterer,
I thank thee for't, and heaven forbid
That kings should let their ears hear their faults hid.
Fit counsellor and servant for a prince,
Who by thy wisdom makes a prince thy servant,
65   What wouldst thou have me do?

HELICANUS   To bear with patience
Such griefs as you do lay upon yourself.

PERICLES   Thou speak'st like a physician, Helicanus,
That ministers a potion unto me
70   That thou wouldst tremble to receive thyself.
Attend me then: I went to Antioch,

---

44 **Signior Sooth** Mister Sycophant   45 **makes . . . life** puts your life in danger   48 **All . . .
else** everyone else leave me   **cares** diligence   **o'erlook** supervise   49 **lading's** cargo is
51 **moved** provoked/angered   52 **brow** appearance/countenance   53 **dart** an arrow or light
spear   54 **move** arouse   58 **ground** sharpened   62 **let . . . hid** allow themselves to listen to
flattery   63 **Fit** fitting/suitable   69 **ministers** provides/dispenses   71 **Attend me** listen to me

Where, as thou know'st, against the face of death
I sought the purchase of a glorious beauty
From whence an issue I might propagate,
75 Are arms to princes, and bring joys to subjects.
Her face was to mine eye beyond all wonder,
The rest — hark in thine ear — as black as incest,
Which by my knowledge found, the sinful father
Seemed not to strike, but smooth. But thou know'st this:
80 'Tis time to fear when tyrants seems to kiss.
Which fear so grew in me I hither fled
Under the covering of a careful night,
Who seemed my good protector, and, being here,
Bethought me what was past, what might succeed.
85 I knew him tyrannous, and tyrants' fears
Decrease not, but grow faster than the years.
And should he doubt — as doubt no doubt he doth —
That I should open to the list'ning air
How many worthy princes' bloods were shed
90 To keep his bed of blackness unlaid ope,
To lop that doubt he'll fill this land with arms,
And make pretence of wrong that I have done him,
When all for mine — if I may call't — offence
Must feel war's blow, who spares not innocence.
95 Which love to all of which thyself art one,
Who now reproved'st me for't—

HELICANUS   Alas, sir—

PERICLES   Drew sleep out of mine eyes, blood from my cheeks,
Musings into my mind, with thousand doubts
100 How I might stop this tempest ere it came,

---

73 purchase benefit/acquisition/prize   **74 an issue** a child/an heir   **75 Are . . . subjects** i.e.
royal heirs (**issue**), which are weapons/protection to princes and bring joy to their subjects
79 Seemed pretended   **smooth** indulge/conciliate   **82 careful** protecting   **83 Who** i.e. the
night   **84 Bethought** considered   **succeed** follow   **87 doubt** suspect   **90 unlaid ope**
undiscovered/concealed   **91 lop** remove/eliminate   **doubt** suspicion   **arms** weapons (i.e.
soldiers)   **93 all** all my subjects   **mine . . . offence** my offense—if I may call it that   **94 who**
which (i.e. war)   **96 now reproved'st** was just rebuking   **99 doubts** fears/anxieties

And finding little comfort to relieve them,
I thought it princely charity to grieve for them.

HELICANUS   Well, my lord, since you have given me leave to
speak,
Freely will I speak. Antiochus you fear —
105 And justly too, I think, you fear the tyrant
Who either by public war or private
Treason will take away your life:
Therefore, my lord, go travel for a while,
Till that his rage and anger be forgot, or till
110 The Destinies do cut his thread of life:
Your rule direct to any, if to me,
Day serves not light more faithful than I'll be.

PERICLES   I do not doubt thy faith.
But should he wrong my liberties in my absence?

115 HELICANUS   We'll mingle our bloods together in the earth
From whence we had our being and our birth.

PERICLES   Tyre, I now look from thee then, and to Tarsus
Intend my travel, where I'll hear from thee,
And by whose letters I'll dispose myself.
120 The care I had and have of subjects' good
On thee I lay, whose wisdom's strength can bear it.
I'll take thy word for faith, not ask thine oath:
Who shuns not to break one, will crack both.
But in our orbs we'll live so round and safe
125 That time of both this truth shall ne'er convince:
Thou showed'st a subject's shine, I a true prince.   *Exeunt*

---

110 The Destinies the three Fates, who control destiny in Greco-Roman mythology
111 direct delegate   **114 should he** what if he (Antiochus) should   **my liberties** my
domains/my royal prerogatives and the rights of my subjects   **115 We'll . . . earth** i.e. we'll die
fighting him   **117 Tarsus** a city on the River Cydnus in Cillicia, present-day Turkey
118 Intend direct   **119 dispose** conduct   **122 not . . . oath** i.e. I won't ask you to swear a
formal oath   **123 Who** whoever   **124 orbs** spheres of activity (i.e. areas of influence)
round straightforwardly/openly   **125 time . . . convince** time shall never disprove (**convince**)
this truth regarding the pair of us   **126 shine** brightness/virtue

[Act 1 Scene 3]

Enter Thaliard alone

THALIARD   So this is Tyre, and this the court. Here must I kill
King Pericles, and if I do it not, I am sure to be hanged at
home: 'tis dangerous. Well, I perceive he was a wise fellow,
and had good discretion, that being bid to ask what he would
5   of the king, desired he might know none of his secrets. Now
do I see he had some reason for't: for if a king bid a man be a
villain, he's bound by the indenture of his oath to be one.
Husht, here comes the lords of Tyre.   *Thaliard stands aside*

Enter Helicanus, Escanes, with other Lords

HELICANUS   You shall not need, my fellow peers of Tyre,
10   Further to question me of your king's departure:
His sealed commission left in trust with me,
Does speak sufficiently he's gone to travel.

THALIARD   How? The king gone?   *Aside*

HELICANUS   If further yet you will be satisfied
15   Why — as it were unlicensed of your loves —
He would depart, I'll give some light unto you.
Being at Antioch—

THALIARD   What, from Antioch?   *Aside*

HELICANUS   Royal Antiochus, on what cause I know not,
20   Took some displeasure at him — at least he judged so —
And doubting lest he had erred or sinned,
To show his sorrow, he'd correct himself:
So puts himself unto the shipman's toil,
With whom each minute threatens life or death.

25   THALIARD   Well, I perceive I shall not be hanged now   *Aside*
although I would. But since he's gone, the king's ears this

1.3   31 . . . **secrets** the poet Philippides reputedly asked this of King Lysimachus of Thrace
4 would of wanted from   **7 indenture** contract between a master and servant   **8 Husht**
hush, be quiet   **11 sealed** bearing the royal seal   **commission** warrant   **12 speak**
sufficiently proclaim satisfactorily   **15 unlicensed . . . loves** without your devoted approval
16 light enlightenment   **21 doubting lest** fearing   **22 he'd correct** he wished to punish
23 puts . . . toil subjects himself to the rigors of the sea   **26 although I would** even if I wished
to be   **the . . . please** the king must be satisfied with this news

must please: he scaped the land to perish at the sea. I'll
present myself.— Peace to the lords of Tyre!   *Aloud*

HELICANUS   Lord Thaliard from Antiochus is welcome.

30   THALIARD   From him I come with message unto princely
Pericles, but since my landing I have understood your lord
has betook himself to unknown travels, now message must
return from whence it came.

HELICANUS   We have no reason to desire it,

35   Commended to our master, not to us,
Yet ere you shall depart, this we desire:
As friends to Antioch we may feast in Tyre.   *Exeunt*

[Act 1 Scene 4]   *running scene 3*

Enter Cleon the governor of Tarsus, with his wife [Dionyza] and others

CLEON   My Dionyza, shall we rest us here
And by relating tales of others' griefs
See if 'twill teach us to forget our own?

DIONYZA   That were to blow at fire in hope to quench it.

5   For who digs hills because they do aspire,
Throws down one mountain to cast up a higher.
O, my distressèd lord, even such our griefs are:
Here they are but felt, and seen with mischief's eyes,
But like to groves, being topped they higher rise.

10   CLEON   O, Dionyza,
Who wanteth food and will not say he wants it,
Or can conceal his hunger till he famish?
Our tongues our sorrows do sound deep,

---

32 betook taken   **message** my message   **34 it** i.e. the message   **35 Commended** (which
has been) directed/addressed   **1.4 Location: Tarsus   5 who digs** whoever digs up (the
image is of someone trying to flatten a hill by digging it up, only to create a bigger pile with the
earth they have removed)   **8 with mischief's eyes** through the eyes of misfortune/misery
9 topped pruned/cut back (making them grow faster than before)   **11 Who wanteth** whoever
lacks/desires   **13 Our . . . them** i.e. we proclaim (**sound**) our misfortunes (**sorrows**) low and
high, then we weep until we have enough breath back (**till . . . breath**) to bewail our sorrows
even more loudly, so that if the gods (**heaven**) are asleep and are oblivious to the suffering of
their creatures, our cries may wake them in order that they can comfort those in need   **sound**
proclaim

Our woes into the air, our eyes to weep
15   Till tongues fetch breath that may proclaim them louder,
That if heaven slumber while their creatures want,
They may awake their helpers to comfort them.
I'll then discourse our woes, felt several years,
And wanting breath to speak, help me with tears.
20   DIONYZA   I'll do my best, sir.
     CLEON   This Tarsus, o'er which I have the government,
A city o'er whom plenty held full hand,
For riches strewed herself even in her streets,
Whose towers bore heads so high they kissed the clouds,
25   And strangers ne'er beheld, but wondered at.
Whose men and dames so jetted and adorned,
Like one another's glass to trim them by,
Their tables were stored full to glad the sight,
And not so much to feed on as delight.
30   All poverty was scorned, and pride so great
The name of help grew odious to repeat.
     DIONYZA   O, 'tis too true.
     CLEON   But see what heaven can do by this our change.
These mouths who but of late earth, sea and air
35   Were all too little to content and please,
Although they gave their creatures in abundance,
As houses are defiled for want of use,
They are now starved for want of exercise.
Those palates who, not yet two summers younger,
40   Must have inventions to delight the taste
Would now be glad of bread and beg for it.

---

18 discourse relate   **19 wanting . . . speak** when I want breath/because you want breath
22 o'er . . . hand over whom plenty poured her gifts   **23 riches** a personification of wealth or
of plenty (from French *richesse*, "plenty")   **25 wondered at** admired/were astonished by
26 jetted strutted/swaggered   **adorned** adorned themselves   **27 Like . . . by** as if they were
like one another's mirror (**glass**) with which to adorn (**trim**) themselves/they mirrored one
another's finery   **28 glad** gladden/make glad   **31 The . . . repeat** even to propose asking for
help became repulsive   **33 by . . . change** through the example of our change in fortune
37 want lack   **39 not . . . younger** only two years ago   **40 inventions** novelties

Those mothers who to nuzzle up their babes
Thought nought too curious, are ready now
To eat those little darlings whom they loved.
45   So sharp are hunger's teeth, that man and wife,
Draw lots who first shall die to lengthen life.
Here stands a lord, and there a lady, weeping.
Here many sink, yet those which see them fall,
Have scarce strength left to give them burial.
50   Is not this true?

DIONYZA   Our cheeks and hollow eyes do witness it.

CLEON   O, let those cities that of plenty's cup
And her prosperities so largely taste
With their superfluous riots, hear these tears!
55   The misery of Tarsus may be theirs.

Enter a Lord

LORD   Where's the lord governor?

CLEON   Here.
Speak out thy sorrows, which thou bring'st in haste,
For comfort is too far for us to expect.

60   LORD   We have descried upon our neighbouring shore,
A portly sail of ships make hitherward.

CLEON   I thought as much.
One sorrow never comes but brings an heir,
That may succeed as his inheritor.
65   And so in ours: some neighbouring nation,
Taking advantage of our misery,
Hath stuffed the hollow vessels with their power,
To beat us down, the which are down already,
And make a conquest of unhappy me,
70   Whereas no glory's got to overcome.

---

42 **nuzzle up** nurture/bring up   43 **curious** elaborate/carefully prepared   46 **shall . . . life**
will die so that the other can survive   53 **largely** abundantly   54 **superfluous riots**
extravagant indulgence   **these tears** this lamentation   60 **descried** spotted/observed
61 **portly** stately/majestic   **sail** fleet   **make hitherward** sail toward us   67 **power** army
69 **unhappy** wretched   70 **Whereas . . . overcome** in whom no glory can be gained in
conquering

LORD   That's the least fear, for by the semblance
            Of their white flags displayed, they bring us peace,
            And come to us as favourers, not as foes.

CLEON   Thou speak'st like him's untutored to repeat:
75   Who makes the fairest show means most deceit.
            But bring they what they will and what they can,
            What need we fear?
            The ground's the lowest, and we are halfway there.
            Go tell their general we attend him here,
80   To know from whence he comes and what he craves.

LORD   I go, my lord.   [Exit]

CLEON   Welcome is peace, if he on peace consist,
            If wars, we are unable to resist.

Enter Pericles with attendants

PERICLES   Lord governor, for so we hear you are,
85   Let not our ships and number of our men
            Be like a beacon fired t'amaze your eyes.
            We have heard your miseries as far as Tyre,
            And seen the desolation of your streets.
            Nor come we to add sorrow to your tears,
90   But to relieve them of their heavy load,
            And these our ships you happily may think
            Are like the Trojan horse was stuffed within
            With bloody veins expecting overthrow,
            Are stored with corn to make your needy bread,
95   And give them life whom hunger starved half dead.

ALL TARSIANS The gods of Greece protect you,   *They kneel*
            And we'll pray for you.

---

71 **least fear** not to be feared in the least   72 **white flags** used to show that a ship had no
hostile intention   73 **favourers** friends   74 **him's . . . repeat** someone who has not learned
(the following maxim)/ someone too inexperienced to comment   75 **Who** he who
78 **The . . . there** i.e. the ground is as far as we can fall, and we are nearly there   82 **on peace
consist** is disposed toward peace   86 **beacon** fire or light placed in a prominent position as an
alarm signal   **t'amaze** to terrify   89 **add . . . tears** i.e. add to your misfortunes
91 **these . . . bread** although you may think that our ship is like the Trojan horse, which was
filled with ferocious warriors (**bloody veins**: a metonymy), it is actually filled with grain to
make bread for your hungry people   **happily** haply/perhaps

PERICLES   Arise, I pray you, rise.   *They rise*

We do not look for reverence but for love,

100   And harbourage for ourself, our ships and men.

CLEON   The which when any shall not gratify,

Or pay you with unthankfulness in thought,

Be it our wives, our children or ourselves,

The curse of heaven and men succeed their evils!

105   Till when — the which, I hope, shall ne'er be seen —

Your grace is welcome to our town and us.

PERICLES   Which welcome we'll accept, feast here awhile,

Until our stars that frown, lend us a smile.   *Exeunt*

[Act 2 Chorus]   *running scene 4*

Enter Gower

GOWER   Here have you seen a mighty king

His child, iwis, to incest bring,

A better prince, and benign lord,

That will prove awful both in deed and word.

5   Be quiet then, as men should be,

Till he hath passed necessity:

I'll show you those in troubles reign,

Losing a mite, a mountain gain.

The good in conversation,

10   To whom I give my benison,

Is still at Tarsus, where each man

Thinks all is writ, he speken can,

And to remember what he does

Build his statue to make him glorious.

---

101 **gratify** show gratitude for/grant   102 **in thought** even in thought   104 **succeed**
inevitably follow   108 **stars** fates/fortunes   **2 Chorus**   2 **iwis** certainly/truly (archaic)
3 **A better prince** i.e. Pericles   4 **awful** awe-inspiring/worthy of respect   6 **passed necessity**
gone through extreme suffering   7 **those . . . reign** those who rule during periods of difficulty
(or, alternatively, "trouble's reign," those who are ruled by trouble)   8 **mite** a tiny particle
9 **The good** i.e. Pericles   **conversation** behavior/manners   10 **benison** blessing   12 **writ**
holy scripture/authoritative command   **he speken can** he (Pericles) is able to speak (**spoken**
is archaic)   13 **remember** commemorate   14 **Build his statue** construct a statue of him
make him glorious glorify his deeds

15 But tidings to the contrary
   Are brought your eyes, what need speak I?
Dumb show
Enter at one door Pericles talking with Cleon, all the train with them.
Enter at another door a Gentleman with a letter to Pericles. Pericles
shows the letter to Cleon. Pericles gives the messenger a reward, and
knights him. Exit Pericles [with his Attendants] at one door, and Cleon
at another [with his Attendants]

GOWER Good Helicane that stayed at home
  Not to eat honey like a drone
  From others' labours: though he strive
20 To killen bad, keeps good alive.
  And to fulfil his prince' desire
  Sends word of all that haps in Tyre:
  How Thaliard came full bent with sin
  And had intent to murder him,
25 And that in Tarsus was not best
  Longer for him to make his rest.
  He doing so, put forth to seas,
  Where when men been there's seldom ease:
  For now the wind begins to blow,
30 Thunder above and deeps below
  Makes such unquiet, that the ship
  Should house him safe is wracked and split,
  And he, good prince, having all lost,
  By waves from coast to coast is tossed.
35 All perishen of man, of pelf,
  Ne aught escapend but himself.
  Till Fortune, tired with doing bad,
  Threw him ashore, to give him glad.
  And here he comes: what shall be next,
40 Pardon old Gower, this 'longs the text.   *[Exit]*

---

15 tidings . . . contrary i.e. adverse news **16 *Dumb show*** a mimed sequence, common in early modern plays ***train*** retinue **17 Helicane** i.e. Helicanus **18 Not to** not intending to **20 killen** kill (archaic) **22 haps** happens **23 full bent** fully determined **27 doing so** doing as advised **28 been** are (archaic) **32 Should** which should **35 perishen** perish (archaic) **pelf** possessions **36 Ne aught escapend** nor did anything escape (archaic) **38 glad** gladness/happiness **40 'longs** belongs to/prolongs

[Act 2 Scene 1]

Enter Pericles wet

PERICLES   Yet cease your ire, you angry stars of heaven!
Wind, rain and thunder, remember earthly man
Is but a substance that must yield to you,
And I, as fits my nature, do obey you.

5   Alas, the seas hath cast me on the rocks,
Washed me from shore to shore, and left my breath
Nothing to think on but ensuing death.
Let it suffice the greatness of your powers
To have bereft a prince of all his fortunes,

10   And having thrown him from your wat'ry grave,
Here to have death in peace is all he'll crave.

Enter three Fishermen

FIRST FISHERMAN   What ho, Pilch!

SECOND FISHERMAN   Ha, come and bring away the nets.

FIRST FISHERMAN   What, Patch-breech, I say!

15   THIRD FISHERMAN   What say you, master?

FIRST FISHERMAN   Look how thou stirr'st now! Come away, or I'll
fetch th' with a wanion.

THIRD FISHERMAN   Faith, master, I am thinking of the poor men
that were cast away before us even now.

20   FIRST FISHERMAN   Alas, poor souls, it grieved my heart to hear
what pitiful cries they made to us to help them when, well-a-
day, we could scarce help ourselves.

THIRD FISHERMAN   Nay, master, said not I as much when I saw the
porpoise how he bounced and tumbled? They say they're

25   half fish, half flesh: a plague on them, they ne'er come but
I look to be washed. Master, I marvel how the fishes live in
the sea.

2.1 *Location: the seashore at Pentapolis*   **1 ire** fury   **6 breath** life   **12 Pilch** leather
coat/jerkin   **14 Patch-breech** patched trousers   **16 Look . . . now!** Get a move on!/Now
you're moving! (ironic)   **17 fetch th'** strike thee   **wanion** vengeance   **21 well-a-day** alas
24 porpoise porpoises were thought to appear before stormy weather   **26 I . . . washed** I
expect to be soaked

FIRST FISHERMAN   Why, as men do a-land: the great ones eat up
the little ones. I can compare our rich misers to nothing so
30   fitly as to a whale: a plays and tumbles, driving the poor fry
before him, and, at last, devours them all at a mouthful.
Such whales have I heard on o'th'land, who never leave
gaping till they swallowed the whole parish: church, steeple,
bells and all.

35   PERICLES   A pretty moral.   *Aside*

THIRD FISHERMAN   But master, if I had been the sexton, I would
have been that day in the belfry.

SECOND FISHERMAN   Why, man?

THIRD FISHERMAN   Because he should have swallowed me too,
40   and when I had been in his belly I would have kept such a
jangling of the bells that he should never have left till he cast
bells, steeple, church and parish up again! But if the good
King Simonides were of my mind—

PERICLES   Simonides?   *Aside*

45   THIRD FISHERMAN   We would purge the land of these drones that
rob the bee of her honey.

PERICLES   How from the finny subject of the sea   *Aside*
These fishers tell the infirmities of men,
And from their wat'ry empire recollect
50   All that may men approve or men detect.—
Peace be at your labour, honest fishermen.   *To Fishermen*

SECOND FISHERMAN   'Honest', good fellow? What's that? If it be a
day fits you, search't out of the calendar and nobody will
look after it!

55   PERICLES   May see the sea hath cast upon your coast —

SECOND FISHERMAN   What a drunken knave was the sea to cast
thee in our way!

---

28 **a-land** on land   30 **fitly** appropriately   **a** he   **fry** young fish   32 **on** of   35 **pretty**
clever/ingenious   **moral** story with a moral point   36 **sexton** church officer whose duties
included bell-ringing   37 **belfry** bell tower   41 **cast** regurgitated   45 **drones . . . honey** i.e.
lazy and unproductive subjects   47 **finny subject** fin-bearing citizens (i.e. fish)   49 **recollect**
gather up   50 **All . . . detect** i.e. everything that might represent men in a positive or negative
light   52 **If . . . it!** i.e. if honesty is a condition that suits a bedraggled creature such as Pericles,
it could be eradicated and no one would miss it (it is possible that a line is missing, in which
Pericles says "good day" to the fishermen)   53 **search't** remove it   55 **May** you may   **hath
cast** has thrown   56 **cast** vomit

PERICLES   A man, whom both the waters and the wind
         In that vast tennis-court hath made the ball
60   For them to play upon, entreats you pity him:
         He asks of you that never used to beg.

FIRST FISHERMAN   No, friend, cannot you beg? Here's them in our
         country of Greece gets more with begging than we can do
         with working.

65 SECOND FISHERMAN   Canst thou catch any fishes then?

PERICLES   I never practised it.

SECOND FISHERMAN   Nay, then thou wilt starve sure, for here's
         nothing to be got nowadays unless thou canst fish for't.

PERICLES   What I have been I have forgot to know,
70   But what I am, want teaches me to think on:
         A man thronged up with cold. My veins are chill,
         And have no more of life than may suffice
         To give my tongue that heat to ask your help,
         Which if you shall refuse, when I am dead,
75   For that I am a man, pray you see me buried.

FIRST FISHERMAN   'Die', quotha? Now gods forbid't, an I have a
         gown here. Come, put it on, keep thee warm: *Gives a gown*
         now, afore me, a handsome fellow! Come, thou   *to Pericles*
         shalt go home, and we'll have flesh for holidays, fish for
80   fasting-days and, moreo'er, puddings and flapjacks, and
         thou shalt be welcome.

PERICLES   I thank you, sir.

SECOND FISHERMAN   Hark you, my friend — you said you could
         not beg?

PERICLES   I did but crave.

85 SECOND FISHERMAN   But crave? Then I'll turn craver too, and so I
         shall scape whipping.

---

59 **that vast tennis-court** i.e. the sea   61 **never used** was never accustomed   62 **Here's
them** there are those   68 **fish for't** get it through fishing/get it by artifice (i.e. begging or
trickery)   71 **thronged up** overwhelmed   75 **For that** because   **pray you** may I ask/please
76 **quotha** says he/indeed   **gods forbid't** i.e. god forbid   **an** if/as long as   78 **afore me** a
mild oath   79 **fish for fasting-days** meat was forbidden during Lent, on Fridays and
Saturdays, and on some other penitential days   80 **puddings** sausages; also carries its
modern meaning of a sweet or savory pudding   **flapjacks** pancakes   84 **crave** request
85 **craver** supplicant/beggar

PERICLES   Why, are your beggars whipped, then?

SECOND FISHERMAN   O, not all, my friend, not all: for if all your
beggars were whipped I would wish no better office than to
90   be beadle. But, master, I'll go draw up the net.

[Exeunt Second and Third Fishermen]

PERICLES   How well this honest mirth becomes their labour!

FIRST FISHERMAN   Hark you, sir, do you know where ye are?

PERICLES   Not well.

FIRST FISHERMAN   Why, I'll tell you: this is called Pentapolis, and
95   our king, the good Simonides.

PERICLES   The good Simonides, do you call him?

FIRST FISHERMAN   Ay, sir, and he deserves so to be called for his
peaceable reign and good government.

PERICLES   He is a happy king, since he gains from
100   His subjects the name of good by his government.
How far is his court distant from this shore?

FIRST FISHERMAN   Marry, sir, half a day's journey. And I'll tell
you, he hath a fair daughter, and tomorrow is her birthday,
and there are princes and knights come from all parts of the
105   world to joust and tourney for her love.

PERICLES   Were my fortunes equal to my desires,
I could wish to make one there.

FIRST FISHERMAN   O, sir, things must be as they may, and what a
man cannot get he may lawfully deal for his wife's soul.

Enter the two Fishermen, drawing up a net

110   SECOND FISHERMAN   Help, master, help! Here's a fish hangs in the
net like a poor man's right in the law: 'twill hardly come out.
Ha, bots on't, 'tis come at last, and 'tis turned to a rusty
armour.   *They pull pieces of armour from the net*

---

90 beadle parish constable, whose duties included whipping vagrants   **91 becomes** suits/is
appropriate for   **94 Pentapolis** seemingly located in Greece, but should probably be identified
with Cyrene in Cyrenaica, the major Greek colony in North Africa   **102 Marry** by the Virgin
Mary (a mild oath)   **105 tourney** take part in a tournament   **107 make one** be one of the
participants   **108 what . . . soul** what a man cannot otherwise obtain he may get by selling
his wife for sex; plays on "wife's soul"/"wife's hole" (i.e. vagina) and puns on **get**: if the man
cannot **get** (beget) children, then he can sell his wife to someone who will father them for him
111 right just claim   **'twill . . . out** the "fish" will not come out of the net/the poor man will
not get the verdict he desires   **112 bots on't** an expletive, equivalent to "a plague on it"
bots a maggot infection in horses

PERICLES   An armour, friends? I pray you let me see it.

115   Thanks Fortune yet, that after all crosses

Thou givest me somewhat to repair myself.

And though it was mine own, part of my heritage,

Which my dead father did bequeath to me

With this strict charge even as he left his life:

120   'Keep it my Pericles, it hath been a shield

'Twixt me and death' — and pointed to this brace —

'For that it saved me, keep it: in like necessity,

The which the gods protect thee from, may't defend thee.'

It kept where I kept, I so dearly loved it,

125   Till the rough seas, that spares not any man,

Took it in rage, though calmed have given't again.

I thank thee for't, my shipwreck now's no ill

Since I have here my father gave in his will.

FIRST FISHERMAN   What mean you, sir?

130   PERICLES   To beg of you, kind friends, this coat of worth,

For it was sometime target to a king:

I know it by this mark. He loved me dearly,

And for his sake I wish the having of it,

And that you'd guide me to your sovereign's court,

135   Where with it I may appear a gentleman.

And if that ever my low fortune's better

I'll pay your bounties, till then rest your debtor.

FIRST FISHERMAN   Why, wilt thou tourney for the lady?

PERICLES   I'll show the virtue I have borne in arms.

140   FIRST FISHERMAN   Why, d'ye take it, and the gods give thee good

on't!   *Pericles puts on the armour*

SECOND FISHERMAN   Ay, but hark you, my friend, 'twas we that

made up this garment through the rough seams of the

---

115 crosses misfortunes/trials   117 heritage inheritance   119 charge command/
responsibility   121 brace vambrace, armor covering the arms   122 For that because   in
like necessity in a similarly dire situation   124 kept dwelled/stayed   126 though . . . again
i.e. now the seas are calm, they have given it back again   128 my father that which my father
130 coat of worth valuable coat (i.e. the armor)   131 sometime once   target shield/
protection   137 pay your bounties repay your generosity   rest remain   138 tourney joust/
take part in a tournament   139 virtue courage/ability   140 d'ye take it do you take it (i.e.
take it)   141 on't of it/from it   143 made up fitted together, as in the making of clothes
seams the furrows of the waves, imagined as the seams of a garment

waters. There are certain condolements, certain vails: I hope,
145   sir, if you thrive you'll remember from whence you had them.

PERICLES   Believe't, I will.

By your furtherance I am clothed in steel,
And spite of all the rapture of the sea
This jewel holds his building on my arm.
150   Unto thy value I will mount myself
Upon a courser, whose delightful steps
Shall make the gazer joy to see him tread.
Only, my friend, I yet am unprovided
Of a pair of bases —

155   SECOND FISHERMAN   We'll sure provide: thou shalt have my best
gown to make thee a pair, and I'll bring thee to the court
myself.

PERICLES   Then honour be but a goad to my will,
This day I'll rise, or else add ill to ill.   [*Exeunt*]

[Act 2 Scene 2]   *running scene 6*

Enter Simonides with attendance, and Thaisa

SIMONIDES   Are the knights ready to begin the triumph?

FIRST LORD   They are, my liege,
And stay your coming to present themselves.

SIMONIDES   Return them we are ready, and our daughter,
5   In honour of whose birth these triumphs are,
Sits here like beauty's child, whom Nature gat
For men to see and, seeing, wonder at.   [*Exit an Attendant*]

---

144 condolements usually means expressions of sympathy: the Second Fisherman either
confuses it with "emoluments" (profits) or with "dole" (portion or share), or he is being
deliberately euphemistic   **vails** tips/gratuities (literally, the remnants of cloth kept by tailors
after a suit is finished)   **147 furtherance** assistance   **148 rapture** seizure/plundering
149 holds his building occupies its proper position   **150 Unto thy value** either a jewel on
Pericles' arm has also survived, with which he will buy the horse, or Pericles will buy a horse
equal to the worth of the piece of armor (described as a jewel)   **151 courser** horse
152 gazer onlooker   **154 bases** knee-length skirts worn by a knight on horseback
158 honour . . . will let honor spur me on   **goad** a rod used for driving cattle
2.2   *Location: Pentapolis*   1 triumph tournament   **3 stay** wait for   **4 Return** answer/
inform   **6 gat** begat: conceived/bred

THAISA   It pleaseth you, my royal father, to express
           My commendations great, whose merit's less.

10 SIMONIDES   It's fit it should be so, for princes are
           A model which heaven makes like to itself:
           As jewels lose their glory if neglected,
           So princes their renowns if not respected.
           'Tis now your honour, daughter, to entertain
15   The labour of each knight in his device.

THAISA   Which to preserve mine honour I'll perform.

The First Knight passes by

His Attendant presents his shield to Thaisa?

SIMONIDES   Who is the first that doth prefer himself?

THAISA   A knight of Sparta, my renownèd father,
           And the device he bears upon his shield
20   Is a black Ethiop reaching at the sun,
           The word: *Lux tua vita mihi.*

SIMONIDES   He loves you well that holds his life of you.

The Second Knight

Passes by and his Attendant presents his shield to Thaisa?

           Who is the second that presents himself?

THAISA   A prince of Macedon, my royal father,
25   And the device he bears upon his shield
           Is an armed knight that's conquered by a lady.
           The motto thus in Spanish: *Piùe per dolcezza che per forza.*

The Third Knight

Passes by and his Attendant presents his shield to Thaisa

SIMONIDES   And with the third?

---

8 express . . . great praise me highly   **10 princes** men and women of high (princely) rank
11 model image   **13 renowns** reputations   **14 honour** honorable duty   **entertain**
accept/receive   **15 device** heraldic design and motto   **17 prefer** present   **18 Sparta**
powerful ancient Greek city-state   **20 Ethiop** used loosely in the seventeenth century to
refer to all black Africans   **21 word** motto   ***Lux . . . mihi*** "Your light is life to me" (Latin)
22 holds . . . of regards his life as being dependent on   **24 Macedon** Macedonia, a kingdom at
the northern end of the Greek peninsula that became a world power under Philip II and
Alexander the Great   **27 in Spanish** puzzling as the motto is closer to Italian than Spanish
Piùe . . . forza "More by gentleness than by force"

THAISA   The third, of Antioch,

30   And his device a wreath of chivalry.

The word: *Me pompae provexit apex.*

The Fourth Knight

> *Passes by and his Attendant presents his shield to Thaisa*

SIMONIDES   What is the fourth?

THAISA   A burning torch that's turnèd upside down,

The word: *Qui me alit me extinguit.*

35   SIMONIDES   Which shows that beauty hath his power and will,

Which can as well inflame as it can kill.

The Fifth Knight

> *Passes by and his Attendant presents his shield to Thaisa*

THAISA   The fifth, an hand environèd with clouds,

Holding out gold, that's by the touchstone tried:

The motto thus: *Sic spectanda fides.*

The Sixth Knight [Pericles]

> *Passes by, wearing the rusty armour*
>
> *He presents his own device to Thaisa*

40   SIMONIDES   And what's the sixth and last, the which the knight

Himself with such a graceful courtesy delivered?

THAISA   He seems to be a stranger, but his present is

A withered branch, that's only green at top.

The motto: *In hac spe vivo.*

45   SIMONIDES   A pretty moral.

From the dejected state wherein he is

He hopes by you his fortunes yet may flourish.

FIRST LORD   He had need mean better than his outward show

Can any way speak in his just commend:

---

30 wreath of chivalry chaplet or garland of leaves or flowers, worn or awarded as a mark of
distinction/the twisted band by which the crest is joined to a knight's helmet   **31 Me . . . apex**
the honor of the contest has led me on   **34 Qui . . . extinguit** "Who feeds me extinguishes me"
37 environèd surrounded   **38 touchstone** smooth black quartz or jasper, used to test the
purity of gold; the touchstone became a symbol of fidelity   **tried** tested   **39 Sic spectanda
fides** "Thus is faithfulness to be tested"   **device** may be a real branch, as Pericles has no shield
42 stranger unfamiliar person/foreigner   **present** offering   **44 In . . . vivo** "In this hope I
live"   **48 He . . . commend** i.e. he must prove that he is better than his appearance would
suggest, because that cannot speak in his favor

50   For by his rusty outside he appears
        To have practised more the whipstock than the lance.

SECOND LORD   He well may be a stranger, for he comes
        To an honoured triumph strangely furnishèd.

THIRD LORD   And on set purpose let his armour rust
55   Until this day, to scour it in the dust.

SIMONIDES   Opinion's but a fool that makes us scan
        The outward habit for the inward man.
        But stay, the knights are coming —
        We will withdraw into the gallery.   [*Exeunt*]

Great shouts, and all cry 'The mean knight!'

[Act 2 Scene 3]   *running scene 6 continues*

Enter the King [*Simonides, Thaisa, Marshal*] *and Knights from tilting*

SIMONIDES   Knights,
        To say you're welcome were superfluous.
        To place upon the volume of your deeds,
        As in a title page, your worth in arms,
5   Were more than you expect, or more than's fit,
        Since every worth in show commends itself.
        Prepare for mirth, for mirth becomes a feast:
        You are princes and my guests.

THAISA   But you, my knight and guest,   *To Pericles*
10   To whom this wreath of victory I give
        And crown you king of this day's happiness.   *Crowns him with*

PERICLES   'Tis more by fortune, lady, than my merit.   *a wreath*

SIMONIDES   Call it by what you will, the day is yours,
        And here, I hope, is none that envies it.
15   In framing artists art hath thus decreed,
        To make some good but others to exceed,

---

51 whipstock handle of a whip **53 strangely** bizarrely (playing on **stranger**) **furnishèd**
equipped/fitted out **54 on set purpose** deliberately **55 scour** clean **56 Opinion's . . .**
man public opinion makes us foolishly examine (**scan**) the external appearance of a man in
search of (**for**) his inner worth **59 mean** humble/poor **2.3** *tilting* jousting **3 place . . .**
arms i.e. advertise your martial ability **6 in show** in action **7 becomes** suits **9 you** you
are **15 framing** making, creating

And you are her laboured scholar. Come, queen
   o'th'feast —
For, daughter, so you are — here take your place.
Marshal, the rest as they deserve their grace.   *To Marshal*

20 KNIGHTS   We are honoured much by good Simonides.

SIMONIDES   Your presence glads our days: honour we love,
For who hates honour hates the gods above.

MARSHAL   Sir, yonder is your place.   *To Pericles*

PERICLES   Some other is more fit.

25 FIRST KNIGHT   Contend not, sir, for we are gentlemen
Have neither in our hearts nor outward eyes
Envies the great, nor shall the low despise.

PERICLES   You are right courteous, knights.

SIMONIDES   Sit, sir, sit.   *They sit*

30   By Jove I wonder, that is king of thoughts,   *Aside*
These cates resist me he but thought upon.

THAISA   By Juno, that is queen of marriage,   *Aside*
All viands that I eat do seem unsavoury,
Wishing him my meat.—
                   Sure, he's a gallant gentleman.   *To Simonides*

35 SIMONIDES   He's but a country gentleman.
He's done no more than other knights have done,
He's broken a staff, or so. So let it pass.

THAISA   To me he seems like diamond to glass.   *Aside?*

PERICLES   Yon king's to me like to my father's picture,   *Aside*
40   Which tells me in that glory once he was,
Had princes sit like stars about his throne,
And he the sun for them to reverence.

---

17 **her laboured scholar** the scholar into whom Art has put most effort/the scholar who has laboriously studied art   **19 Marshal** arrange, position **as . . . grace** according to their merit **22 who** whoever   **25 Contend not** do not argue **26 Have** who have **outward eyes** eyes that see outward/eyes on the outside of the body   **27 Envies** that which envies **28 right** very   **30 By . . . upon** by Jove, who is aware of everything, I marvel that these delicacies (**cates**) become unappetizing to me when I think of him   **33 viands** foodstuffs **unsavoury** tasteless/unappetizing   **34 meat** food/object of my sexual attention **gallant** fine/brave   **37 a staff** i.e. his opponent's lance in the tournament   **38 to** compared with   **39 Yon** that   **40 tells me** announces or discloses (him to) me   **41 Had** when he had   **42 reverence** pay homage to

None that beheld him, but like lesser lights
Did vail their crowns to his supremacy,
45 Where now his son's like a glow-worm in the night,
The which hath fire in darkness, none in light.
Whereby I see that time's the king of men,
He's both their parent and he is their grave,
And gives them what he will, not what they crave.

50 SIMONIDES   What, are you merry, knights?

KNIGHTS   Who can be other in this royal presence?

SIMONIDES   Here, with a cup that's stored unto the brim,
As you do love, fill to your mistress' lips:
We drink this health to you.   *Drinks a toast*

55 KNIGHTS   We thank your grace.

SIMONIDES   Yet pause awhile. Yon knight doth sit too
        melancholy,
As if the entertainment in our court
Had not a show might countervail his worth.
Note it not you, Thaisa?

60 THAISA   What is't to me, my father?

SIMONIDES   O, attend, my daughter,
Princes in this should live like gods above,
Who freely give to everyone that come to honour them,
And princes not doing so are like to gnats,
65 Which make a sound, but killed are wondered at.
Therefore to make his entertain more sweet,
Here, say we drink this standing bowl of wine   *Drinks a toast*
        to him.

THAISA   Alas, my father, it befits not me
Unto a stranger knight to be so bold:
He may my proffer take for an offence,
70 Since men take women's gifts for impudence.

---

44 **vail** lower   45 **Where . . . light** i.e. like a glowworm, Pericles is best seen at night; in the
light of his father's glory he would not seem to glow at all   **Where** whereas   52 **stored** filled
53 **fill . . . lips** i.e. drink a full cup in honor of your mistress   56 **Yon** that   58 **countervail**
match, equal   59 **Note . . . you** don't you observe it   64 **like . . . at** like gnats, which when
they are dead seem very small considering how noisy they were   66 **entertain** entertainment
67 **standing bowl** bowl/goblet with a stem or legs   69 **stranger knight** knight who is a
stranger/foreign knight   **bold** shameless/immodest   70 **proffer** offering

SIMONIDES   How? Do as I bid you, or you'll move me else.

THAISA   Now by the gods, he could not please me   *Aside*
    better.

SIMONIDES   And, further, tell him we desire to know
75   Of whence he is, his name and parentage?

THAISA   The king my father, sir, has drunk to you—   *To Pericles*

PERICLES   I thank him.

THAISA   Wishing it so much blood unto your life.

PERICLES   I thank both him and you, and pledge him freely.

80   THAISA   And, further, he desires to know of you
    Of whence you are, your name and parentage?

PERICLES   A gentleman of Tyre, my name Pericles,
    My education being in arts and arms,
    Who, looking for adventures in the world,
85   Was by the rough seas reft of ships and men,
    And after shipwreck driven upon this shore.

THAISA   He thanks your grace,   *To Simonides*
    Names himself Pericles, a gentleman of Tyre,
    Who only by misfortune of the seas
90   Bereft of ships and men, cast on this shore.

SIMONIDES   Now by the gods, I pity his misfortune,
    And will awake him from his melancholy.
    Come, gentlemen, we sit too long on trifles   *To Knights*
    And waste the time which looks for other revels:
95   Even in your armours as you are addressed,
    Will well become a soldier's dance.
    I will not have excuse with saying this:
    'Loud music is too harsh for ladies' heads',
    Since they love men in arms as well as beds.

    They dance

100   So, this was well asked, 'twas so well performed.

---

72 move me provoke me   **78 blood** spirit/health   **79 pledge him** drink his health   **83 arts and arms** artistic/scholarly pursuits and martial skills   **85 reft** robbed/deprived   **90 cast** was cast   **93 sit** dwell   **trifles** trivialities   **95 addressed** dressed/attired   **96 Will** you will **become** suit/be appropriate for   **97 I . . . beds** i.e. I won't have anyone excuse themselves by saying that women don't like the loud music of a soldier's dance, as I know that they like men in arms (i.e. knights) as well as men in their beds   **100 this . . . asked** i.e. I did well to ask for this

Come, sir, here's a lady that wants breathing too,   *To Pericles*
And I have heard you knights of Tyre
Are excellent in making ladies trip,
And that their measures are as excellent.

105 PERICLES   In those that practise them they are, my lord.

SIMONIDES   O, that's as much as you would be denied
Of your fair courtesy!

They dance

Unclasp, unclasp!
Thanks, gentlemen, to all: all have done well,
But you the best. Pages and lights to conduct   *To Pericles*
110 These knights unto their several lodgings!
Yours, sir, we have given order be next our own.

PERICLES   I am at your grace's pleasure.

SIMONIDES   Princes, it is too late to talk of love,
And that's the mark, I know, you level at:
115 Therefore each one betake him to his rest,
Tomorrow all for speeding do their best.   [*Exeunt*]

[Act 2 Scene 4]   *running scene 7*

Enter Helicanus and Escanes

HELICANUS   No, Escanes, know this of me:
Antiochus from incest lived not free,
For which the most high gods not minding longer
To withhold the vengeance that they had in store,
5 Due to this heinous capital offence,
Even in the height and pride of all his glory —
When he was seated in a chariot
Of inestimable value, and his daughter with him —
A fire from heaven came and shrivelled up
10 Those bodies even to loathing. For they so stunk

---

101 **breathing** exercising   103 **trip** dance/step lightly/fall sexually   104 **measures** formal
dance steps/strategies in wooing   105 **practise them** put them to use   106 **that's . . .**
courtesy i.e. you are too modest   110 **several** various   114 **level** aim   115 **betake him** take
himself   116 **speeding** success   **2.4**   *Location: Tyre*   3 **not minding longer** intending no
longer   5 **capital** punishable by death

That all those eyes adored them ere their fall
Scorn now their hand should give them burial.

ESCANES   'Twas very strange.

HELICANUS   And yet but justice: for though this king were great,

15   His greatness was no guard to bar heaven's shaft,
But sin had his reward.

ESCANES   'Tis very true.

Enter two or three Lords

FIRST LORD   See, not a man in private conference
Or council has respect with him but he.

20   SECOND LORD   It shall no longer grieve without reproof.

THIRD LORD   And cursed be he that will not second it.

FIRST LORD   Follow me then.— Lord Helicane, a word.   *To Helicanus*

HELICANUS   With me? And welcome. Happy day, my lords.

FIRST LORD   Know that our griefs are risen to the top,

25   And now at length they overflow their banks.

HELICANUS   Your griefs, for what? Wrong not your prince, you
    love.

FIRST LORD   Wrong not yourself then, noble Helicane,
But if the prince do live let us salute him,
Or know what ground's made happy by his breath.

30   If in the world he live, we'll seek him out,
If in his grave he rest, we'll find him there.
We'll be resolved he lives to govern us,
Or dead, give's cause to mourn his funeral
And leave us to our free election.

35   SECOND LORD   Whose death's indeed the strongest in our
    censure.
And knowing this kingdom is without a head —
Like goodly buildings left without a roof,
Soon fall to ruin — your noble self,

---

11 **eyes adored** eyes that adored   15 **bar** prevent   **shaft** arrow (i.e. vengeance)   16 **his** its
19 **respect** influence   20 **grieve** cause grievance   23 **Happy day** i.e. "good day"   24 **griefs**
grievances   26 **you love** i.e. that you love   29 **what . . . breath** what country he is living in
32 **resolved** reassured/persuaded   **he lives** if/that he lives   33 **give's** i.e. it will give us
mourn his funeral mourn at his funeral/regret his death   34 **to . . . election** to choose
another ruler   35 **Whose** i.e. Pericles'   **strongest . . . censure** most likely (probability) in our
assessment   37 **left** which, if left

That best know how to rule and how to reign,
40 We thus submit unto: our sovereign.
ALL   Live, noble Helicane!
HELICANUS Try honour's cause, forbear your suffrages!
If that you love Prince Pericles, forbear.
Take I your wish, I leap into the seas,
45 Where's hourly trouble, for a minute's ease.
A twelvemonth longer let me entreat you
To forbear the absence of your king.
If in which time expired he not return,
I shall with agèd patience bear your yoke.
50 But if I cannot win you to this love,
Go search like nobles, like noble subjects,
And in your search spend your adventurous worth,
Whom if you find, and win unto return,
You shall like diamonds sit about his crown.
55 FIRST LORD To wisdom he's a fool that will not yield.
And since Lord Helicane enjoineth us,
We with our travels will endeavour it.
HELICANUS Then you love us, we you, and we'll clasp hands:
When peers thus knit, a kingdom ever stands.   [*Exeunt*]

[Act 2 Scene 5]

running scene 8

Enter the King [Simonides] reading of a letter at one door, the Knights meet him

FIRST KNIGHT Good morrow to the good Simonides.
SIMONIDES Knights, from my daughter this I let you know:
That for this twelvemonth she'll not undertake
A married life.

---

42 Try honour's cause try being honorable   **forbear your suffrages** refrain from voting
(for me)/avoid electing (another ruler)   **43 forbear** leave off/have patience   **47 forbear** to
endure with patience   **48 not** does not   **49 yoke** harness (i.e. the servitude of the ruler to
the people)   **50 love** demonstration of your affection   **52 spend . . . worth** demonstrate
your courageous nobility   **53 Whom** i.e. Pericles   **win unto** persuade to   **56 enjoineth**
instructs/urges   **57 travels** journeys (or **travails**, endeavors)   **59 knit** unite
2.5 *Location: Pentapolis*

5   Her reason to herself is only known,
     Which from her by no means can I get.

SECOND KNIGHT   May we not get access to her, my lord?

SIMONIDES   Faith, by no means, she hath so strictly
     Tied her to her chamber that 'tis impossible.

10   One twelvemoons more she'll wear Diana's livery:
     This by the eye of Cynthia hath she vowed
     And on her virgin honour will not break it.

THIRD KNIGHT   Loath to bid farewell, we take our leaves.

                                            [Exeunt Knights]

SIMONIDES   So, they are well dispatched.

15   Now, to my daughter's letter:
     She tells me here she'll wed the stranger knight,
     Or never more to view nor day nor light.
     'Tis well, mistress, your choice agrees with mine:
     I like that well! Nay, how absolute she's in't,

20   Not minding whether I dislike or no.
     Well, I do commend her choice
     And will no longer have it be delayed.
     Soft, here he comes — I must dissemble it.

Enter Pericles

PERICLES   All fortune to the good Simonides.

25 SIMONIDES   To you as much. Sir, I am beholding to you
     For your sweet music this last night: I do
     Protest, my ears were never better fed
     With such delightful pleasing harmony.

PERICLES   It is your grace's pleasure to commend,

30   Not my desert.

SIMONIDES   Sir, you are music's master.

PERICLES   The worst of all her scholars, my good lord.

SIMONIDES   Let me ask you one thing:
     What do you think of my daughter, sir?

---

9 Tied her confined herself   **10 twelvemoons** twelve months   **Diana** goddess of hunting, virginity, and the moon; also associated with childbirth and with witchcraft   **livery** uniform (i.e. Thaisa will remain a virgin)   **11 the . . . Cynthia** the moon   **Cynthia** Diana as moon goddess   **14 dispatched** dismissed   **17 nor day nor** either day or   **19 absolute** certain   **23 Soft** be quiet   **25 beholding** indebted   **30 desert** merit

35	PERICLES	A most virtuous princess.
	SIMONIDES	And she is fair, too, is she not?
	PERICLES	As a fair day in summer: wondrous fair.
	SIMONIDES	Sir, my daughter thinks very well of you,
		Ay, so well that you must be her master
40		And she will be your scholar, therefore look to it.
	PERICLES	I am unworthy for her schoolmaster.
	SIMONIDES	She thinks not so: peruse this writing *Gives a letter*
		else.
	PERICLES	What's here? *Aside*
		A letter that she loves the knight of Tyre?
45		'Tis the king's subtlety to have my life! *Reads*
		O, seek not to entrap me, gracious lord, *To Simonides*
		A stranger and distressèd gentleman
		That never aimed so high to love your daughter,
		But bent all offices to honour her.
50	SIMONIDES	Thou hast bewitched my daughter,
		And thou art a villain.
	PERICLES	By the gods I have not!
		Never did thought of mine levy offence,
		Nor never did my actions yet commence
55		A deed might gain her love, or your displeasure.
	SIMONIDES	Traitor, thou liest.
	PERICLES	Traitor?
	SIMONIDES	Ay, traitor.
	PERICLES	Even in his throat, unless it be the king
60		That calls me traitor, I return the lie.
	SIMONIDES	Now by the gods, I do applaud his courage. *Aside*
	PERICLES	My actions are as noble as my thoughts,
		That never relished of a base descent:
		I came unto your court for honour's cause,
65		And not to be a rebel to her state.

---

42 else if you don't believe it   **44 that** saying that   **45 subtlety** trick   **48 to** as to   **49 bent**
directed   **offices** service   **53 levy** raise/intend; possibly misused for **level**, aim   **55 might**
that might   **63 relished** tasted   **base** ignoble/common   **65 state** kingdom/rule

And he that otherwise accounts of me,
This sword shall prove he's honour's enemy.

SIMONIDES   No?

Here comes my daughter, she can witness it.

Enter Thaisa

70   PERICLES   Then as you are as virtuous as fair,   *To Thaisa*
Resolve your angry father if my tongue
Did e'er solicit or my hand subscribe
To any syllable that made love to you?

THAISA   Why, sir, say if you had,

75   Who takes offence at that, would make me glad?

SIMONIDES   Yea, mistress, are you so peremptory?
I am glad on't with all my heart!—   *Aside*
I'll tame you, I'll bring you in subjection.   *To Thaisa*
Will you, not having my consent,

80   Bestow your love and your affections
Upon a stranger?— Who, for aught I know,   *Aside*
May be — nor can I think the contrary —
As great in blood as I myself.—
Therefore hear you, mistress, either frame your will   *To Thaisa*

85   To mine — and you sir, hear you — either be
Ruled by me, or I'll make you man and wife!   *Joins their hands*
Nay, come, your hands and lips must seal it too,
And being joined I'll thus your hopes destroy,   *Pulls their hands apart*
And for further grief — God give you joy!   *Joins their hands again*

90   What, are you both pleased?

THAISA   Yes, if you love me, sir?

PERICLES   Even as my life my blood that fosters it.

SIMONIDES   What, are you both agreed?

BOTH   Yes, if't please your majesty.

95   SIMONIDES   It pleaseth me so well that I will see you wed,
And then with what haste you can, get you to bed.   *Exeunt*

---

66 **accounts of me** thinks me   71 **Resolve** assure   72 **subscribe** sign   73 **made love to**
courted   75 **that, would** that which would   76 **peremptory** determined   81 **aught**
anything   84 **frame** adapt/accommodate   **will** intentions (puns on **will**, sexual desire)
92 **fosters** nourishes

[Act 3 Chorus]

Enter Gower

GOWER   Now sleep y-slackèd hath the rouse,
No din but snores about the house,
Made louder by the o'erfed breast
Of this most pompous marriage feast.
5 The cat with eyne of burning coal
Now couches from the mouse's hole,
And crickets sing at the oven's mouth
Are the blither for their drouth.
Hymen hath brought the bride to bed,
10 Where by the loss of maidenhead
A babe is moulded. Be attent,
And time that is so briefly spent
With your fine fancies quaintly eche.
What's dumb in show, I'll plain with speech.   *Dumb show*

Enter Pericles and Simonides at one door with Attendants. A
Messenger meets them, kneels and gives Pericles a letter. Pericles shows
it Simonides, the Lords kneel to him. Then enter Thaisa, with child,
with Lychorida, a nurse. The King shows her the letter, she rejoices: she
and Pericles take leave of her father, and depart [with Lychorida and
their Attendants. Exeunt Simonides and his train]

15 GOWER   By many a dern and painful perch,
Of Pericles the careful search
By the four opposing coigns
Which the world together joins,
Is made with all due diligence
20 That horse and sail and high expense
Can stead the quest. At last from Tyre —

---

3 Chorus   **1 y-slackèd** reduced to inactivity (archaic)   **rouse** carousing/mirth   **3 breast** stomach   **4 pompous** magnificent/ceremonious   **5 eyne** eyes   **6 couches** lies asleep **from** away from   **7 crickets sing** i.e. crickets that sing   **8 blither** more happy   **drouth** the dryness of their position (crickets were thought to like heat)   **9 Hymen** Greek god of marriage   **10 maidenhead** virginity   **11 Be attent** listen   **12 briefly** quickly   **13 fancies** imaginations   **eche** eke out/supplement   **14 plain** explain   **15 dern** dreary/secret   **painful** laborious   **perch** a measure of land: 30.5 square yards or 25.3 square meters   **16 Of** for **17 coigns** corners   **21 stead** help, assist

Fame answering the most strange inquire —
To th'court of King Simonides
Are letters brought, the tenor these:
25   Antiochus and his daughter dead,
The men of Tyrus on the head
Of Helicanus would set on
The crown of Tyre, but he will none.
The mutiny he there hastes t'appease,
30   Says to 'em, if King Pericles
Come not home in twice six moons,
He, obedient to their dooms,
Will take the crown. The sum of this
Brought hither to Pentapolis
35   Y-ravishèd the regions round,
And everyone with claps can sound,
'Our heir apparent is a king:
Who dreamt? Who thought of such a thing?'
Brief, he must hence depart to Tyre.
40   His queen, with child, makes her desire —
Which who shall cross? — along to go:
Omit we all their dole and woe.
Lychorida her nurse she takes,
And so to sea. Their vessel shakes
45   On Neptune's billow, half the flood
Hath their keel cut, but Fortune, moved,
Varies again. The grizzled north
Disgorges such a tempest forth
That as a duck for life that dives,
50   So up and down the poor ship drives.
The lady shrieks and, well-a-near,

---

22 **Fame** rumor   **most . . . inquire** inquiries from the most distant places   **24 tenor**
substance/content   **25 dead** being dead   **28 will none** will have none of it   **29 t'appease** to
pacify/relieve   **31 moons** months   **32 dooms** decisions, judgments   **33 sum** summary/
essence   **35 Y-ravishèd** entranced/enraptured (archaic)   **36 claps** applause   **can** began
sound declare   **37 heir apparent** next in line to the throne   **39 Brief** in short   **41 cross**
contradict   **42 dole** grief/sorrow   **43 nurse** nurse/midwife   **45 Neptune's billow** the waves
Neptune god of the oceans   **half . . . cut** they are halfway there   **flood** waves/rushing water
46 moved provoked   **47 grizzled** grisly/horrible/gray   **north** north wind (thought to raise
storms)   **50 drives** is propelled   **51 well-a-near** alas

Does fall in travail with her fear.
And what ensues in this fell storm
Shall for itself, itself perform:
55   I nill relate, action may
Conveniently the rest convey,
Which might not what by me is told.
In your imagination hold
This stage the ship, upon whose deck
60   The sea-tossed Pericles appears to speak.   [*Exit*]

[Act 3 Scene 1]   *running scene 10*

Enter Pericles on shipboard

PERICLES   The god of this great vast, rebuke these surges
Which wash both heaven and hell, and thou that hast
Upon the winds command, bind them in brass,
Having called them from the deep! O, still
5   Thy deaf'ning dreadful thunders, gently quench
Thy nimble sulphurous flashes!— O, how, Lychorida!   *Calls*
How does my queen? — Thou stormest venomously,
Wilt thou spit all thyself? The seaman's whistle
Is as a whisper in the ears of death,
10   Unheard. Lychorida!— Lucina, O   *Calls*
Divinest patroness, and midwife gentle
To those that cry by night, convey thy deity
Aboard our dancing boat, make swift the pangs
Of my queen's travails!— Now, Lychorida!

Enter Lychorida   *With the baby*

52 Does . . . travail goes into labor   53 fell cruel   55 nill will not (archaic)   action
performance   56 Conveniently suitably   57 Which . . . told i.e. which my story might not be
able to convey   58 hold consider/retain   60 appears to speak appears and speaks
3.1   *Location: a ship*   1 The god i.e. Neptune   vast immense space, i.e. the sea   rebuke
repress   surges violent waves   2 thou Aeolus, god of the winds   3 bind . . . brass in
Homer's *Odyssey*, Aeolus' island was surrounded by walls of brass   4 still calm   5 Thy
Pericles may now address Jove, who controlled thunder   6 nimble sudden   sulphurous
flashes lightning   8 Wilt . . . thyself i.e. will you spit out all of your thunder and lightning at
once   seaman's whistle used to give orders   9 as . . . Unheard as silent as a whisper to the
dead   10 Lucina goddess of childbirth   14 travails labor, with a pun on "travels"

15   LYCHORIDA   Here is a thing too young for such a place,
           Who if it had conceit would die,
           As I am like to do. Take in your arms
           This piece of your dead queen.
    PERICLES   How? How, Lychorida?
20   LYCHORIDA   Patience, good sir, do not assist the storm.
           Here's all that is left living of your queen:
           A little daughter. For the sake of it,
           Be manly and take comfort.   *Gives him the baby*
    PERICLES   O you gods!
25   Why do you make us love your goodly gifts
           And snatch them straight away? We here below
           Recall not what we give, and therein may
           Use honour with you.
    LYCHORIDA   Patience, good sir, even for this charge.
30   PERICLES   Now, mild may be thy life,   *To the baby*
           For a more blusterous birth had never babe.
           Quiet and gentle thy conditions, for
           Thou art the rudeliest welcome to this world
           That ever was prince's child. Happy what follows:
35   Thou hast as chiding a nativity
           As fire, air, water, earth and heaven can make
           To herald thee from the womb.
           Even at the first, thy loss is more than can
           Thy portage quit with all thou can'st find here.
40   Now the good gods throw their best eyes upon't!
    Enter two Sailors
    FIRST SAILOR   What courage, sir? God save you!
    PERICLES   Courage enough. I do not fear the flaw,
           It hath done to me the worst: yet for the love

---

16 conceit understanding   **17 like** likely   **18 piece** fragment/masterpiece   **20 assist** i.e. by ranting or weeping   **27 Recall not** do not demand the return of   **therein** in that respect
28 Use . . . you deal honorably with you/deserve to be treated honorably by you   **29 charge** responsibility   **30 mild . . . life** i.e. may your life be mild   **32 conditions** way of life
33 rudeliest most roughly   **34 Happy what follows** may what follows be happy   **35 chiding** noisy/tumultuous   **38 thy . . . here** i.e. the cost of losing her mother is so great that in coming into the world Marina has already lost more than the world can ever repay her   **39 portage** porterage or freight charges   **quit** repay   **40 best eyes** most favorable aspect   **42 flaw** gust, squall

Of this poor infant, this fresh new seafarer,

45   I would it would be quiet.

FIRST SAILOR   Slack the bowlines there! Thou wilt not, wilt thou,
blow and split thyself.

SECOND SAILOR   But sea-room an the brine and cloudy billow
kiss the moon, I care not.

50   FIRST SAILOR   Sir, your queen must overboard. The sea works
high, the wind is loud, and will not lie till the ship be cleared
of the dead.

PERICLES   That's your superstition.

FIRST SAILOR   Pardon us, sir. With us at sea it hath been still
55   observed, and we are strong in custom. Therefore briefly
yield 'er, for she must overboard straight.

PERICLES   As you think meet. Most wretched queen!

LYCHORIDA   Here she lies, sir.   *Reveals the body*

PERICLES   A terrible childbed hast thou had, my dear.   *To Thaisa*
60   No light, no fire, th'unfriendly elements
Forgot thee utterly. Nor have I time
To give thee hallowed to thy grave, but straight
Must cast thee, scarcely coffined, in the ooze,
Where, for a monument upon thy bones
65   And aye-remaining lamps, the belching whale
And humming water must o'erwhelm thy corpse,
Lying with simple shells. O Lychorida,
Bid Nestor bring me spices, ink and paper,
My casket and my jewels, and bid Nicander
70   Bring me the satin coffer. Lay the babe   *Gives her the baby*
Upon the pillow. Hie thee, whiles I say
A priestly farewell to her. Suddenly, woman!

[*Exit Lychorida*]

---

46 Slack slacken   bowlines ropes used to steady the sails   Thou the storm   48 But sea-
room if we have room to maneuver the ship   brine sea   cloudy billow sea spray   50 works
high is turbulent   54 still always   55 strong in custom adhere strongly to our traditions
briefly quickly/immediately   56 straight immediately   57 meet suitable   62 hallowed with
religious ceremony   64 for a monument instead of a tomb   65 aye-remaining lamps ever-
burning votive lights   belching spouting   66 humming murmuring   68 Nestor the name
of an old and wise king in classical mythology   69 Nicander the name of a Greek poet,
physician, and grammarian   70 satin satin-lined   coffer box, chest   71 Hie thee go quickly
72 Suddenly immediately

SECOND SAILOR   Sir, we have a chest beneath the hatches, caulked
and bitumed ready.

75   PERICLES   I thank thee. Mariner, say, what coast is this?

FIRST SAILOR   We are near Tarsus.

PERICLES   Thither, gentle mariner,
Alter thy course for Tyre. When can'st thou reach it?

FIRST SAILOR   By break of day, if the wind cease.

80   PERICLES   O, make for Tarsus!
There will I visit Cleon, for the babe
Cannot hold out to Tyrus. There I'll leave it
At careful nursing. Go thy ways, good mariner,
I'll bring the body presently.   *Exeunt*

[Act 3 Scene 2]

Enter Lord Cerimon with a Servant

And another survivor of the storm

CERIMON   Philemon, ho!

Enter Philemon

PHILEMON   Doth my lord call?

CERIMON   Get fire and meat for these poor men.

[*Exit Philemon*]

'T has been a turbulent and stormy night.

5   SERVANT   I have been in many, but such a night as this
Till now, I ne'er endured.

CERIMON   Your master will be dead ere you return,   *To Servant*
There's nothing can be ministered to nature
That can recover him.— Give this to the   *To the other*
'pothecary,

10   And tell me how it works.   [*Exeunt all but Cerimon*]

Enter two Gentlemen

FIRST GENTLEMAN   Good morrow.

---

73 **beneath the hatches** belowdecks   **caulked** sealed   74 **bitumed** made waterproof with
bitumen (pitch)   78 **Alter . . . Tyre** alter your direction (**course**), which is currently toward
Tyre   83 **Go thy ways** go ahead/go about it   84 **presently** at once   **3.2 Location:**
Ephesus   8 **ministered** given in assistance   **nature** a person's physical strength or
constitution   9 **'pothecary** apothecary, who prepares and sells drugs for medicinal purposes

SECOND GENTLEMAN   Good morrow to your lordship.

CERIMON   Gentlemen, why do you stir so early?

FIRST GENTLEMAN   Sir, our lodgings standing bleak upon the sea
15 Shook as the earth did quake:
The very principals did seem to rend
And all to topple. Pure surprise and fear
Made me to quit the house.

SECOND GENTLEMAN   That is the cause we trouble you so early,
20 'Tis not our husbandry.

CERIMON   O, you say well.

FIRST GENTLEMAN   But I much marvel that your lordship, having
Rich tire about you, should at these early hours,
Shake off the golden slumber of repose.
25 'Tis most strange nature should be so conversant with pain,
Being thereto not compelled.

CERIMON   I hold it ever
Virtue and cunning were endowments greater
Than nobleness and riches. Careless heirs
30 May the two latter darken and expend,
But immortality attends the former,
Making a man a god. 'Tis known, I ever
Have studied physic, through which secret art,
By turning o'er authorities, I have,
35 Together with my practice, made familiar
To me and to my aid the blest infusions
That dwells in vegetives, in metals, stones,
And I can speak of the disturbances
That nature works and of her cures, which doth give me
40 A more content in course of true delight

---

14 bleak upon exposed to/in an exposed position next to   bleak windswept   15 as as if
16 principals main rafters, posts, or braces of a building   rend tear apart   20 husbandry
industriousness   21 O . . . well an ironic dismissal responding to the gentleman's self-
depreciation   23 tire furnishings   24 repose sleep   25 conversant familiar   pain labor
27 hold it ever have always believed   28 cunning skill/cleverness/knowledge   29 Careless
prodigal/reckless   30 darken sully/dishonor   33 physic medicine   34 turning o'er
authorities reading learned books   35 practice practical investigations   36 to my aid to
assist me in healing   blest infusions medicinal properties   37 vegetives plants, herbs
39 works causes   40 more content truer happiness   in course in the pursuit

Than to be thirsty after tottering honour,
Or tie my pleasure up in silken bags
To please the fool and death.

SECOND GENTLEMAN   Your honour has
45   Through Ephesus poured forth your charity,
And hundreds call themselves your creatures, who
By you have been restored. And not your knowledge,
Your personal pain, but even your purse still open,
Hath built Lord Cerimon such strong renown,
50   As time shall never—

Enter two or three with a chest

CERIMON'S SERVANT   So, lift there.

CERIMON   What's that?

CERIMON'S SERVANT   Sir, even now
Did the sea toss up upon our shore this chest.
55   'Tis of some wreck.

CERIMON   Set't down, let's look upon't.

SECOND GENTLEMAN   'Tis like a coffin, sir.

CERIMON   What e'er it be,
'Tis wondrous heavy. Wrench it open straight:
60   If the sea's stomach be o'ercharged with gold,
'Tis a good constraint of fortune it belches upon us.

SECOND GENTLEMAN   'Tis so, my lord.

CERIMON   How close 'tis caulked and bitumed!
Did the sea cast it up?
65 CERIMON'S SERVANT   I never saw so huge a billow, sir,
As tossed it upon shore.

CERIMON   Wrench it open.
Soft! It smells most sweetly in my sense.

---

41 **tottering honour** unstable reputation   42 **tie . . . bags** draw all my pleasure from the
acquisition of wealth   43 **To . . . death** i.e. which would please only a fool, or death, who will
inherit in the end   45 **Ephesus** ancient city on the western coast of Asia Minor (in present-
day Turkey), famous for its temple to Diana; also the setting of Shakespeare's *Comedy of Errors*
46 **call . . . creatures** acknowledge that they owe their lives to you   **creatures** dependents
47 **not** not only   48 **pain** labor   **your . . . open** i.e. your generosity   60 **o'ercharged**
overfilled   61 **constraint of fortune** act commanded by fortune   63 **close** tightly   **caulked**
sealed   **bitumed** smeared with bitumen (pitch)   65 **billow** wave   68 **Soft!** Wait a moment!

SECOND GENTLEMAN   A delicate odour.

70   CERIMON   As ever hit my nostril. So, up with it.   *They open the chest*
O you most potent gods! What's here, a corpse?

SECOND GENTLEMAN   Most strange!

CERIMON   Shrouded in cloth of state, balmed and entreasured
With full bags of spices, a passport too!

75   Apollo, perfèct me in the characters:
'Here I give to understand,   *Reads*
If e'er this coffin drives a-land,
I, King Pericles, have lost
This queen, worth all our mundane cost.

80   Who finds her, give her burying:
She was the daughter of a king.
Besides this treasure for a fee,
The gods requite his charity.'
If thou livest, Pericles, thou hast a heart

85   That even cracks for woe. This chanced tonight?

SECOND GENTLEMAN   Most likely, sir.

CERIMON   Nay, certainly tonight,
For look how fresh she looks: they were too rough
That threw her in the sea. Make a fire within,

90   Fetch hither all my boxes in my closet.   [*Exit a Servant*]
Death may usurp on nature many hours,
And yet the fire of life kindle again
The o'er-pressed spirits. I heard of an Egyptian
That had nine hours lain dead, who was

95   By good appliance recoverèd.

Enter one with napkins and fire

---

70 it i.e. the lid   **73 cloth of state** material fit for a queen (literally refers to the canopy over a
throne)   **balmed** embalmed/anointed   **entreasured** kept as in a treasury   **74 passport**
document providing identification/guaranteeing admission   **75 Apollo** Greco-Roman god of
medicine, learning, and music   **perfèct me** help me to understand   **characters**
handwriting/writing   **77 drives a-land** is driven ashore   **79 mundane cost** worldly wealth
80 Who whoever   **85 even** just now/fully   **This chanced tonight?** This happened last night?
88 rough hasty/careless   **90 closet** private room/inner chamber   **93 o'er-pressed**
overwhelmed   **spirits** vital powers or energies (in medieval and early modern medicine,
substances or fluids thought to permeate the blood and organs)   **95 appliance** attention,
treatment

Well said, well said — the fire and cloths. The rough and
Woeful music that we have, cause it to sound,
    beseech you.   *Music*

The viol once more — how thou stirr'st, thou block!
The music there! I pray you give her air.   *Music again*
100   Gentlemen, this queen will live,
Nature awakes a warm breath out of her!
She hath not been entranced above five hours:
See how she 'gins to blow into life's flower again.

FIRST GENTLEMAN   The heavens through you increase our
    wonder,
105   And sets up your fame for ever.

CERIMON   She is alive! Behold her eyelids, cases
To those heavenly jewels which Pericles hath lost,
Begin to part their fringes of bright gold.
The diamonds of a most praisèd water
110   Doth appear, to make the world twice rich. Live,
And make us weep to hear your fate, fair creature,
Rare as you seem to be.   *She moves*

THAISA   O dear Diana, where am I? Where's my lord?
What world is this?

115   SECOND GENTLEMAN   Is not this strange?

FIRST GENTLEMAN   Most rare.

CERIMON   Hush, my gentle neighbours.
Lend me your hands, to the next chamber bear her.
Get linen. Now this matter must be looked to,
120   For her relapse is mortal. Come, come,
And Aesculapius guide us.   *They carry her away. Exeunt*

---

96 **Well said** well done   **cloths** the Quarto text's spelling could indicate cloths or clothes
98 **viol** a stringed instrument   **how thou stirr'st** how slow you are   **block** blockhead, idiot
101 **Nature . . . her** i.e. Nature sets her breathing again   102 **above** more than   103 **'gins**
begins   **blow** blossom/bloom   107 **heavenly jewels** Thaisa's eyes   108 **fringes . . . gold**
Thaisa's eyelashes   109 **diamonds . . . water** Thaisa's eyes   **water** luster/quality   112 **Rare**
marvelous/exceptional   116 **Most rare** most unusual/extraordinary   120 **is mortal** would
be fatal   121 **Aesculapius** Greco-Roman god of healing (the son of Apollo)

[Act 3 Scene 3]

Enter Pericles [and Lychorida with Marina] at Tarsus, with Cleon and Dionyza

PERICLES   Most honoured Cleon, I must needs be gone:
My twelve months are expired, and Tyrus stands
In a litigious peace. You and your lady
Take from my heart all thankfulness, the gods
5   Make up the rest upon you.

CLEON   Your shakes of fortune, though they haunt you
       mortally
Yet glance full wond'ringly on us.

DIONYZA   O, your sweet queen!
That the strict fates had pleased you had brought her
10   Hither to have blessed mine eyes with her.

PERICLES   We cannot but obey the powers above us.
Could I rage and roar as doth the sea she lies in,
Yet the end must be as 'tis. My gentle babe Marina,
Whom, for she was born at sea, I have named so,
15   Here I charge your charity withal, leaving her
The infant of your care, beseeching you to give her
Princely training, that she may be mannered as she is born.

CLEON   Fear not, my lord, but think
Your grace that fed my country with your corn —
20   For which the people's prayers still fall upon you —
Must in your child be thought on. If neglection
Should therein make me vile, the common body
By you relieved, would force me to my duty,
But if to that my nature need a spur,

3.3   *Location: Tarsus*   3 litigious contentious   **4 Take . . . you** i.e. I cannot thank you
enough, the gods will fully reward you   **6 shakes of fortune** damaging shocks delivered by
fortune   **haunt you mortally** pursue you with lethal intent   **7 glance . . . us** touch us and
amaze us   **13 Marina** "child of the sea" (from Latin *mare*)   **15 charge . . . withal** entrust to
your kindness/burden your kindness with   **16 of** in   **17 she . . . born** her behavior may
match her high status   **20 for . . . fall** the people constantly bless Pericles/the people should
always bless Pericles   **21 neglection** negligence   **22 common body** people of Tarsus
24 that i.e. that duty   **a spur** encouragement

25   The gods revenge it upon me and mine,
        To the end of generation.

PERICLES   I believe you: your honour and your goodness
        Teach me to't without your vows. Till she be married,
        Madam, by bright Diana whom we honour all,
30   Unscissored shall this hair of mine remain,
        Though I show ill in't. So I take my leave:
        Good madam, make me blessèd in your care
        In bringing up my child.

DIONYZA   I have one myself,
35   Who shall not be more dear to my respect
        Than yours, my lord.

PERICLES   Madam, my thanks and prayers.

CLEON   We'll bring your grace e'en to the edge o'th'shore,
        Then give you up to the masked Neptune, and
40   The gentlest winds of heaven.

PERICLES   I will embrace your offer. Come, dearest madam.—
        O, no tears, Lychorida, no tears!   *To Lychorida*
        Look to your little mistress, on whose grace
        You may depend hereafter.— Come, my lord.   [*Exeunt*]

[Act 3 Scene 4]   *running scene 13*

Enter Cerimon and Thaisa

CERIMON   Madam, this letter and some certain jewels
        Lay with you in your coffer, which are
        At your command. Know you the character?   *Shows the letter*

THAISA   It is my lord's. That I was shipped at sea
5   I well remember, even on my eaning time,
        But whether there delivered, by the holy gods
        I cannot rightly say. But since King Pericles,

---

26 To . . . generation until all procreation stops/until Cleon's descendants die out   **28 to't** to do it   **31 show ill in't** (shall) look unattractive   **32 blessèd** fortunate   **35 respect** esteem, fondness/care, attention   **39 masked** deceptively calm/withdrawn   **3.4** *Location: Ephesus*   **2 coffer** coffin   **3 character** handwriting   **4 shipped at** sent to   **5 even on** just at   **eaning time** time of giving birth (**eaning** means "lambing," but writers also use it of humans)   **6 whether there delivered** whether I gave birth there   **7 rightly** accurately

My wedded lord, I ne'er shall see again,
A vestal livery will I take me to
10   And never more have joy.

CERIMON   Madam, if this you purpose as ye speak,
Diana's temple is not distant far,
Where you may abide till your date expire.
Moreover, if you please, a niece of mine
15   Shall there attend you.

THAISA   My recompense is thanks, that's all,
Yet my good will is great, though the gift small.   *Exeunt*

[Act 4 Chorus]   *running scene 14*

Enter Gower

GOWER   Imagine Pericles arrived at Tyre,
Welcomed and settled to his own desire.
His woeful queen we leave at Ephesus,
Unto Diana there's a votaress.
5   Now to Marina bend your mind,
Whom our fast-growing scene must find
At Tarsus, and by Cleon trained
In music's letters, who hath gained
Of education all the grace,
10   Which makes her both the heart and place
Of general wonder. But, alack,
That monster envy, oft the wrack
Of earnèd praise, Marina's life
Seeks to take off by treason's knife,
15   And in this kind: our Cleon hath
One daughter and a full grown wench

---

9 **vestal livery** a virgin priestess's clothing; Vestal Virgins tended the sacred fire in the temple of Vesta, Roman goddess of the hearth   11 **this . . . speak** you mean to do as you say
13 **abide . . . expire** stay for the rest of your life   16 **recompense** payment   **4 Chorus   2 to** in accordance with   **4 there's** there is/there as   **votaress** priestess   5 **bend** direct, turn
6 **fast-growing** i.e. because fourteen years have passed   8 **music's letters** the study of music
10 **heart and place** focal point   12 **wrack** ruin, destruction   13 **earnèd** justified   15 **kind** manner

Even ripe for marriage-rite. This maid
Hight Philoten, and it is said
For certain in our story she
20 Would ever with Marina be,
Be't when they weaved the sleided silk,
With fingers long, small, white as milk,
Or when she would with sharp nee'le wound
The cambric which she made more sound
25 By hurting it, or when to th'lute
She sung, and made the night-bird mute
That still records with moan, or when
She would with rich and constant pen,
Vail to her mistress Dian. Still
30 This Philoten contends in skill
With absolute Marina: so
With dove of Paphos might the crow
Vie feathers white. Marina gets
All praises, which are paid as debts
35 And not as given. This so darks
In Philoten all graceful marks
That Cleon's wife with envy rare
A present murder does prepare
For good Marina, that her daughter
40 Might stand peerless by this slaughter.
The sooner her vile thoughts to stead,
Lychorida, our nurse, is dead,
And cursèd Dionyza hath

---

17 **ripe** mature/sexually available   18 **Hight** is called (deliberately archaic)   **Philoten** the
name is taken from Gower's *Confessio Amantis*   19 **For certain** assuredly   21 **sleided** variant
of "sleaved": (of silk) separated into threads to be used in weaving or embroidery   22 **small**
slender   23 **nee'le** needle   24 **cambric** fine white linen originally made in Cambrai, France
sound strong (the embroidery covers the fabric, making it stronger)   26 **night-bird**
nightingale   27 **records with moan** sings in a mournful fashion/recalls sadly; alludes to the
classical legend of Philomela, raped by her brother-in-law Tereus and eventually transformed
into a nightingale   28 **rich** eloquent   **constant** consistent/loyal   29 **Vail** pay homage
31 **absolute** incomparable   32 **dove of Paphos** white dove sacred to Venus, who rose from
the waves near Paphos in Cyprus   33 **Vie feathers white** compete to see which had the whiter
feathers   35 **as given** as compliments   **darks** eclipses   36 **graceful marks** attractive
characteristics/signs of virtue   37 **rare** exceptional   38 **present** immediate   41 **stead** assist

The pregnant instrument of wrath
45 Pressed for this blow. The unborn event
I do commend to your content,
Only I carry wingèd Time,
Post on the lame feet of my rhyme,
Which never could I so convey
50 Unless your thoughts went on my way.
Dionyza does appear
With Leonine a murderer.   *Exit*

[Act 4 Scene 1]   *running scene 15*

Enter Dionyza with Leonine

DIONYZA   Thy oath remember, thou hast sworn to do't.
'Tis but a blow, which never shall be known,
Thou canst not do a thing in the world so soon
To yield thee so much profit. Let not conscience,
5 Which is but cold, inflame love in thy bosom,
Nor let pity, which even women have cast off,
Melt thee, but be a soldier to thy purpose.

LEONINE   I will do't, but yet she is a goodly creature.

DIONYZA   The fitter then the gods should have her.
10 Here she comes weeping for her only mistress' death —
Thou art resolved?

LEONINE   I am resolved.

Enter Marina with a basket of flowers

MARINA   No: I will rob Tellus of her weed
To strew thy green with flowers, the yellows, blues,
15 The purple violets, and marigolds,

---

44 **pregnant** ready/compliant   45 **Pressed** pushed forward/forced into service   46 **content**
pleasure (in watching the play)   47 **wingèd Time** Time was represented as an old man with
wings   48 **Post** quickly   **lame . . . rhyme** halting verse   **feet** metrical units   49 **never . . .
way** I could not express (**convey**) without the help of your imaginations   **4.1   *Location:***
Tarsus   3 **soon** quickly   5 **love** i.e. love for Marina   7 **be . . . purpose** behave like a soldier
and do your job   8 **goodly** attractive   9 **fitter** more appropriate   10 **only** one and only
11 **Thou art resolved** you have decided   13 **Tellus** Roman goddess of the earth   **weed**
garment, clothing; plays on sense of "plant"   14 **green** the green grass of the grave

Shall as a carpet hang upon thy grave
While summer days doth last. Ay me, poor maid,
Born in a tempest when my mother died,
This world to me is as a lasting storm,
20   Whirring me from my friends.

DIONYZA   How now, Marina, why do you keep alone?
How chance my daughter is not with you?
Do not consume your blood with sorrowing,
Have you a nurse of me! Lord, how your favour's
25   Changed with this unprofitable woe!
Come, give me your flowers, o'er the sea margent
Walk with Leonine. The air is quick there
And it pierces and sharpens the stomach.
Come, Leonine, take her by the arm, walk with her.
30   MARINA   No, I pray you, I'll not bereave you of your servant.

DIONYZA   Come, come.
I love the king your father and yourself
With more than foreign heart. We every day
Expect him here: when he shall come and find
35   Our paragon, to all reports, thus blasted,
He will repent the breadth of his great voyage,
Blame both my lord and me, that we have taken
No care to your best courses. Go, I pray you,
Walk and be cheerful once again, reserve
40   That excellent complexion, which did steal
The eyes of young and old. Care not for me,
I can go home alone.

MARINA   Well, I will go,
But yet I have no desire to it.

---

17 **Ay me** alas   19 **lasting** perpetual   20 **Whirring** rushing/whirling   21 **How now** what is
the matter   **keep** remain   22 **How chance** how does it happen that   23 **sorrowing** sighing
(thought to waste the blood and cause ill-health)   24 **Have . . . me** make me your nurse
favour's appearance is   26 **o'er . . . margent** along the edge of the sea (i.e. on the seashore)
27 **quick** invigorating   28 **stomach** appetite   33 **With . . . heart** i.e. as if we were relatives/of
the same nation   35 **Our . . . reports** our unequaled beauty, as all agree (**paragon** plays on
sense of "rival")   **blasted** blighted/withered   38 **courses** interests   39 **reserve** preserve

45   **DIONYZA**   Come, come, I know 'tis good for you.

               Walk half an hour, Leonine, at the least.

               Remember what I have said.

  LEONINE   I warrant you, madam.

  DIONYZA   I'll leave you, my sweet lady, for a while.

50   Pray walk softly, do not heat your blood.

               What, I must have care of you!

  MARINA   My thanks, sweet madam.—   [*Exit Dionyza*]

               Is this wind westerly that blows?

  LEONINE   South-west.

55   **MARINA**   When I was born the wind was north.

  LEONINE   Was't so?

  MARINA   My father, as nurse says, did never fear,

               But cried 'Good seamen' to the sailors,

               Galling his kingly hands haling ropes,

60   And clasping to the mast endured a sea

               That almost burst the deck.

  LEONINE   When was this?

  MARINA   When I was born.

               Never was waves nor wind more violent,

65   And from the ladder tackle washes off

               A canvas climber. 'Ha,' says one, 'wolt out?'

               And with a dropping industry they skip

               From stem to stern, the boatswain whistles, and

               The master calls and trebles their confusion.

70   **LEONINE**   Come, say your prayers.

  MARINA   What mean you?

  LEONINE   If you require a little space for prayer,

               I grant it. Pray, but be not tedious,

               For the gods are quick of ear and I am sworn

75   To do my work with haste.

  MARINA   Why will you kill me?

---

48 warrant promise/assure   **50 softly** slowly/gently   **heat your blood** overexert yourself
59 Galling chafing, rubbing   **haling** pulling, hauling   **65 ladder tackle** ropes or a rope ladder in the rigging of the ship   **66 canvas climber** sailor climbing in the rigging   **wolt out?** are you going?   **67 dropping** dripping   **industry** toil, labor   **68 stem to stern** from the front to the back of the ship   **boatswain** ship's chief officer

LEONINE	To satisfy my lady.
MARINA	Why, would she have me killed, now?

       As I can remember, by my troth,

80   I never did her hurt in all my life.

       I never spake bad word, nor did ill turn

       To any living creature. Believe me, la,

       I never killed a mouse nor hurt a fly.

       I trod upon a worm against my will,

85   But I wept for't. How have I offended,

       Wherein my death might yield her any profit

       Or my life imply her any danger?

LEONINE   My commission

       Is not to reason of the deed, but do't.

90 MARINA   You will not do't for all the world, I hope.

       You are well favoured, and your looks foreshow

       You have a gentle heart. I saw you lately

       When you caught hurt in parting two that fought.

       Good sooth, it showed well in you. Do so now:

95   Your lady seeks my life, come you between

       And save poor me, the weaker.

LEONINE   I am sworn and will dispatch.   *Seizes her*

Enter Pirates   *Leonine runs away*

FIRST PIRATE   Hold, villain!

SECOND PIRATE   A prize, a prize!

100 THIRD PIRATE   Half part, mates, half part! Come, let's have her

       aboard suddenly.   *Exeunt [Pirates with Marina]*

Enter Leonine

LEONINE   These roguing thieves serve the great pirate Valdes,

       And they have seized Marina. Let her go,

       There's no hope she will return — I'll swear she's dead,

105   And thrown into the sea. But I'll see further.

---

79 by my troth a mild expletive, meaning "by my faith"   **troth** truth   **82 la** an exclamation
(like "indeed")   **88 commission** order   **91 well favoured** of a good appearance/pleasant-
looking   **foreshow** indicate   **93 caught hurt** received an injury   **94 Good sooth** in good
truth (a mild expletive)   **99 prize** ship or property captured at sea   **100 Half part** fair shares
(either in selling Marina or in raping her)   **have** carry   **101 suddenly** immediately
102 roguing villainous   **Valdes** may refer to Pedro de Valdes, a Spanish admiral in the
Armada fleet of 1588

> Perhaps they will but please themselves upon her,
> Not carry her aboard. If she remain,
> Whom they have ravished must by me be slain.   *Exit*

[Act 4 Scene 2]

Enter the three bawds: [*Pander, Bawd and Bolt*]

PANDER Bolt.

BOLT Sir.

PANDER Search the market narrowly. Mytilene is full of gallants, we lost too much money this mart by being too
5 wenchless.

BAWD We were never so much out of creatures. We have but poor three, and they can do no more than they can do, and they with continual action are even as good as rotten.

PANDER Therefore let's have fresh ones, whate'er we pay for
10 them. If there be not a conscience to be used in every trade, we shall never prosper.

BAWD Thou say'st true. 'Tis not our bringing up of poor bastards — as I think, I have brought up some eleven—

BOLT Ay, to eleven, and brought them down again. But
15 shall I search the market?

BAWD What else, man? The stuff we have, a strong wind will blow it to pieces, they are so pitifully sodden.

---

106 please themselves upon i.e. rape   **108 ravished** abducted/raped   **4.2** *Location:* **Mytilene**   **three bawds** the term "bawd" (one who sells another person for sex) could still be used of both sexes   ***Pander*** a stereotypical name for a male bawd, derived from Pandarus, who brought Troilus and Cressida together   ***Bolt*** a projectile or a pin for fastening (both with phallic associations), "to bolt" means "to sift"   **3 narrowly** carefully   **Mytilene** chief town of the Greek island of Lesbos   **4 gallants** fashionable young men   **mart** market   **6 creatures** servants (i.e. whores)   **7 but poor three** only three   **8 action** sexual action   **rotten** diseased ("rot" means venereal disease)   **9 fresh** inexperienced/undiseased   **10 If . . . trade** if we don't conscientiously provide our customers with good products (**conscience** also carries sexual puns: to have a ready **conscience** is to have an erection, and **con** is a slang term for the vagina)   **12 'Tis . . . bastards** i.e. bringing up the prostitutes' bastard children does not make us a profit   **14 to . . . again** and lowered them to prostitution as soon as they turned eleven   **16 stuff** prostitutes (used to refer to the genitals and to goods)   **17 blow . . . pieces** make them fall apart/disintegrate as a result of syphilis   **sodden** suffering from syphilis (i.e. stewed, as if in a sweating tub)

PANDER   Thou say'st true, they're too unwholesome, o'conscience: the poor Transylvanian is dead that lay with
20   the little baggage.

BOLT   Ay, she quickly pooped him, she made him roast meat for worms. But I'll go search the market.   *Exit*

PANDER   Three or four thousand chequins were as pretty a proportion to live quietly, and so give over.

25   BAWD   Why to give over, I pray you? Is it a shame to get when we are old?

PANDER   O, our credit comes not in like the commodity, nor the commodity wages not with the danger. Therefore, if in our youths we could pick up some pretty estate, 'twere not amiss
30   to keep our door hatched. Besides, the sore terms we stand upon with the gods will be strong with us for giving o'er.

BAWD   Come, other sorts offend as well as we.

PANDER   As well as we, ay, and better too. We offend worse: neither is our profession any trade, it's no calling. But here
35   comes Bolt.

Enter Bolt with the Pirates and Marina

BOLT   Come your ways, my masters. You say she's a virgin?

FIRST PIRATE   O, sir, we doubt it not.

BOLT   Master, I have gone through for this piece you see. If you like her, so. If not, I have lost my earnest.

40   BAWD   Bolt, has she any qualities?

---

18 unwholesome diseased   **19 o'conscience** on my conscience (a mild expletive)
20 baggage slut   **21 pooped** infected or killed with venereal disease ("poop" is a slang term
for female genitals)   **roast . . . worms** a meal for worms   **roast meat** a body corrupted by
venereal disease   **23 chequins** Italian gold coins (*zecchini*), worth between seven shillings and
nine shillings and sixpence   **24 proportion** portion/fortune   **give over** i.e. retire   **25 get**
gain/make money (can also mean breed/copulate)   **27 our . . . danger** a good reputation isn't
gained as easily as profits (**commodity**), nor do the profits measure up to the risks (with a pun
on **commodity**, referring to the whores)   **28 if . . . hatched** if we could earn enough while we
were young, it would not be a mistake to close our door to business   **30 sore** severe
31 the . . . o'er the gods' disapproval should encourage us to retire   **32 sorts** kinds/social
ranks/professions   **as . . . we** in addition to us; Pander takes it to mean "as skillfully as we do"
34 profession career; puns on "profession" in the sense of "declaration of love"   **calling**
vocation   **36 Come your ways** come along   **38 gone through** bargained (puns on "go," to
copulate)   **piece** piece of flesh: a pejorative term for a woman or girl   **39 so** well and good
earnest deposit   **40 qualities** accomplishments

BOLT   She has a good face, speaks well, and has excellent
good clothes: there's no further necessity of qualities can
make her be refused.

BAWD   What's her price, Bolt?

45 BOLT   I cannot be bated one doit of a thousand pieces.

PANDER   Well, follow me, my masters, you shall have your
money presently. Wife, take her in, instruct her what she has
to do, that she may not be raw in her entertainment.

[Exeunt Pander and the Pirates]

BAWD   Bolt, take you the marks of her — the colour of her
50 hair, complexion, height, her age — with warrant of her
virginity, and cry: 'He that will give most shall have her first.'
Such a maidenhead were no cheap thing, if men were as
they have been. Get this done as I command you.

BOLT   Performance shall follow.   *Exit*

55 MARINA   Alack that Leonine was so slack, so slow:
He should have struck, not spoke. Or that these pirates,
Not enough barbarous, had but o'erboard thrown me,
For to seek my mother.

BAWD   Why lament you, pretty one?

60 MARINA   That I am pretty.

BAWD   Come, the gods have done their part in you.

MARINA   I accuse them not.

BAWD   You are light into my hands, where you are like to
live.

MARINA   The more my fault,
65 To scape his hands, where I was like to die.

BAWD   Ay, and you shall live in pleasure.

MARINA   No.

---

42 there's . . . refused i.e. these are all the qualities she needs   **45 be bated** get it reduced (by)
doit a small Dutch coin, worth around one-eighth of a penny (i.e. a negligible amount)
pieces gold pieces (often refers to the *unite* of James I, worth about twenty shillings)
47 presently immediately   **48 raw** unpolished   **entertainment** reception of her clients
49 marks characteristics   **50 warrant** assurance/guarantee   **54 Performance shall follow** I
will do as you say (puns on sexual **performance**)   **61 done their part** done well by you/fulfilled
their obligations in you   **63 are light** have fallen (**light** can also mean wanton/promiscuous)
like likely   **64 fault** misfortune

BAWD   Yes indeed shall you, and taste gentlemen of all
fashions. You shall fare well, you shall have the difference of
70   all complexions. What, do you stop your ears?

MARINA   Are you a woman?

BAWD   What would you have me be, an I be not a woman?

MARINA   An honest woman, or not a woman.

BAWD   Marry, whip the gosling! I think I shall have
75   something to do with you. Come, you're a young foolish
sapling and must be bowed as I would have you.

MARINA   The gods defend me!

BAWD   If it please the gods to defend you by men, then men
must comfort you, men must feed you, men stir you up.

[*Enter Bolt*]

80   Bolt's returned. Now, sir, hast thou cried her through the
market?

BOLT   I have cried her almost to the number of her hairs, I
have drawn her picture with my voice.

BAWD   And I prithee tell me, how dost thou find the
85   inclination of the people, especially of the younger sort?

BOLT   Faith, they listened to me as they would have
hearkened to their fathers' testament. There was a Spaniard's
mouth watered, and he went to bed to her very description.

BAWD   We shall have him here tomorrow with his best
90   ruff on.

BOLT   Tonight, tonight! But mistress, do you know the
French knight, that cowers i'th'hams?

BAWD   Who, Monsieur Veroles?

---

68 taste have sexual knowledge of   **of all fashions** of all kinds/manners   **69 difference**
range/variety   **70 complexions** constitutions/appearances   **72 an** if   **73 honest** chaste/
respectable   **74 Marry** by the Virgin Mary (a mild oath)   **whip the gosling** confound the little
fool; prostitutes were called geese, so a **gosling** might be a young or inexperienced prostitute
75 something . . . you have some trouble with you (with a sexual pun on do)   **76 sapling** a
young tree   **bowed** made to bend   **78 by** by means of   **79 comfort** give (sexual pleasure) to
feed sexually gratify   **stir you up** arouse you   **80 cried her** advertised her   **82 almost . . .
hairs** in minute detail/any number of times   **87 testament** will   **88 went . . . to** was aroused
by   **89 his best ruff** may indicate the Spaniard's pleasure at the report of Marina and has
further sexual connotations: ruff was frequently used to refer to the female genitalia, and a
torn ruff could be an emblem of the wearer's moral frailty   **91 Tonight, tonight!** i.e. he'll be
here tonight   **92 cowers i'th'hams** is bowlegged, indicating his sexual debility   **93 Veroles**
from French *vérole*, "syphilis"

BOLT   Ay, he. He offered to cut a caper at the proclamation,
95   but he made a groan at it, and swore he would see her
tomorrow.

BAWD   Well, well. As for him, he brought his disease hither,
here he does but repair it. I know he will come in our shadow
to scatter his crowns in the sun.

100   BOLT   Well, if we had of every nation a traveller, we
should lodge them with this sign.

BAWD   Pray you, come hither awhile. You have   *To Marina*
fortunes coming upon you. Mark me, you must seem to do
that fearfully which you commit willingly, despise profit
105   where you have most gain. To weep that you live as ye do
makes pity in your lovers. Seldom but that pity begets you a
good opinion, and that opinion a mere profit.

MARINA   I understand you not.

BOLT   O, take her home, mistress, take her home! These
110   blushes of hers must be quenched with some present practice.

BAWD   Thou say'st true, i'faith, so they must, for your bride
goes to that with shame which is her way to go with warrant.

BOLT   Faith, some do, and some do not. But mistress, if I
have bargained for the joint—

115   BAWD   Thou mayst cut a morsel off the spit.

BOLT   I may so.

BAWD   Who should deny it?— Come, young one,   *To Marina*
I like the manner of your garments well.

BOLT   Ay, by my faith, they shall not be changed yet.

---

94 offered attempted   cut a caper leap or dance for joy; to caper can also mean to
fornicate   95 he . . . it the attempt made him groan in pain   97 he . . . hither he was
already suffering from syphilis   98 repair cure/renew   in our shadow under our roof
99 scatter . . . sun refers to the baldness caused by syphilis and to French gold coins
100 traveller visitor (puns on "travail," painful or laborious effort, used as a euphemism for
sexual activity)   101 lodge house/intercept   this sign either the sign of the brothel or
Marina herself   102 You . . . you i.e. you will earn a lot of money (with a sexual pun on
coming upon)   104 despise seem to despise   106 makes encourages   107 mere clear
109 take her home talk plainly to her   110 present immediate   practice sexual activity
112 shame modesty/reluctance   which . . . warrant which she is entitled to do (may refer to
the bride or to Marina)   113 Faith . . . not i.e. some of the brides are bashful, others are not
115 cut . . . spit cut some meat from the joint while it is still roasting/have sex with Marina
before the customers do   118 manner fashion

| 120 | BAWD | Bolt, spend thou that in the town.   *Gives money* |

Report what a sojourner we have, you'll lose nothing by custom. When Nature framed this piece, she meant thee a good turn, therefore say what a paragon she is, and thou hast the harvest out of thine own report.

| 125 | BOLT | I warrant you, mistress, thunder shall not so awake the beds of eels as my giving out her beauty stirs up the lewdly inclined. I'll bring home some tonight.   [*Exit*] |

| | BAWD | Come your ways, follow me.   *To Marina* |

	MARINA	If fires be hot, knives sharp or waters deep,
130		Untried I still my virgin knot will keep.
		Diana, aid my purpose!

| | BAWD | What have we to do with Diana? Pray you, will you go with us?   *Exeunt* |

[Act 4 Scene 3]
running scene 17

Enter Cleon and Dionyza

	DIONYZA	Why, are you foolish, can it be undone?
	CLEON	O Dionyza, such a piece of slaughter
		The sun and moon ne'er looked upon.
	DIONYZA	I think you'll turn a child again.
5	CLEON	Were I chief lord of all this spacious world,
		I'd give it to undo the deed. O lady,
		Much less in blood than virtue, yet a princess
		To equal any single crown o'th'earth
		I'th'justice of compare. O villain
10		Leonine, whom thou hast poisoned too,

---

121 **sojourner** guest   **you'll . . . custom** i.e. the greater number of customers they have, the more Bolt will earn in tips   122 **this piece** i.e. Marina   **piece** girl/masterpiece   123 **good turn** favor/good sexual experience   **paragon** embodiment of perfection   125 **warrant** promise/assure   **thunder . . . inclined** just as thunder rouses eels from the mud, the description of Marina will (sexually) arouse the brothel's customers (the phallic **eels** are paralleled with the customers' penises)   126 **giving out** advertising   **stirs up** arouses   127 **lewdly inclined** lecherous   128 **Come your ways** come along   130 **Untried . . . keep** i.e. I will protect my virginity   131 **aid my purpose** i.e. help me   **4.3** *Location: Tarsus*   7 **blood** rank/social status   8 **crown** ruler   9 **I'th'justice of compare** in a fair comparison

If thou hadst drunk to him 't'ad been a kindness
Becoming well thy face. What canst thou say
When noble Pericles shall demand his child?

DIONYZA   That she is dead. Nurses are not the Fates,
15   To foster it, not ever to preserve.
She died at night, I'll say so — who can cross it
Unless you play the impious innocent,
And for an honest attribute, cry out
'She died by foul play.'

20 **CLEON**   O, go to! Well, well,
Of all the faults beneath the heavens, the gods
Do like this worst.

DIONYZA   Be one of those that thinks
The petty wrens of Tarsus will fly hence
25   And open this to Pericles. I do shame
To think of what a noble strain you are,
And of how coward a spirit.

CLEON   To such proceeding
Whoever but his approbation added,
30   Though not his prime consent, he did not flow
From honourable courses.

DIONYZA   Be it so, then.
Yet none does know but you how she came dead,
Nor none can know, Leonine being gone.
35   She did disdain my child, and stood between
Her and her fortunes: none would look on her,
But cast their gazes on Marina's face,
Whilst ours was blurted at and held a malkin
Not worth the time of day. It pierced me through,

---

11 **drunk . . . face** if Dionyza had merely toasted him, sparing his life, it would have been an act
that suited her appearance better   14 **Nurses . . . preserve** those who look after a child
cannot control its destiny as the Fates can, to raise it is not to make it live forever   16 **cross**
deny   18 **for . . . attribute** to get a reputation for honesty   20 **go to** an expression of
irritation   24 **petty . . . Pericles** alludes to the folklore tradition in which secret murders are
revealed by birds   **petty** small/weak   **hence** from here   25 **open** reveal   29 **but . . .**
consent merely gave his approval, not his initial consent   **approbation** expression of approval
30 **did not** would not   **flow . . . courses** derive from honorable origins (**courses**)   33 **came**
dead i.e. came to be dead   38 **blurted at** derided   **malkin** wench/slut   39 **Not . . . day** not
worth greeting

40   And though you call my course unnatural,
      You not your child well loving, yet I find
      It greets me as an enterprise of kindness
      Performed to your sole daughter.

CLEON   Heavens forgive it!

45 DIONYZA   And as for Pericles, what should he say?
      We wept after her hearse, and yet we mourn.
      Her monument is almost finished, and her epitaphs
      In glitt'ring golden characters express
      A general praise to her, and care in us
50   At whose expense 'tis done.

CLEON   Thou art like the harpy,
      Which to betray, dost with thine angel's face
      Seize with thine eagle's talons.

DIONYZA   Ye're like one that superstitiously
55   Do swear to th'gods that winter kills the flies.
      But yet I know, you'll do as I advise.   [*Exeunt*]

[Act 4 Second Chorus]   *running scene 18*

Enter Gower

GOWER   Thus time we waste and long leagues make short,
      Sail seas in cockles, have and wish but for't,
      Making to take our imagination,
      From bourn to bourn, region to region.

5   By you being pardoned we commit no crime
      To use one language in each several clime

---

40 course course of action   **41 You . . . loving** i.e. because you don't love your own child very much   **42 greets me** presents itself to me   **enterprise of kindness** action motivated by natural affection   **46 yet** still   **47 epitaphs** inscriptions on her tomb   **48 characters** letters **49 general** universal   **51 like . . . talons** like the treacherous harpy, which uses its angelic face to deceive its victims, giving it the opportunity to seize them with its eagle's talons   **harpy** mythological creature with a woman's face and torso and a bird of prey's wings and claws **55 swear . . . flies** complain to the gods about something as natural as the winter killing flies/ blame the death of flies on winter, rather than acknowledging your own guilt   **4 Second Chorus   1 waste** quickly pass over   **leagues** distances (a **league** is around three miles) **2 cockles** seashells/small shell-shaped boats   **and . . . for't** just by wishing for it   **3 Making to** proceeding to (usually applied to ships)   **4 bourn** boundary/limit   **6 several** different **clime** country/region

Where our scenes seems to live. I do beseech you
To learn of me, who stand i'th'gaps to teach you
The stages of our story. Pericles
10   Is now again thwarting the wayward seas,
Attended on by many a lord and knight,
To see his daughter, all his life's delight.
Old Helicanus goes along: behind
Is left to govern, if you bear in mind,
15   Old Escanes, whom Helicanus late
Advanced in time to great and high estate.
Well-sailing ships and bounteous winds have brought
This king to Tarsus. Think his pilot thought,
So with his steerage shall your thoughts go on
20   To fetch his daughter home, who first is gone.
Like motes and shadows see them move awhile,
Your ears unto your eyes I'll reconcile.

Dumb show

Enter Pericles at one door with all his train, Cleon and Dionyza at the
other. Cleon shows Pericles the tomb, whereat Pericles makes
lamentation, puts on sack-cloth, and in a mighty passion departs.

[*Exeunt Cleon and Dionyza*]

GOWER   See how belief may suffer by foul show:
This borrowed passion stands for true old woe.
25   And Pericles in sorrow all devoured,
With sighs shot through and biggest tears o'ershowered,
Leaves Tarsus and again embarks. He swears
Never to wash his face nor cut his hairs.
He puts on sackcloth, and to sea he bears
30   A tempest which his mortal vessel tears,
And yet he rides it out. Now please you wit

8 i'th'gaps in time gaps (between the scenes represented)   9 stages . . . story i.e. both the
periods of time and the places in which events occurred   10 thwarting crossing/defying
wayward contrary/hostile   15 late recently   16 time due time   18 Think . . . on imagine
that thought pilots Pericles, and let your imagination go with the steering of his ship
21 motes specks of dust/particles   shadows spirits/illusions   22 Your . . . reconcile i.e. I'll
explain what you see   23 foul show hypocrisy   24 borrowed pretended/assumed   stands
for stands in for   29 bears carries (with him/inside him)   30 tempest i.e. raging emotions
mortal vessel i.e. his body   31 rides it out survives it   wit understand/be assured (perhaps
archaic)

The epitaph is for Marina writ
By wicked Dionyza:
'The fairest, sweetest and best lies here,   *Reads*
35   Who withered in her spring of year:
She was of Tyrus the king's daughter
On whom foul death hath made this slaughter.
Marina was she called, and at her birth
Thetis, being proud, swallowed some part o'th'earth.
40   Therefore the earth, fearing to be o'erflowed,
Hath Thetis' birth-child on the heavens bestowed.
Wherefore she does, and swears she'll never stint,
Make raging batt'ry upon shores of flint.'
No visor does become black villainy
45   So well as soft and tender flattery.
Let Pericles believe his daughter's dead,
And bear his courses to be orderèd
By Lady Fortune, while our scene must play
His daughter's woe and heavy well-a-day
50   In her unholy service. Patience, then,
And think you now are all in Mytilene.   *Exit*

[Act 4 Scene 4]   *running scene 19*

Enter two Gentlemen   *From the brothel*

FIRST GENTLEMAN   Did you ever hear the like?

SECOND GENTLEMAN   No, nor never shall do in such a place as
this, she being once gone.

FIRST GENTLEMAN   But to have divinity preached there — did you
5   ever dream of such a thing?

---

32 **is** that is   39 **Thetis . . . bestowed** the sea (**Thetis**—a sea nymph and the mother of the
Greek hero Achilles, often confused [as here] with Tethys, the sister and wife of Oceanus)
swelled with pride at the birth of Marina (**Thetis' birth-child**), and the land, afraid of being
swamped (**o'erflowed**), decided to give Marina to the heavens   42 **she** i.e. Thetis   **stint** cease
43 **Make . . . flint** furiously beating against the rocky shore   44 **visor** mask   47 **bear** permit
courses life (with a nautical pun: a **course** is the direction in which a ship sails)   **orderèd**
managed/dictated   48 **scene** stage   49 **heavy** sorrowful   **well-a-day** lamentation, grief
4.4   ***Location: Mytilene***   4 **divinity** moral statements/talk about divine things

SECOND GENTLEMAN　No, no. Come, I am for no more bawdy houses, shall's go hear the vestals sing?

FIRST GENTLEMAN　I'll do anything now that is virtuous, but I am out of the road of rutting for ever.　　*Exeunt*

[Act 4 Scene 5]

running scene 19 continues

Enter three bawds [Pander, Bawd and Bolt]

PANDER　Well, I had rather than twice the worth of her she had ne'er come here.

BAWD　Fie, fie upon her, she's able to freeze the god Priapus and undo a whole generation! We must either get her

5　ravished or be rid of her. When she should do for clients her fitment, and do me the kindness of our profession, she has me her quirks, her reasons, her master reasons, her prayers, her knees, that she would make a puritan of the devil if he should cheapen a kiss of her.

10　BOLT　Faith, I must ravish her, or she'll disfurnish us of all our *cavalleria* and make our swearers priests.

PANDER　Now the pox upon her green-sickness for me.

BAWD　Faith, there's no way to be rid on't but by the way to the pox — here comes the lord Lysimachus disguised.

15　BOLT　We should have both lord and loon, if the peevish baggage would but give way to customers.

Enter Lysimachus

---

6 bawdy houses brothels　**7 shall's** shall we ("shall us")　**vestals** Vestal Virgins　**9 road** path; also a euphemism for the vagina　**rutting** sexual activity　**4.5　1 I . . . here** I would rather have lost twice what she is worth than have had her come here　**3 Priapus** god of fertility and lechery　**4 undo . . . generation** prevent the conception of the next generation/ make a whole generation unhappy/ruin us financially　**5 do . . . fitment** do that which is fitting/proper (with a sexual pun on fit)　**6 kindness** goodness/sexual favor　**7 quirks** verbal tricks/quibbles　**master** main/principal　**8 puritan** person with strict (or apparently strict) religious or moral convictions　**9 cheapen** bargain for　**10 disfurnish** strip/deprive　**11 *cavalleria*** society of knights/gentlemen (from Italian), i.e. the regular customers of the brothel　**swearers** people who use bad language/delinquents　**12 green-sickness** chlorosis, an anemic disease (a metaphor for female sexual squeamishness)　**for me** as far as I'm concerned　**13 rid on't** rid of it　**the . . . pox** i.e. sexual intercourse　**15 loon** rogue/ commoner　**peevish** silly/spiteful/perverse/coy　**16 baggage** a worthless or immoral woman/slut　**give way** yield sexually

LYSIMACHUS   How now, how a dozen of virginities?

BAWD   Now the gods to bless your honour!

BOLT   I am glad to see your honour in good health.

20   LYSIMACHUS   You may, so: 'tis the better for you that your resorters stand upon sound legs. How now? Wholesome iniquity have you, that a man may deal withal and defy the surgeon?

BAWD   We have here one, sir, if she would — but there

25   never came her like in Mytilene.

LYSIMACHUS   If she'd do the deeds of darkness, thou wouldst say.

BAWD   Your honour knows what 'tis to say well enough.

LYSIMACHUS   Well, call forth, call forth.

[Exit Pander]

BOLT   For flesh and blood, sir, white and red, you shall see

30   a rose, and she were a rose indeed, if she had but —

LYSIMACHUS   What, prithee?

BOLT   O, sir, I can be modest.

LYSIMACHUS   That dignifies the renown of a bawd, no less than it gives a good report to a number to be chaste.

[Enter Pander with Marina]

35   BAWD   Here comes that which grows to the stalk — never plucked yet, I can assure you. Is she not a fair creature?

LYSIMACHUS   Faith, she would serve after a long voyage at sea. Well, there's for you. Leave us.   *Gives money*

BAWD   I beseech your honour, give me leave: a word, and

40   I'll have done presently.

17 how how much for   18 the . . . bless I pray the gods to bless/may the gods bless entirely
20 that . . . legs if your clients (**resorters**) appear healthy (**sound**) (with a sexual pun on **stand**)
21 Wholesome iniquity healthy sin   22 deal withal have sexual dealings with   26 deeds of
darkness sexual acts (a common euphemism)   27 what . . . say what I am saying   29 flesh
woman in a sexual capacity/whore/penis   blood seat of sexual appetite/semen/may also
refer to menstrual or hymeneal blood   white and red a conventional description of female
beauty   30 rose maid/maidenhead   if . . . but— the missing words are probably "a thorn";
Bolt says that Marina is sexually inexperienced: she would be a true rose if only she would have
(i.e. accept) a thorn (i.e. a penis)   32 modest decorous/chaste   33 That . . . chaste i.e.
modesty gives a bawd a good reputation (**renown**), no less than it gives a good character
(**report**) to any number of (probably unchaste) people   35 that . . . yet is a still virgin; Bolt
reduces Marina to her virginity, which is a **rose** whose **stalk** has not yet been broken in being
plucked   37 she . . . sea she would satisfy a sex-starved traveler   40 have done presently be
done soon

LYSIMACHUS   I beseech you, do.

BAWD   First, I would have you note this is an   *To Marina*
honourable man.

MARINA   I desire to find him so, that I may worthily note him.

45 BAWD   Next, he's the governor of this country, and a man
whom I am bound to.

MARINA   If he govern the country you are bound to him
indeed, but how honourable he is in that, I know not.

BAWD   Pray you, without any more virginal fencing, will
50 you use him kindly? He will line your apron with gold.

MARINA   What he will do graciously, I will thankfully receive.

LYSIMACHUS   Ha' you done?

BAWD   My lord, she's not paced yet, you must take some
pains to work her to your manage.— Come, we will leave his
55 honour and her together. Go thy ways.   *To Bolt and Pander*

[*Exeunt Bawd, Bolt and Pander*]

LYSIMACHUS   Now, pretty one, how long have you been at this
trade?

MARINA   What trade, sir?

LYSIMACHUS   Why, I cannot name't but I shall offend.

60 MARINA   I cannot be offended with my trade. Please you to
name it.

LYSIMACHUS   How long have you been of this profession?

MARINA   E'er since I can remember.

LYSIMACHUS   Did you go to't so young? Were you a gamester at
65 five, or at seven?

MARINA   Earlier too, sir, if now I be one.

LYSIMACHUS   Why, the house you dwell in proclaims you to be a
creature of sale.

---

42 note pay attention to the fact that   **44 worthily note** pay due respect to   **46 bound** obliged
47 bound subject   **48 in that** i.e. in his government   **49 virginal fencing** quibbling about/
defense of your virginity   **50 use him kindly** treat him pleasantly/acquiesce to his sexual
needs   **He . . . gold** he will reward you financially and (it is implied) sexually (**line**, copulate
with; white **aprons** were associated with whores)   **51 graciously** virtuously/through divine
grace   **53 she's . . . yet** she hasn't yet been trained sexually   **paced** smooth in her gait (used
of a horse)   **54 work . . . manage** train her   **manage** training of a horse   **55 Go thy ways**
go along   **57 trade** profession, i.e. prostitution (euphemistically referred to as **trade**)   **64 go
to't** i.e. have sexual intercourse   **gamester** prostitute   **68 creature of sale** whore

MARINA   Do you know this house to be a place of such resort,
70   and will come into't? I hear say you're of honourable parts,
         and are the governor of this place.

LYSIMACHUS   Why, hath your principal made known unto you
         who I am?

MARINA   Who is my principal?

75 LYSIMACHUS   Why, your herb-woman, she that sets seeds and
         roots of shame and iniquity. O, you have heard something of
         my power, and so stand aloof for more serious wooing! But I
         protest to thee, pretty one, my authority shall not see thee, or
         else look friendly upon thee. Come, bring me to some private
80   place. Come, come.

MARINA   If you were born to honour, show it now,
         If put upon you, make the judgement good
         That thought you worthy of it.

LYSIMACHUS   How's this? How's this? Some more, be sage.

85 MARINA   For me
         That am a maid, though most ungentle fortune
         Have placed me in this sty, where, since I came,
         Diseases have been sold dearer than physic.
         That the gods
90   Would set me free from this unhallowed place,
         Though they did change me to the meanest bird
         That flies i'th'purer air!

LYSIMACHUS   I did not think thou couldst have spoke so well,
         Ne'er dreamt thou couldst!
95   Had I brought hither a corrupted mind,
         Thy speech had altered it. Hold, here's gold for thee: *Gives gold*

---

69 resort attracting such clientele; "house of resort" is a euphemistic term for a brothel
70 parts qualities   **72 principal** mistress (i.e. the Bawd)   **75 herb-woman** a euphemistic title
for the Bawd, playing on the sexual associations of **seed** and **root** in the following lines
sets . . . iniquity plants and nurtures sinful activities, with sexual puns on **seed** (semen) and
root (penis)   **78 my . . . thee** i.e. I will wink at your offenses   **81 If . . . now** if you were born
to rule, prove it   **82 If . . . it** if you were appointed to rule/have risen to noble status, validate
the judgment of those who thought you worthy of that position   **84 sage** wise/discreet
87 sty brothel   **88 Diseases . . . physic** i.e. it costs more to buy a venereal disease (through
buying a whore) than it does to pay for the treatment   **91 meanest** most humble

Persevere in that clear way thou goest
And the gods strengthen thee!

MARINA   The good gods preserve you.

100   LYSIMACHUS   For me be you thoughten, that I came
With no ill intent, for to me the very doors
And windows savour vilely. Fare thee well —
Thou art a piece of virtue, and I doubt not
But thy training hath been noble.

105   Hold, here's more gold for thee.   *Gives gold*
A curse upon him, die he like a thief
That robs thee of thy goodness. If thou dost
Hear from me it shall be for thy good.

[*Enter Bolt*]

BOLT   I beseech your honour, one piece for me?

110   LYSIMACHUS   Avaunt, thou damned doorkeeper!
Your house, but for this virgin that doth prop it,
Would sink and overwhelm you. Away!   [*Exit*]

BOLT   How's this? We must take another course with you!
If your peevish chastity, which is not worth a breakfast in
115   the cheapest country under the cope, shall undo a whole
household, let me be gelded like a spaniel. Come your ways.

MARINA   Whither would you have me?

BOLT   I must have your maidenhead taken off, or the
common hangman shall execute it. Come your ways, we'll
120   have no more gentlemen driven away. Come your ways, I say.

Enter bawds [*Bawd and Pander*]

BAWD   How now, what's the matter?

BOLT   Worse and worse, mistress. She has here spoken
holy words to the Lord Lysimachus.

BAWD   O, abominable!

---

97 clear blameless/unstained   **100 be you thoughten** assure yourself   **102 savour** smell/
reek   **103 piece of virtue** virtuous woman/outstanding example   **104 training** upbringing/
education   **110 Avaunt** begone/go away   **doorkeeper** pander   **111 prop it** hold it up
113 course course of action   **114 peevish** silly/spiteful/perverse/coy   **115 cope** canopy (the
sky)   **116 spaniel** proverbially submissive dog   **117 Whither . . . me?** what do you want of
me, plays on sexual sense of "have"   **119 hangman . . . it** or I'll have you executed (pun on
maidenhead makes a common equation between sex and death)

125	BOLT	He makes our profession as it were to stink afore the face of the gods.
	BAWD	Marry, hang her up for ever!
	BOLT	The nobleman would have dealt with her like a nobleman, and she sent him away as cold as a snowball,
130		saying his prayers, too.
	BAWD	Bolt, take her away, use her at thy pleasure: crack the glass of her virginity and make the rest malleable.
	BOLT	An if she were a thornier piece of ground than she is, she shall be ploughed.
135	MARINA	Hark, hark you gods!
	BAWD	She conjures! Away with her, would she had never come within my doors. Marry, hang you! She's born to undo us. Will you not go the way of womankind? Marry, come up, my dish of chastity with rosemary and bays!

[*Exeunt Bawd and Pander*]

140	BOLT	Come, mistress, come your way with me.
	MARINA	Whither wilt thou have me?
	BOLT	To take from you the jewel you hold so dear.
	MARINA	Prithee, tell me one thing first.
	BOLT	Come now, your one thing?
145	MARINA	What canst thou wish thine enemy to be?
	BOLT	Why, I could wish him to be my master, or rather my mistress.
	MARINA	Neither of these are so bad as thou art,
		Since they do better thee in their command.
150		Thou hold'st a place for which the painèd'st fiend

---

128 dealt . . . nobleman i.e. liberally (in his sexual behavior and/or his financial reward)
131 crack . . . virginity take her virginity by force (**glass** alludes to the fragility of the hymen and of women's sexual reputation)   **133 An if** if/even if   **thornier . . . ground** i.e. an even more resistant victim (**ground**, woman as land vulnerable to tillage)   **134 ploughed** penetrated/raped   **136 conjures** invokes supernatural aid   **138 Marry, come up** an exclamation used to express indignant or amused surprise or contempt   **139 rosemary** used in cooking and as a decoration at weddings and funerals; recommended by some herbalists to induce menstruation or abortion   **bays** bay leaves are also used in cooking (perhaps puns on bay, vagina)   **142 the jewel** i.e. her virginity   **144 thing** with leering innuendo (**thing** can mean female genitalia)   **145 What . . . be?** i.e. what is the worst thing you could wish upon your enemy   **149 do . . . command** have the advantage of having authority over you   **150 place** position/ job   **painèd'st** most tormented

Of hell would not in reputation change:
Thou art the damned doorkeeper to every
Coistrel that comes inquiring for his Tib.
To the choleric fisting of every rogue
155   Thy ear is liable, thy food is such
As hath been belched on by infected lungs.

BOLT   What would you have me do? Go to the wars,
would you? Where a man may serve seven years for the loss
of a leg, and have not money enough in the end to buy him
160   a wooden one?

MARINA   Do anything but this thou dost. Empty
Old receptacles or common shores of filth,
Serve by indenture to the common hangman:
Any of these ways are yet better than this,
165   For what thou professest a baboon, could he speak,
Would own a name too dear. O, that the gods
Would safely deliver me from this place!
Here, here's gold for thee. If that thy master would
    gain   *Gives gold*
By me, proclaim that I can sing, weave, sew, and dance,
170   With other virtues which I'll keep from boast,
And will undertake all these to teach.
I doubt not but this populous city will
Yield many scholars.

BOLT   But can you teach all this you speak of?

175 MARINA   Prove that I cannot, take me home again
And prostitute me to the basest groom
That doth frequent your house.

BOLT   Well, I will see what I can do for thee.
If I can place thee, I will.

---

151 **change** exchange   152 **doorkeeper** pander   153 **Coistrel** knave, scoundrel   **Tib** whore
(a pet form of "Isabel," a general name for prostitutes)   154 **To . . . liable** you are vulnerable
to the angry attack (**choleric fisting**) of any rogue   155 **thy . . . lungs** i.e. you take nourishment
from something that is unhealthy   158 **would you** would you have me   **for . . . leg** only to
end up losing a leg   162 **receptacles** containers/vessels   **shores** waterside rubbish dumps or
sewage channels   163 **by indenture** on a contract/as an apprentice   165 **professest** make a
profession of   **baboon** baboons were proverbially lustful   166 **own . . . dear** value his
reputation too highly   170 **virtues** accomplishments   176 **basest groom** lowest scoundrel

180 MARINA   But amongst honest women.

BOLT   Faith, my acquaintance lies little amongst them.
          But since my master and mistress hath bought you, there's
          no going but by their consent. Therefore I will make them
          acquainted with your purpose, and I doubt not but I shall
185   find them tractable enough. Come, I'll do for thee what I can.
          Come your ways.   *Exeunt*

[Act 5 Chorus]   *running scene 20*

Enter Gower

GOWER   Marina thus the brothel scapes, and chances
          Into an honest house, our story says.
          She sings like one immortal, and she dances
          As goddess-like to her admirèd lays.
5   Deep clerks she dumbs, and with her nee'le composes
          Nature's own shape of bud, bird, branch or berry,
          That even her art sisters the natural roses,
          Her inkle, silk, twin with the rubied cherry.
          That pupils lacks she none of noble race,
10   Who pour their bounty on her, and her gain
          She gives the cursèd bawd. Here we her place,
          And to her father turn our thoughts again,
          Where we left him on the sea. We there him lost,
          Whence, driven before the winds, he is arrived
15   Here where his daughter dwells, and on this coast
          Suppose him now at anchor. The city strived
          God Neptune's annual feast to keep, from whence
          Lysimachus our Tyrian ship espies,
          His banners sable, trimmed with rich expense,
20   And to him in his barge with fervour hies.

---

180 **honest** virtuous/chaste   181 **my . . . little** I have few friends   185 **tractable** compliant/
cooperative   186 **Come your ways** come along   **5 Chorus**   3 **she . . . goddess-like** i.e. she
dances as well as she sings   4 **lays** songs   5 **Deep** learned/erudite   **clerks** scholars
dumbs reduces to silence   **nee'le** needle   7 **sisters** closely resembles   8 **inkle** linen tape/
linen thread   **silk** silk thread or the silk on which she embroiders   **twin** are identical to
rubied red   19 **His** its   **sable** black (used in heraldry)   20 **hies** hurries

In your supposing once more put your sight
Of heavy Pericles: think this his bark,
Where what is done in action, more if might,
Shall be discovered, please you sit and hark.   *Exit*

[Act 5 Scene 1]   *running scene 21*

Enter Helicanus, to him two Sailors   *One of Tyre and one of Mytilene*

SAILOR OF TYRE   Where is Lord Helicanus? He   *To Sailor of Mytilene*
    can resolve you—
    O, here he is.—
    Sir, there is a barge put off from Mytilene,   *To Helicanus*
    And in it is Lysimachus, the governor,
5 Who craves to come aboard. What is your will?
HELICANUS   That he have his. Call up some gentlemen.
SAILOR OF TYRE   Ho, gentlemen, my lord calls!
Enter two or three Gentlemen   *Of Tyre*
FIRST GENTLEMAN   Doth your lordship call?
HELICANUS   Gentlemen, there is some of worth would come
    aboard.
10   I pray, greet him fairly.
Enter Lysimachus   *And a Lord*
SAILOR OF MYTILENE   Sir,   *To Lysimachus*
    This is the man that can in aught you would
    Resolve you.
LYSIMACHUS   Hail, reverent sir, the gods preserve you.
15 **HELICANUS**   And you, to outlive the age I am
    And die as I would do.
LYSIMACHUS   You wish me well.
    Being on shore, honouring of Neptune's triumphs,
    Seeing this goodly vessel ride before us,
20   I made to it, to know of whence you are.

21 **supposing** imagination   22 **heavy** sorrowful   **bark** ship   23 **what . . . action** i.e. what is
acted   **if might** if it were possible   **5.1** *Location: off the shore of Mytilene*   1 **resolve**
satisfy/answer   9 **some of worth** someone of rank/value   10 **fairly** cordially/politely
12 **aught you would** anything you would like to know   14 **reverent** worthy of respect
16 **die . . . do** i.e. die honorably   18 **triumphs** festivities

HELICANUS   First, what is your place?

LYSIMACHUS   I am the governor of this place you lie before.

HELICANUS   Sir, our vessel is of Tyre, in it the king,

A man, who for this three months hath not spoken

25   To anyone, nor taken sustenance

But to prorogue his grief.

LYSIMACHUS   Upon what ground is his distemperature?

HELICANUS   'Twould be too tedious to repeat,

But the main grief springs from the loss of a

30   Belovèd daughter and a wife.

LYSIMACHUS   May we not see him?

HELICANUS   You may, but bootless is your sight: he will

Not speak to any.

LYSIMACHUS   Yet let me obtain my wish.

35   HELICANUS   Behold him. This was a goodly person.   *Reveals Pericles*

Till the disaster that one mortal night

Drove him to this.

LYSIMACHUS   Sir king, all hail, the gods preserve you!   *To Pericles*

Hail, royal sir!

40   HELICANUS   It is in vain, he will not speak to you.

LORD   Sir, we have a maid in Mytilene, I durst wager

Would win some words of him.

LYSIMACHUS   'Tis well bethought.

She questionless with her sweet harmony

45   And other chosen attractions, would allure

And make a battery through his deafened parts,

Which now are midway stopped,

She is all happy as the fairest of all,

And with her fellow maid is now upon

50   The leafy shelter that abuts against

The island's side.   [*Exit Lord*]

---

21 **place** position/rank   24 **this** the past   26 **prorogue** prolong   27 **Upon . . .
distemperature?** What is the cause of his mental disturbance?   28 **tedious** painful/tiresome
32 **bootless** fruitless/unavailing   36 **mortal** fatal   45 **chosen** choice/special   **allure** win
over   46 **make . . . stopped** i.e. penetrate the parts of his body which are currently so
deafened that attempts to communicate can get only halfway in   48 **all happy** endowed with
all good qualities

HELICANUS   Sure all effectless, yet nothing we'll omit
        That bears recovery's name. But since your kindness
        We have stretched thus far, let us beseech you
55   That for our gold we may provision have,
        Wherein we are not destitute for want
        But weary for the staleness.

LYSIMACHUS   O, sir, a courtesy
        Which if we should deny, the most just gods
60   For every graft would send a caterpillar
        And so inflict our province. Yet once more
        Let me entreat to know at large the cause
        Of your king's sorrow.

HELICANUS   Sit, sir, I will recount it to you—

[*Enter Lord with Marina and her companion*]

65   But see, I am prevented.

LYSIMACHUS   O, here's the lady that I sent for!—
        Welcome, fair one— is't not a goodly present?

HELICANUS   She's a gallant lady.

LYSIMACHUS   She's such a one that, were I well assured
70   Came of a gentle kind and noble stock,
        I'd wish no better choice, and think me rarely wed.
        Fair one, all goodness that consists in beauty
        Expect even here, where is a kingly patient.
        If that thy prosperous and artificial feat
75   Can draw him but to answer thee in aught,
        Thy sacred physic shall receive such pay
        As thy desires can wish.

MARINA   Sir, I will use my utmost skill in his
        Recovery, provided that none but
80   I and my companion maid be suffered
        To come near him.

---

52 **effectless** useless   53 **bears recovery's name** can be called a cure   60 **graft** grafted plant
61 **inflict** afflict (with famine)   62 **at large** without restraint/in detail   67 **present** i.e. gift
which may restore Pericles to health   68 **gallant** fine/splendid   70 **gentle kind** honorable/
descent   **stock** family/ancestry   71 **rarely wed** i.e. married to an exceptional person
72 **consists** is embodied/resides   74 **prosperous** beneficial   **artificial feat** skillful
accomplishment   75 **aught** anything   76 **physic** treatment/medicine   80 **suffered** allowed

LYSIMACHUS   Come, let us leave her, and the gods make her
prosperous.

The Song   *All men except Pericles stand aside while Marina sings*

LYSIMACHUS   Marked he your music?   *Comes forward*

85 MARINA   No, nor looked on us.

LYSIMACHUS   See, she will speak to him.   *Steps back*

MARINA   Hail, sir! My lord, lend ear.

PERICLES   Hum, ha.   *Pushes Marina away*

MARINA   I am a maid,
90 My lord, that ne'er before invited eyes,
But have been gazed on like a comet. She speaks,
My lord, that maybe hath endured a grief
Might equal yours, if both were justly weighed.
Though wayward Fortune did malign my state,
95 My derivation was from ancestors
Who stood equivalent with mighty kings,
But time hath rooted out my parentage,
And to the world and awkward casualties
Bound me in servitude.— I will desist,   *Aside*
100 But there is something glows upon my cheek
And whispers in mine ear, 'Go not till he speak.'

PERICLES   My fortunes — parentage — good parentage —
To equal mine? Was it not thus? What say you?

MARINA   I said, my lord, if you did know my parentage
105 You would not do me violence.

PERICLES   I do think so. Pray you, turn your eyes upon me.
You're like something that — What countrywoman?
Here of these shores?

MARINA   No, nor of any shores,
110 Yet I was mortally brought forth and am
No other than I appear.

---

83 *The Song* see text at end of Textual Notes, p. 97   84 **Marked he** did he notice   93 **justly
weighed** assessed equally   94 **wayward** hostile/erratic   **did . . . state** was hostile toward
my welfare   97 **rooted out** torn up   98 **awkward casualties** perverse mishaps
100 **something . . . ear** i.e. something tells me   **glows** flushes with expectation   107 **What
countrywoman?** i.e. what is your nationality

PERICLES   I am great with woe, and shall deliver weeping.
My dearest wife was like this maid, and such a one
My daughter might have been. My queen's square brows,
115   Her stature to an inch, as wand-like straight,
As silver-voiced, her eyes as jewel-like,
And cased as richly, in pace another Juno,
Who starves the ears she feeds, and makes them hungry
The more she gives them speech. Where do you live?

120   MARINA   Where I am but a stranger: from the deck
You may discern the place.

PERICLES   Where were you bred?
And how achieved you these endowments which
You make more rich to owe?

125   MARINA   If I should tell my history, it would seem
Like lies disdained in the reporting.

PERICLES   Prithee speak,
Falseness cannot come from thee, for thou look'st
Modest as justice, and thou seem'st a palace
130   For the crowned truth to dwell in. I will believe thee
And make senses credit thy relation
To points that seem impossible, for thou look'st
Like one I loved indeed. What were thy friends?
Did'st thou not say when I did push thee back —
135   Which was when I perceived thee — that thou cam'st
From good descending?

MARINA   So indeed I did.

PERICLES   Report thy parentage. I think thou saidst
Thou hadst been tossed from wrong to injury,
140   And that thou thought'st thy griefs might equal mine,
If both were opened.

---

112 **great** pregnant/heavy   **deliver** give birth/speak   114 **square brows** high and broad
forehead   115 **as wand-like straight** as straight as a rod   117 **cased** enclosed   **pace** gait,
movement   **Juno** Roman goddess, wife of Jupiter, renowned for stately beauty
118 **starves . . . speech** i.e. the more she says, the more they want to hear   124 **to owe** by
owning them   129 **Modest as justice** alludes to the virginal goddess of justice, Astraea
thou . . . in i.e. you seem to be virtuous enough for truth to make its home in you
131 **relation** story   132 **To** even to   133 **friends** relatives   141 **opened** revealed/made plain

MARINA   Some such thing I said,
And said no more but what my thoughts
Did warrant me was likely.

145 PERICLES   Tell thy story.
If thine considered prove the thousand part
Of my endurance, thou art a man, and I
Have suffered like a girl. Yet thou dost look
Like Patience, gazing on kings' graves and smiling
150 Extremity out of act. What were thy friends?
How lost thou them? Thy name, my most kind virgin?
Recount, I do beseech thee. Come, sit by me.

MARINA   My name is Marina.   *Sits*

PERICLES   O, I am mocked,
155 And thou by some incensèd god sent hither
To make the world to laugh at me!

MARINA   Patience,
Good sir, or here I'll cease.

PERICLES   Nay, I'll be patient.
160 Thou little know'st how thou dost startle me
To call thyself Marina.

MARINA   The name
Was given me by one that had some power:
My father, and a king.

165 PERICLES   How! A king's daughter?
And called Marina?

MARINA   You said you would believe me,
But not to be a troubler of your peace,
I will end here.

170 PERICLES   But are you flesh and blood?
Have you a working pulse, and are no fairy?
Motion? Well, speak on. Where were you born?
And wherefore called Marina?

MARINA   Called Marina,
175 For I was born at sea.

---

144 warrant tell/assure   **likely** appropriate   **147 my endurance** what I have endured
149 Patience i.e. a statue of Patience on a tomb   **150 Extremity** hardship   **act** action
172 Motion? i.e. can you move

PERICLES   At sea? What mother?

MARINA   My mother was the daughter of a king,
Who died the minute I was born,
As my good nurse Lychorida hath oft
180   Delivered weeping.

PERICLES   O, stop there a little!
This is the rarest dream that e'er dulled sleep
Did mock sad fools withal. This cannot be
My daughter, buried. Well, where were you bred?
185   I'll hear you more, to th'bottom of your story,
And never interrupt you.

MARINA   You scorn. Believe me, 'twere best I did give o'er.

PERICLES   I will believe you by the syllable
Of what you shall deliver. Yet give me leave —
190   How came you in these parts? Where were you bred?

MARINA   The king my father did in Tarsus leave me,
Till cruel Cleon, with his wicked wife,
Did seek to murder me, and wooed a villain
To attempt it, who having drawn to do't,
195   A crew of pirates came and rescued me,
Brought me to Mytilene. But, good sir,
Whither will you have me? Why do you weep? It may be
You think me an imposture. No, good faith.
I am the daughter to King Pericles,
200   If good King Pericles be.

PERICLES   Ho, Helicanus!   *Calls*

HELICANUS   Calls my lord?   *Helicanus, Lysimachus and*

PERICLES   Thou art a grave and noble counsellor,   *Attendants come*
Most wise in general. Tell me if thou canst,   *forward*
205   What this maid is, or what is like to be,
That thus hath made me weep.

---

180 **Delivered weeping** said tearfully   182 **dulled** gloomy/lethargic   183 **withal** with
184 **buried** who I thought was buried   188 **by the syllable** in every word   194 **drawn** drawn
his sword   197 **Whither . . . me?** i.e. where are your questions leading   198 **imposture**
impostor   **good faith** truly   200 **be** lives   204 **general** all things   205 **like** likely

HELICANUS   I know not,
But here's the regent, sir, of Mytilene,
Speaks nobly of her.

210 LYSIMACHUS   She never would tell
Her parentage, being demanded that,
She would sit still and weep.

PERICLES   O, Helicanus, strike me!— Honoured sir,   *To Lysimachus*
Give me a gash! Put me to present pain,
215 Lest this great sea of joys rushing upon me
O'erbear the shores of my mortality,
And drown me with their sweetness. O, come hither,   *To Marina*
Thou that beget'st him that did thee beget,
Thou that wast born at sea, buried at Tarsus,
220 And found at sea again! O Helicanus,
Down on thy knees, thank the holy gods as loud
As thunder threatens us: this is Marina!
What was thy mother's name? Tell me but that,
For truth can never be confirmed enough
225 Though doubts did ever sleep.

MARINA   First, sir, I pray, what is your title?

PERICLES   I am Pericles of Tyre. But tell me now
My drowned queen's name, as in the rest you said
Thou hast been god-like perfect, the heir of kingdoms,
230 And another life to Pericles thy father.

MARINA   Is it no more to be your daughter than
To say my mother's name was Thaisa?
Thaisa was my mother, who did end
The minute I began.

235 PERICLES   Now blessing on thee! Rise, th'art my
child.—   *She rises*
Give me fresh garments.— Mine own, Helicanus!   *To Attendants*
She is not dead at Tarsus, as she should have been,
By savage Cleon. She shall tell thee all,

---

209 Speaks who speaks   **212 still** silent/motionless   **214 Give . . . gash** wound me
present immediate   **216 O'erbear** overwhelm   **218 beget'st** gives life to   **221 as . . . us**
with shouts as loud as the thunder with which they threaten us   **225 did ever sleep** were laid
to rest

When thou shalt kneel and justify in knowledge

240   She is thy very princess. Who is this?

HELICANUS   Sir, 'tis the governor of Mytilene,

Who hearing of your melancholy state

Did come to see you.

PERICLES   I embrace you.—   *To Lysimachus*

245   Give me my robes. I am wild in my beholding.   *To Attendants*

O heavens, bless my girl! But hark, what music?

Tell Helicanus, my Marina, tell him

O'er point by point, for yet he seems to doubt

How sure you are my daughter. But what music?

250   HELICANUS   My lord, I hear none.

PERICLES   None?

The music of the spheres! List, my Marina.

LYSIMACHUS   It is not good to cross him, give him way.

PERICLES   Rarest sounds, do ye not hear?

255   LYSIMACHUS   Music, my lord? I hear.

PERICLES   Most heavenly music.

It nips me unto list'ning, and thick slumber

Hangs upon mine eyes. Let me rest.   *Sleeps*

LYSIMACHUS   A pillow for his head. So, leave him all.   *To Attendants*

260   Well, my companion friends,

If this but answer to my just belief,

I'll well remember you.   *All except Pericles stand back*

[*Enter*] Diana

DIANA   My temple stands in Ephesus. Hie thee thither

And do upon mine altar sacrifice.

265   There when my maiden priests are met together,

Before the people all

Reveal how thou at sea didst lose thy wife,

---

239 When whereupon   justify in knowledge assure yourself beyond all doubt   245 wild . . .
beholding made delirious by what I see   248 doubt have suspicions about   249 sure
certainly   252 music . . . spheres harmony supposedly produced by the movement of stars
and planets on the concentric spheres thought to surround the earth   List listen   253 cross
contradict/challenge   254 Rarest most splendid/exceptional   257 nips compels
261 answer . . . belief prove true, as I expect   262 well remember recall you vividly/reward
you handsomely   263 Hie thee thither go there quickly   265 maiden virginal, chaste

To mourn thy crosses with thy daughter's. Call,
And give them repetition to the life.

270 Perform my bidding, or thou liv'st in woe:
Do it, and happy, by my silver bow.
Awake and tell thy dream.   [*Exit Diana*]

PERICLES   Celestial Dian, goddess argentine.
I will obey thee.— Helicanus!

Helicanus, Lysimachus

275 HELICANUS   Sir.

and Marina come

PERICLES   My purpose was for Tarsus, there to strike   *forward*
The inhospitable Cleon, but I am
For other service first. Toward Ephesus
Turn our blown sails, eftsoons I'll tell thee why.

280 Shall we refresh us, sir, upon your shore   *To Lysimachus*
And give you gold for such provision
As our intents will need?

LYSIMACHUS   Sir, with all my heart,
And when you come ashore I have another suit.

285 PERICLES   You shall prevail, were it to woo my daughter,
For it seems you have been noble towards her.

LYSIMACHUS   Sir, lend me your arm.

PERICLES   Come, my Marina.   *Exeunt*

[Act 5 Second Chorus]

running scene 22

Enter Gower

GOWER   Now our sands are almost run,
More a little, and then dumb.
This my last boon give me,
For such kindness must relieve me:
5   That you aptly will suppose
What pageantry, what feats, what shows,
What minstrelsy, and pretty din,

---

268 crosses trials/misfortunes   **Call** speak out loudly/declare   **269 give . . . life** describe
them faithfully   **271 silver bow** i.e. crescent moon   **273 argentine** silvery   **276 purpose
was for** intention was to go to   **279 blown** swollen/wind-driven   **eftsoons** shortly
5 Second Chorus   2 More a little a little more   **3 boon** request/favor   **5 aptly** easily/
readily   **7 minstrelsy** noisy music   **pretty din** pleasing noise

The regent made in Mytilene
To greet the king. So he thrived
10   That he is promised to be wived
To fair Marina, but in no wise
Till he had done his sacrifice
As Dian bade, whereto being bound,
The interim, pray you, all confound.
15   In feathered briefness sails are filled,
And wishes fall out as they're willed.
At Ephesus the temple see
Our king and all his company.
That he can hither come so soon,
20   Is by your fancies' thankful doom.   [*Exit*]

[Act 5 Scene 2]   *running scene 23*

[*Enter Pericles, Marina, Lysimachus, Helicanus and Attendants, and
Thaisa, Cerimon and the Priests of Diana*]

PERICLES   Hail Dian! To perform thy just command,
I here confess myself the King of Tyre,
Who frighted from my country did wed
At Pentapolis, the fair Thaisa.
5   At sea in childbed died she, but brought forth
A maid-child called Marina whom, O goddess,
Wears yet thy silver livery. She at Tarsus
Was nursed with Cleon, who at fourteen years
He sought to murder, but her better stars
10   Brought her to Mytilene, against whose shore
Riding, her fortunes brought the maid aboard us,
Where by her own most clear remembrance she
Made known herself my daughter.

---

11 **wise** way   12 **he** i.e. Pericles   13 **bound** i.e. by his promise to Diana/on his way
14 **interim . . . confound** make the intervening time seem as nothing   15 **feathered briefness**
the speed of a bird in flight   20 **by . . . doom** thanks to the consent of your imagination
5.2 *Location: Ephesus*   1 just righteous/exact   2 **confess** admit/proclaim
7 **Wears . . . livery** i.e. is still a virgin   9 **stars** fortune, destiny   10 **against . . . Riding** as we
were anchored

THAISA	Voice and favour!	

15   You are, you are, O royal Pericles!   *She faints*

PERICLES   What means the nun? She dies — help, gentlemen!

CERIMON   Noble sir, if you have told Diana's altar true,
This is your wife.

PERICLES   Reverend appearer, no.

20   I threw her overboard with these very arms.

CERIMON   Upon this coast, I warrant you.

PERICLES   'Tis most certain.

CERIMON   Look to the lady. O, she's but o'erjoyed.
Early one blustering morn this lady was

25   Thrown upon this shore. I oped the coffin,
Found there rich jewels, recovered her, and placed her
Here in Diana's temple.

PERICLES   May we see them?

CERIMON   Great sir, they shall be brought you to my house,

30   Whither I invite you. Look, Thaisa is recovered.

THAISA   O, let me look!   *Rises*
If he be none of mine, my sanctity
Will to my sense bend no licentious ear,
But curb it, spite of seeing. O my lord,

35   Are you not Pericles? Like him you spake,
Like him you are. Did you not name a tempest,
A birth and death?

PERICLES   The voice of dead Thaisa!

THAISA   That Thaisa am I,

40   Supposèd dead and drowned.

PERICLES   Immortal Dian!

THAISA   Now I know you better.
When we with tears parted Pentapolis,
The king my father gave you such a ring.   *Points to his ring*

45   PERICLES   This, this! No more, you gods, your present kindness
Makes my past miseries sports! You shall do well

---

14 favour appearance   19 reverend appearer person who appears reverend   32 sanctity i.e.
religious vows   33 sense i.e. desire   bend direct   licentious lustful   34 curb restrain
spite of seeing in spite of what I see   46 sports amusements/entertainments

That on the touching of her lips I may melt
And no more be seen. O, come, be buried
A second time within these arms.   *Embraces her*

50 MARINA   My heart   *Kneels*
Leaps to be gone into my mother's bosom.

PERICLES   Look who kneels here, flesh of thy flesh, Thaisa,
Thy burden at the sea, and called Marina
For she was yielded there.

55 THAISA   Blest, and mine own.   *They embrace*

HELICANUS   Hail, madam, and my queen.

THAISA   I know you not.

PERICLES   You have heard me say, when I did fly from Tyre,
I left behind an ancient substitute.

60 Can you remember what I called the man?
I have named him oft.

THAISA   'Twas Helicanus then.

PERICLES   Still confirmation.
Embrace him, dear Thaisa, this is he.   *They embrace*

65 Now do I long to hear how you were found,
How possibly preserved, and who to thank,
Besides the gods, for this great miracle?

THAISA   Lord Cerimon, my lord: this man
Through whom the gods have shown their power, that can

70 From first to last resolve you.

PERICLES   Reverend sir,   *To Cerimon*
The gods can have no mortal officer
More like a god than you, will you deliver
How this dead queen relives?

75 CERIMON   I will, my lord,
Beseech you, first go with me to my house,
Where shall be shown you all was found with her,
How she came placèd here in the temple,
No needful thing omitted.

---

54 yielded born   **59 substitute** deputy   **66 How possibly preserved** by what possible means
you were preserved   **72 officer** agent   **77 all** all that   **78 came placèd** came to be placed

80   PERICLES   Pure Dian,
        I bless thee for thy vision, and will offer
        Night oblations to thee. Thaisa,
        This prince, the fair betrothèd of your daughter,
        Shall marry her at Pentapolis,
85   And now this ornament
        Makes me look dismal will I clip to form,
        And what this fourteen years no razor touched
        To grace thy marriage-day I'll beautify.
    THAISA   Lord Cerimon hath letters of good credit,
90   Sir, my father's dead.
    PERICLES   Heavens make a star of him! Yet there my queen,
        We'll celebrate their nuptials, and ourselves
        Will in that kingdom spend our following days.
        Our son and daughter shall in Tyrus reign.
95   Lord Cerimon, we do our longing stay
        To hear the rest untold. Sir, lead's the way.   [*Exeunt*]

[Epilogue]

[*Enter Gower*]

    GOWER   In Antiochus and his daughter you have heard
        Of monstrous lust the due and just reward.
        In Pericles, his queen and daughter seen,
        Although assailed with fortune fierce and keen,
5   Virtue preserved from fell destruction's blast,
        Led on by heaven and crowned with joy at last.
        In Helicanus may you well descry
        A figure of truth, of faith, of loyalty.
        In reverend Cerimon there well appears
10   The worth that learnèd charity aye wears.

---

82 Night oblations nightly/evening prayers   83 fair handsome   85 this ornament i.e.
Pericles' beard and long hair   86 Makes which makes   to form into shape   89 of good
credit credible   91 there in Pentapolis   94 son i.e. Lysimachus   95 do . . . stay i.e. frustrate
our longing   96 untold that is untold   Epilogue   4 keen harsh/cruel   5 fell cruel/savage
7 descry see/discover   8 figure emblem   10 aye always/forever

For wicked Cleon and his wife, when fame
Had spread his cursèd deed to th'honoured name
Of Pericles, to rage the city turn,
That him and his they in his palace burn.

15   The gods for murder seemèd so content
To punish, although not done, but meant.
So, on your patience evermore attending,
New joy wait on you. Here our play has ending.   [*Exit*]

---

11 fame report/rumor   **12 to** against   **13 to . . . turn** the citizens become angry   **15 so** in
this manner   **16 although . . . meant** even though it was not done, but only intended

TEXTUAL NOTES

Q = First Quarto text of 1609
Q2 = a correction introduced in the Second Quarto text of 1609
Q3 = a correction introduced in the Third Quarto text of 1611
Q4 = a correction introduced in the Fourth Quarto text of 1619
Q5 = a correction introduced in the Fifth Quarto text of 1630
F3 = a correction introduced in the Third Folio text, second issue, of 1664
F4 = a correction introduced in the Fourth Folio text of 1685
PA = a reading in George Wilkins' novel, *The Painfull Adventures of Pericles, Prince of Tyre* (1608)
Ed = a correction introduced by a later editor
SD = stage direction
SH = speech heading (i.e. speaker's name)

List of parts = Ed. *Not in* Q

Prologue 4 SH GOWER = Ed. *Not in* Q **6 holidays** = Q. *Sometimes emended to* holy-ales **11 these** = Q2. Q = those **30 account'** = Ed. Q = account'd **39 a** = F3. Q = of

1.1.18 razed = Ed. Q = racte **25 boundless** = Ed. Q = bondlesse **41 From** = Ed. Q = For **50 Grip** *spelled* Gripe *in* Q **57 SH ANTIOCHUS** = Ed. Q *prints* (Antiochus) *at the end of the preceding line. Some editors, noting Pericles' frequent repetition of the king's name, print* I wait the sharpest blow, Antiochus *followed by Antiochus' reply.* **60, 61 'ssayed** = Ed. Q = sayd **114 cancel** = Q3. Q = counsell **128 you're** = Q3. Q = you **137 'schew** = Ed. Q = shew **172 SH ANTIOCHUS** = Ed. *Not in* Q

1.2.4 Be my = Ed. Q = By me **6 should** = Ed. Q = stould **17 me. The** = Ed. Q = me the **26 th'ostent** = Ed. Q = the stint **31 am** = Ed. Q = once **36 And . . . comfortable** = Ed. Q = And keepe your mind till you returne to vs peacefull and comfortable **41 breath** = Ed. Q = sparke. *Sometimes emended to* wind **46 pardon** = Ed. Q = paadon **61 heaven** = Ed. Q = heaue **67 Such . . . yourself** = Ed. Q = such griefes as you your selfe doe lay vpon your selfe **72 Where, as** = Ed. Q = Whereas **84 me** = Ed. *Not in* Q **85 fears** = F4. Q = feare **87 he doubt** = Ed. Q = he doo't **as doubt no** = Ed. Q = as no **93 call't** = Ed. Q = call **124 we'll** = Ed. Q = will

1.3.1 SH THALIARD = Ed. *Not in* Q **26 king's ears this** = Ed. Q = Kings seas. *Sometimes emended to* king's ears it **27 sea** = Q. *Sometimes emended*

to seas **29 SH HELICANUS** = Ed. *Not in* Q **32 betook** = Ed. Q = betake
travels *spelled* trauailes *in* Q
1.4.13 our = Ed. Q = and **do** = Ed. Q = to **22 o'er** = Ed. Q = on **36 they** =
Ed. Q = thy **39 two summers** = Ed. Q = too sauers. *Sometimes emended*
to two savours. *The analogous passage in* PA *reads:* this their City . . . not
two summers younger, did so excell in pompe **58 thou** = Q4. Q = thee
67 Hath = Ed. Q = That **74 him's** = Ed. Q = himnes **77 fear** = Q4. Q =
leaue **78 The** = Q4. Q = our **80 from . . . craves** = Ed. Q = for what he
comes, and whence / he comes, and what he craues **96 SH ALL**
TARSIANS = Ed. Q = Omnes.
2 Chorus 1 SH GOWER = Q4. *Not in* Q **11 Tarsus** = Ed. Q = *Tharstill*
12 speken = Ed. Q = spoken **17 SH GOWER** = Ed. *Not in* Q **Helicane** =
Ed. Q = *Helicon* **19 though** = Ed. Q = for though. *Sometimes emended to*
forthy *or* for that **20 keeps** = Ed. Q = keepe **22 Sends word** = Ed. Q =
Sau'd one. *Sometimes emended to* Sent word **24 had intent** = Q
(corrected). Q = hid in Tent **to murder** = Q *(corrected).* Q = murdred.
Sometimes emended to murdren **25 Tarsus** = Ed. Q = *Tharsis* **34 tossed**
= Ed. Q = tost **40 'longs** = Ed. Q = long's
2.1.12 What ho, Pilch! = Ed. Q = What, to pelch **31 devours** = Ed. Q =
deuowre **39 SH THIRD FISHERMAN** = Ed. Q = I. **47 finny subject** =
Ed. Q = fenny subiect. PA = finny subjects **53 search't** = Ed. Q = Search
nobody will = Ed. Q = no body **76 quotha** = Ed. Q = ke-tha **an** = Ed. Q
= and **79 holidays** = Ed. Q = all day **80 moreo'er** = Ed. Q = more; or
87 your = Ed. Q = you **94 is called Pentapolis** = Q2. Q = I cald
Pantapoles **105 joust** = Ed. Q = Iust **123 thee from, may't** = Ed. Q =
thee, Fame may. *Sometimes emended to* the Gods forfend, the same
140 d'ye = Ed. Q *(corrected)* = do'e. Q *(uncorrected)* = di'e **141 on't** = Ed.
Q = an't **148 rapture** = Ed. Q = rupture. PA = a Iewel, whom all the
raptures of the sea could not bereaue from his arme **151 delightful** =
Ed. Q = delight. *Sometimes emended to* delightsome **158 goad** = Ed. Q =
Goale. *Sometimes emended to* equal
2.2.1 SH SIMONIDES = Ed. Q = *King (throughout)* **4 daughter** = Ed. Q =
daughter heere **27 *Più per dolcezza che per forza*** = Ed. Q = *Pue Per*
doleera kee per forsa. Sometimes emended to Piu per dulcura que per fuerça
30 chivalry = Ed. Q = Chiually **31 *Me pompae provexit apex*** = Ed. Q =
Me Pompey prouexit apex **57 for** = Ed. Q = by. PA = as Uertue was not to
be approoued by wordes, but by actions, so the outward habite was the
least table of the inward minde
2.3.3 To = F4. Q = I **13 yours** = Q3. Q = your **15 artists** = Ed. Q = an Artist
31 but = Ed. Q = not **36 He's** = Ed. Q = ha's **39 Yon** = Q2. Q = You
40 me = Q4. *Not in* Q **45 son's** = Ed. Q = sonne **52 stored** = Ed. Q =
stur'd. F3 = stirr'd **53 you do** = Q4. Q = do you **66 entertain** = Ed. Q =

entraunce **74 And, further** = Ed. Q = And furthermore. *Sometimes emended to* Furthermore   **know** = Ed. Q = know of him   **83 education being** = Q5. Q = education beene. *Sometimes emended to* education's been *or* education has been   **113 SH SIMONIDES** = Ed. *Not in* Q

2.4.8 Of = Ed. Q = of an   **19 council has** = Ed. Q = counsaile, ha's   **27 Helicane** *spelled* Hellican *in* Q   **32 We'll** = Ed. Q = And   **35 death's indeed** = Ed. Q = death in deed. *Sometimes emended to* death indeed's   **57 endeavour it** = Ed. Q = endeauour. *Sometimes emended to* endeavour us

2.5.77 SD *Aside* printed on the following line in Q   **94 SH BOTH** *spelled* Ambo *in* Q

3 Chorus 1 SH GOWER = Ed. *Not in* Q   **rouse** = Ed. Q = rout   **7 crickets sing** = Ed. Q = Cricket sing. *Sometimes emended to* crickets   **13 eche** = Ed. Q = each   **15 SH GOWER** = Ed. *Not in* Q   **17 coigns** = Ed. Q = Crignes   **29 t'appease** = Ed. Q = t'oppresse. PA = appeased the stubborne mutiny of the *Tyrians*   **34 Pentapolis** *spelled* Penlapolis *in* Q   **35 Y-ravishèd** = Ed. Q = Iranyshed   **46 Fortune, moved** = Ed. Q = fortune mou'd. *Sometimes emended to* fortune's mood   **57 not what** = Ed. Q = not? what   **60 sea-tossed** = Ed. Q = seas tost

3.1.0 SD *on* = Q4. Q = a   **7 Thou stormest** = Ed. Q = then storme   **8 spit** = Ed. Q = speat. F3 = spet. *Sometimes emended to* split, spite, *or* speak   **11 midwife** = Ed. Q = my wife   **46 Slack** = Q *(corrected)*. Q *(uncorrected)* = Slake   **bowlines** = Ed. Q = bolins   **55 custom** = Ed. Q = easterne. *Sometimes emended to* In ease *or* in earnest   **63 the ooze** = Ed. Q = oare. *Sometimes emended to* care   **65 And** = Ed. Q = The   **aye-remaining** = Ed. Q = ayre remayning. *Sometimes emended to* e'er remaining   **68 paper** = Q2. Q = Taper   **70 coffer** = Ed. Q = Coffin   **76 SH FIRST SAILOR** = Ed. Q = 2.

3.2.4 'T has = Ed. Q = T'as   **18 quit** = Ed. Q = quite   **38 I** = Ed. *Not in* Q   **51 SD** *chest* = Ed. Q = Chist   **SH CERIMON'S SERVANT** = Ed. Q = Seru. *(throughout)*   **54 chest** = Ed. Q = Chist   **63 bitumed** = Ed. Q = bottomed   **71 corpse** = Ed. Q = Corse   **74–75 too! Apollo** = Ed. Q = to *Apollo*   **85 even** = Q4. Q = ever. PA = thou hast a body even drowned with woe   **94 lain** *spelled* lien *in* Q   **96 cloths** = Ed. Q = clothes. Q4 = cloathes   **101 warm** = Q2. Q = warmth

3.3.0 SD *at Tarsus* spelled Atharsus in Q   **6 haunt** = Ed. Q = hant. *Sometimes emended to* hurt   **29–30 all . . . remain** = Ed. Q = All vnsisterd shall this heyre of mine remayne. PA = his head should grow unscissored   **31 ill** = Ed. Q = will   **42 Lychorida** *spelled* Licherida *in* Q

3.4.0 SD *Thaisa* spelled Tharsa in Q   **5 eaning** = F3. Q = learning. *Sometimes emended to* groaning, bearing, yearning, *or* yielding   **9 vestal** = Ed. Q = vastall   **16 SH THAISA** = Ed. Q = Thin.

4 Chorus 1 SH GOWER = Q4. *Not in* Q   **8 music's letters** = Q. *Sometimes emended to* music, letters   **10 her** = Ed. Q = hie. *Sometimes emended to* high   **heart** = Ed. Q = art   **14 Seeks** = Ed. Q = Seeke   **17 ripe** = Ed. Q = right   **marriage-rite** = Ed. Q = marriage light   **21 Be't** *spelled* Beet *in* Q   **23 nee'le** = Ed. Q = needle   **26 night-bird** = Ed. Q = night bed   **32 With** = Ed. Q = The. *Sometimes emended to* With the   **the** = Ed. Q = with the   **38 murder** = Ed. Q = murderer   **47 carry** = Ed. Q = carried   **48 on** = Ed. Q = one

4.1.5 inflame . . . bosom = Ed. Q = in flaming, thy loue bosome, enflame too nicelie. *Sometimes emended to* inflaming love in thy bosom, / Inflame *or* or fanning love thy bosom / Unflame *or* or flaming love thy bosom / Enslave *or* in flaming, thy love-bosom / Inflame   **19 as** = Ed. *Not in* Q   **26 o'er . . . margent** = Ed. Q = ere the sea marre it   **68 stem** = Ed. Q = sterne   **82 la** = Ed. Q = law   **84 trod** *spelled* trode *in* Q

4.2.4 much = Q2. Q = much much   **18 they're too** = Ed. Q = ther's two   **23 chequins** *spelled* Checkins *in* Q   **37 SH FIRST PIRATE** = Ed. Q = Sayler   **56 struck** = Ed. Q = strooke   **57 but** = Ed. Q = not   **65 like** = Q4. *Not in* Q   **92 i'th'** = Ed. Q = ethe   **93 Veroles** *spelled* Verollus *in* Q   **106 lovers. Seldom** = Ed. Q = Louers sel-dome   **111 SH BAWD** = F3. Q = *Mari*.   **130 Untried** = Ed. Q = Vntide

4.3.1 are = Q4. Q = ere   **4 child** = Ed. Q = chidle   **30 prime** = Ed. Q = prince. Q4 = whole   **38 malkin** = Ed. Q = Mawkin   **39 through** *spelled* thorow *in* Q   **53 talons** *spelled* talents *in* Q   **54 Ye're** = Ed. Q = Yere

4 Second Chorus 8 i'th' = Ed. Q = with. Q4 = in   **10 the** = Q2. Q = thy   **12 life's** = Ed. Q = liues   **13 along: behind** = Ed. Q = along behind,   **14 if** = Ed. Q = it   **18 his** = Ed. Q = this   **19 go on** = Ed. Q = grone. *Sometimes emended to* groan *or* grow on   **29 puts** = Ed. Q = put   **48 scene** = Ed. Q = Steare. *Sometimes emended to* stir

4.5.11 cavalleria = Ed. Q = Caualereea   **15 loon** = Ed. Q = Lowne   **33 dignifies** = Q4. Q = dignities   **53 paced** *spelled* pac'ste *in* Q   **59 name't** = Ed. Q = name. *Sometimes emended to* name it   **77 aloof** = Ed. Q = aloft. *Sometimes emended to* off aloof   **116 ways** = Ed. Q = way   **138 womankind** = Ed. Q = wemen-kinde   **153 Coistrel** = Ed. Q = custerell   **166 O, that** = Q4. Q = that   **180 women** = Q3. Q = woman

5 Chorus 1 SH GOWER = Ed. *Not in* Q   **5 nee'le** = Ed. Q = neele   **8 twin** = Ed. Q = Twine   **10 pour** = Ed. Q = powre   **13 We . . . lost** = Ed. Q = wee there him left. Q4 = tumbled and tost. *Sometimes emended to* Waves there him tossed   **14 Whence** = Ed. Q = Where. Q4 = And

5.1.1 SH SAILOR OF TYRE = Ed. Q = *1. Say*.   **7 SH SAILOR OF TYRE** = Ed. Q = *2. Say*.   **11 SH SAILOR OF MYTILENE** = Ed. Q = *1. Say*.   **34 SH LYSIMACHUS** = Q4. *Not in* Q (*this line is part of Helicanus' speech*)   **35 SH HELICANUS** = Q4. Q = *Lys*   **36 Till** = Ed. Q = SH *Hell*. Till   **night** = Ed. Q = wight   **46 deafened** = Ed. Q = defend   **48–49 She . . . upon** =

Ed. Q = shee is all happie as the fairest of all, and her fellow maides, now vpon. *Sometimes emended to* She in all happy, / As the fair'st of all, among her fellow maids / Dwells now i'th **50 leafy** = Ed. Q = leauie **59 gods** = Ed. Q = God **60 graft** = Ed. Q = graffe **71 I'd** = Ed. Q = I do **wed** = Ed. Q = to wed **72 one** = Ed. Q = on **74 feat** = Ed. Q = fate **84 Marked** = Ed. Q = Marke **98 awkward** = Ed. Q = augward **107 You're** = Ed. Q = your **countrywoman** = Ed. Q = Countrey women **108 Here** = Ed. Q = heare **shores** = Ed. Q = shewes **117 cased** = Ed. Q = caste **129 seem'st** *spelled* seemest *in* Q **palace** = Ed. Q = *Pallas* **132 look'st** *spelled* lookest *in* Q **134 say** = Ed. Q = stay **139 tossed** *spelled* tost *in* Q **140 thought'st** = Ed. Q = thoughts **148 dost** = Ed. Q = doest **151 them? Thy** = Ed. Q = thy **172 Motion? Well,** = Ed. Q = Motion well, *Sometimes emended to* Motion as well? **193 and wooed** = Ed. Q = and hauing wooed **201 SH PERICLES** = Ed. Q = *Hell.* **230 another** = Ed. Q = an other **life** = Ed. Q = like **236 garments . . . Helicanus** = Ed. Q = garments, mine owne *Hellicanus* **240 princess** = Ed. Q = Princes **248 doubt** = Ed. Q = doat. *Sometimes emended to* dote **269 life** = Ed. Q = like **270 Perform** = Ed. Q = or performe **271 Do it** = Ed. Q = doo't **284 suit** = Ed. Q = sleight

5 Second Chorus 16 willed = Ed. Q = wild

5.2.10 against = Ed. Q = gainst **16 nun** = Ed. Q = mum **19 Reverend** = Q2. Q = Reuerent **23 o'erjoyed** *spelled* ouer-joyde *in* Q **24 one** = Ed. Q = in **41 Immortal** = Ed. Q = I mortall **58 SH PERICLES** = Q4. Q = *Hell* **71 Reverend** = F3. Q = Reuerent **81 I bless** = Ed. Q = blesse

Epilogue = Ed. Q = *FINIS.* **5 preserved** = Ed. Q = preferd **12 deed to th'honoured** = Ed. Q = deede, the honor'd

Marina's Song in Act 5 Scene 1

Wilkins' Painfull Adventures *provides the following words for the song (spelling modernized):*

> Amongst the harlots foul I walk,
> Yet harlot none am I:
> The rose amongst the thorns doth grow,
> And is not hurt thereby.
> The thief that stole me, sure I think,
> Is slain before this time.
> A bawd me bought, yet am I not
> Defiled by fleshly crime:
> Nothing were pleasanter to me,

Than parents mine to know.
I am the issue of a king,
My blood from kings doth flow.
In time the heavens may mend my state,
And send a better day,
For sorrow adds unto our griefs,
But helps not any way:
Show gladness in your countenance,
Cast up your cheerful eyes,
That God remains, that once of nought
Created earth and skies.

SCENE-BY-SCENE ANALYSIS

PROLOGUE

The play's Chorus, Gower, enters and tells the audience that he has returned from the grave and taken mortal form again to tell the story "that old was sung" of Pericles. It begins in Antioch in Syria, where the widowed King Antiochus has entered into an incestuous relationship with his daughter, and, to prevent her numerous suitors from winning her, has devised a riddle that they must answer correctly or be put to death. Gower points to numerous severed heads onstage as evidence that none has yet succeeded.

ACT 1 SCENE 1

Lines 1–64: Pericles, Prince of Tyre, enters the palace of Antiochus to undertake the challenge, resolving that death is a small price to pay to win Antiochus' daughter's hand in marriage. The girl is brought in wearing a bridal gown and Antiochus reminds Pericles of the perils he faces. Undeterred, Pericles resolves to face the trial, and Antiochus' daughter wishes that "Of all 'ssayed yet" Pericles may prove "prosperous."

Lines 65–143: Pericles reads the riddle and understands its meaning: the king is both father and lover to the girl, and the "I" of the puzzle is incest. When pressed for an answer, Pericles states that he knows the truth but that it were better kept concealed. Antiochus knows that Pericles knows the truth, but does not confess as much, claiming that as Pericles has failed to solve the riddle he must die, but he grants him a further forty days to solve it. Antiochus and the others exit, and Pericles, in soliloquy, speaks with disgust about the king's incestuous love for his daughter, revealing that he knows his life is in danger and resolving to leave the city. He exits.

Lines 144–173: Antiochus returns, and privately admits that he knows Pericles has discovered the secret and "therefore instantly this prince must die." Thaliard enters and Antiochus offers him gold to kill Pericles, but a Messenger arrives informing them of Pericles' escape. Antiochus orders Thaliard after him, and Thaliard promises to do what he has been commanded. Antiochus states that he can never be calm until he knows Pericles is dead.

ACT 1 SCENE 2

Back in Tyre (a city in modern-day Lebanon), Pericles reveals in soliloquy that he is consumed by melancholy and by the fear that Antiochus, not content with Pericles' silence about his dark secret, will make war against him and his people, against whom they will not be able to offer resistance. Helicanus, Pericles' trusted counselor, enters with other Lords, whom he chastises for offering flattery to Pericles when plain, truthful advice is what is needed. Pericles sends the Lords away and confides everything he has experienced at Antiochus' court to Helicanus. They agree that war is likely, and Helicanus urges Pericles to leave Tyre until the danger is past, leaving the throne to Helicanus' stewardship. Pericles agrees, believing Helicanus trustworthy, and resolves to go to Tarsus (an ancient city in modern-day Turkey).

ACT 1 SCENE 3

Thaliard arrives in Tyre, and though he speaks well of Pericles, he knows that he will be hanged upon his return to Antioch if he does not fulfill his task. He hears Helicanus and other Lords entering and withdraws to overhear their conversation. Helicanus tells the Lords that Pericles has displeased Antiochus, and so has gone to live the dangerous life of a sailor as penance. Thaliard resolves to tell Antiochus that Pericles has perished at sea, and comes forward to greet Helicanus. He says he has a message for Pericles, but has heard that the Prince has gone on "unknown travels" and so he will return to Antioch. Helicanus asks him to stay and feast with them before he goes.

ACT 1 SCENE 4

Cleon, the governor of Tarsus, and his wife, Dionyza, bewail the famine that has gripped their city for the last two years. A Lord enters to tell them that a ship has been spotted off the coast, and Cleon fears it is "some neighbouring nation, / Taking advantage of our misery." The Lord, however, says that the ship was flying the white flag of peace, and Cleon sends him to greet its crew. Pericles enters with his shipmates to deliver corn to the starving city. Cleon and the citizens of Tarsus kneel to Pericles with their thanks, but he humbly asks them to rise, seeking "love" rather than "reverence," asking for safe harborage for his ships and men. Cleon welcomes them and Pericles resolves to stay until "our stars that frown, lend us a smile."

ACT 2 CHORUS

Gower reenters and tells us of Pericles' enormous popularity among the people of Tarsus, who have made a statue of him. In a dumb show, Pericles receives a letter, which he shows to Cleon. Gower goes on to tell us that Helicanus has been as good as his word, and sends Pericles regular letters relating all that goes on in Tyre. Helicanus' letter tells Pericles of Thaliard's journey to Tyre to murder him, and advises him to leave Tarsus for a safer place. While at sea, Gower tells us, Pericles' ship is wrecked in a storm and Pericles himself is stranded alone on the perilous ocean until at last he is washed up on a strange shore.

ACT 2 SCENE 1

Lines 1–109: Pericles enters alone and begs the elements to cease their anger and leave him to die in peace. Three Fishermen enter and speak of the storm and the boat they saw shipwrecked, before going on to discuss how the food chain in the sea resembles life in human communities: "the great ones eat up the little ones." Pericles, impressed with them and the metaphor through which they "tell the infirmities of men," comes forward and greets them. He asks for their help, and tells them he is not used to begging. They ask him if he can fish, and he tells them no, asking that if they will not help him that they will at least see him buried when he is dead. They offer him warm hospitality, and tell him he is in Pentapolis in Greece, which is ruled by the benevolent King Simonides. They tell Pericles that tomorrow is the king's daughter's birthday, and many princes and knights will come to joust in a tournament to win her love. Pericles wishes he could take part in it.

Lines 110–159: Two of the Fishermen reenter with a suit of armor that they found caught in their nets and Pericles thanks the goddess Fortune, telling them he had lost it in the wreck, and that it was given to him by his late father. He asks them for it so that he might wear it and try his luck in the tournament. They agree, asking only that he remember their kindness and reward them if he is successful, which he promises to do. He resolves to buy as good a horse as the bracelet on his arm will afford, and the Fishermen agree to help supply him in all other points of clothing and weaponry.

ACT 2 SCENE 2

Simonides and his daughter, Thaisa, view the knights who come to joust in the tournament as they pass by in turn, each bearing a shield with a motto in Latin or Italian, which Simonides translates. The sixth of these knights is Pericles, in his rusty armor, with a Latin motto that translates as "In this hope I live." Some Lords mock Pericles for his lowly appearance, but Simonides argues that "Opinion's but a fool that makes us scan / The outward habit for the inward man."

ACT 2 SCENE 3

All return from the joust, and Simonides bids the entire assembly to sit and feast. Thaisa crowns Pericles, the champion, with a wreath, and the knights treat him with the highest respect, asking him to sit at the table with them despite his feeling that his lowly appearance ought to prevent him from doing so. Simonides and Thaisa both reveal in private asides that they are smitten with this mysterious, humble knight, even to the extent of losing their appetites. Pericles notes in an aside how Simonides and his happy reign reminds him of his own father, and reflects that he himself, like all men, is subject to time and fortune. Simonides sees Pericles sitting alone in melancholy, and sends Thaisa to him, asking her to toast to him and inquire about his parentage. She pretends to object, but in an aside reveals that she is glad to have the chance to talk to him. He tells her he is the Prince of Tyre, and of the shipwreck he has suffered. She relates this to Simonides, who pities Pericles and resolves to be a friend to him. After the feast there is dancing, following which Simonides urges the knights to rest so they may continue wooing Thaisa the next day.

ACT 2 SCENE 4

Back in Tyre, Helicanus tells Escanes—another wise counselor from Pericles' court—that Antiochus and his daughter, while "seated in a chariot / Of inestimable value," were killed by a "fire from heaven." Both men reflect on the divine punishment of sin. Three Lords enter in some perturbation and broach their griefs with Helicanus. They ask him to tell them where Pericles is, or at least to tell them if he is still alive, pleading that if he is not that they be allowed to choose a new ruler, preferring Helicanus himself as their choice. He asks them to wait for twelve months, after which time he will accept the crown, but urges them, if they cannot wait, to go and look for Pericles themselves. They decide to do so, and they all part in amity.

ACT 2 SCENE 5

Simonides enters reading a letter, which he tells the knights is from Thaisa, saying that she will not marry for the next year and that she gives no reason for this. Dejected, the knights nonetheless accept and leave the court, and Simonides reveals that the letter really says that she has decided to marry Pericles, which pleases him greatly. Pericles enters and Simonides says in an aside he will pretend to be angry about the matter. He greets Pericles and asks him what he thinks of Thaisa, then shows him the letter. Pericles denies giving her any cause to feel so strongly, but Simonides calls him a traitor, accusing him of bewitching his daughter. Pericles defends himself forcefully, yet still respectfully, against the king, and Simonides lauds his courage in an aside. Thaisa enters and Pericles asks her to confirm that he has never attempted to woo her; she protests that no one could take offense at something that would make her glad. Simonides takes each of them by the hand and continues to pretend to chastise them both, ending by saying that if they don't obey him he'll make them man and wife. With an equal measure of surprise and joy both accept and Simonides leads them off to be married.

ACT 3 CHORUS

Gower tells us that the court is asleep after the marriage celebrations, and that Pericles and Thaisa that night conceive a child. In a dumb show, Pericles receives a letter which he shows to Simonides, and then he, his pregnant wife, and Lychorida, their nursemaid, leave Pentapolis. Gower goes on to explain that Pericles has heard of the deaths of Antiochus and his daughter, and that the people of Tyre want to crown the unwilling Helicanus, who wants to wait another six months for the rightful king's return. Pericles and his family set off for Tyre to halt a mutiny, and the people of Pentapolis send him on his way, joyous to learn that the strange knight who has married their princess is in fact a king. At sea, Pericles' ship is struck by another terrible storm.

ACT 3 SCENE 1

On board the ship Pericles calls to the gods to allay the storm. Lychorida enters carrying Pericles' newborn daughter and tells him that Thaisa has died in childbirth. He cries to the gods for taking away the loves they give us, and tells the baby that its life will be gentle and mild as her birth amid the storm was so rough. Some Sailors come on deck and tell Pericles that according to their seafaring superstition Thaisa's body must be thrown overboard or the storm will never abate. He agrees, and speaks poignantly over her body, calling for spices, ink, paper, and his casket and jewels to perform a "priestly farewell" to her. One of the Sailors offers him a watertight chest in which to inter the body and another tells him they are near the coast of Tarsus. Pericles orders them to dock there so that he might entrust the baby to Cleon's care, fearing that the child will not survive all the way to Tyre.

ACT 3 SCENE 2

In Ephesus (an ancient Greek city in modern-day Turkey), Cerimon, a kindly doctor, administers to men who have suffered in the storm. Two Gentlemen enter and reveal that they have been driven out of their storm-battered coastal houses through fear, and ask why Cerimon, whose clothes signify wealth, should take the trouble to help the poor and the sick. Cerimon answers that "Virtue and cunning" (divine power and knowledge) are far more precious than money, and that he values his knowledge of medicine and natural drugs highly. The Gentlemen attest that he is highly thought of as a charitable healer in Ephesus. Cerimon's servant and others enter carrying Thaisa's coffin, which they found washed up on the shore. They open it and find Pericles' letter and jewels, the latter offered in the letter as payment for anyone who will do the charitable office of giving Thaisa, a king's daughter, proper burial. Cerimon perceives that she is actually still alive, and has the servant make a fire and bring him his medicines, ordering music to be played too. Thaisa revives, and they take her "to the next chamber" to nurse her fully back to health.

ACT 3 SCENE 3

In Tarsus Pericles tells Cleon that he must return to Tyre, and shows a patient, albeit sad, fortitude in his acceptance of what has happened to him. He asks Cleon to raise his daughter, named Marina because she was born at sea, as an aristocrat, "that she may be mannered as she is born." Cleon agrees, wishing to repay Pericles for his kindness to him and his people during the famine. Pericles thanks him and Dionyza and vows never to cut his hair until Marina is married, leaving Lychorida to stay and help rear the child.

ACT 3 SCENE 4

In Ephesus Cerimon shows Thaisa the jewels and the letter that were found with her in her coffin, and she recognizes Pericles' handwriting. Believing she will never see him again, she decides to take holy orders and become a vestal virgin. Cerimon offers to help her and to take her to the temple of Diana, the goddess of chastity.

ACT 4 CHORUS

Gower tells us of the passage of time, with Pericles a king, settled at Tyre, Thaisa at Diana's temple, and Marina, now aged fourteen (see 5.2.87), living in Tarsus, best friends with Cleon and Dionyza's daughter, Philoten. Marina, whom Cleon educated and bred as a princess according to his promise, is so full of natural graces and talents that all praise her, disregarding Philoten. This fills Dionyza with an envious rage, and so after Lychorida's (natural) death she hires a murderer, Leonine, to kill Marina.

ACT 4 SCENE 1

Dionyza tells Leonine to do the deed without conscience or remorse and he will be rewarded well. Marina enters with flowers to strew on Lychorida's grave, lamenting that the world to her "is as a lasting storm, / Whirring me from my friends." Dionyza pretends to comfort her, and tells her to walk along the seafront with Leonine, saying that the sea air will do her good. Marina does not want to, but consents. She tells Leonine of the storm in which she was born, and of her father's bravery and resolve through it. Leonine tells her that he means to kill her, offering her the chance to pray first, and she pleads with him. Suddenly, a group of Pirates enter and scare Leonine away. They kidnap Marina, and Leonine notes that they "serve the great pirate Valdes." Believing that Marina will never be seen again, he resolves to tell Dionyza that she is dead and thrown into the sea, but notes that there is a chance they may want to rape her and leave her, and he will then have to kill her after all.

ACT 4 SCENE 2

At a brothel in Mytilene (a town on the island of Lesbos, Greece), three bawds—Pander, Bawd, and their man, Bolt—bemoan the fact that trade is slow, blaming their lack of prostitutes for the problem (Bawd says they have "but poor three," and that they are disease-ridden). Pander sends Bolt out into the market to find "fresh ones," and he and Bawd discuss the prospect of retirement. Bolt returns with Marina and the Pirates, who tell them that she is a virgin and ask one thousand marks for her. Pander leaves with the Pirates to pay them, and Bawd tells Bolt to go out and advertise her features and virginity in the marketplace. Marina wishes that Leonine or the Pirates had killed her. Bawd tries to coax Marina into accepting her new life, even suggesting that she will grow to enjoy it in time, but Marina is horrified, thinking Bawd so inhuman she asks her if she is a woman. Bolt returns and tells the Bawd of all the men who were virtually queuing up to sleep with Marina, noting that one "Spaniard's mouth watered." Bolt and Bawd decide that Marina must be forced, the Bawd telling her not to weep as it will put their customers off. She also promises Bolt that he may also "cut a morsel off the spit," and sends him out to advertise her further. Marina swears that she will serve the goddess Diana, and keep her chastity, even if she must take her own life.

ACT 4 SCENE 3

In Tarsus, Dionyza tells Cleon what she thinks is true: that Leonine has killed Marina at her behest. Cleon is outraged, but Dionyza is unrepentant, explaining how she was driven to it by Marina's constant eclipsing of their own daughter, and accusing Cleon of cowardice and hypocrisy. Cleon wonders what he can say to Pericles, and worries that the gods will be angry.

ACT 4 SECOND CHORUS

Gower apologizes for the device of so many imaginary leaps across time and place, and that the play uses "one language in each several clime." He tells us that Pericles is making his way to Tarsus with Helicanus to see Marina, having left Escanes to rule temporarily in Tyre. In a dumb show, Cleon and Dionyza show Pericles Marina's tomb; he dons sackcloth and leaves "*in a mighty passion.*" Gower remarks on villainy and deception, and tells us that Pericles has sworn never to wash his face or cut his hair, setting sail once more on his travels, and encountering another storm at sea. Gower reads Marina's epitaph, written by Dionyza, and tells us that we are now returning to Marina in Mytilene.

ACT 4 SCENE 4

Two Gentlemen leave the brothel, vowing to lead virtuous lives after having tried to sleep with Marina and been converted to goodness by the "divinity" of her persuasive oratory.

ACT 4 SCENE 5

Lines 1–55: Pander and the Bawd are bemoaning being saddled with Marina as she is even worse for business than their previous predicament, able to "freeze the god Priapus" with her chaste goodness. Bolt decides that he must "ravish her" to break her in to her duties in the brothel. Lysimachus, the governor of Mytilene, arrives in disguise and asks for a girl without any venereal disease, that a man may "deal withal and defy the surgeon." They tell him of Marina, a virgin, but insinuate that she will not be tempted into bed for any amount of money. The Bawd brings Marina out and instructs her to do whatever the governor—a powerful and influential customer—wants her to do, saying that he is "an honourable man." Marina retorts that she hopes "to find him so."

Lines 56–112: Left alone with her, Lysimachus asks Marina how long she has been in this "trade." Perhaps willfully, she does not understand him, and interprets the meaning as the trade she has lived by her whole life: her virtue and honor. He tells her that he is the governor of the town and tries to use his power to seduce her, but she pleads that she is only in this "sty" by cruel chance, and wishes that the gods would change her to "the meanest bird / That flies i'th'purer air" so that she could escape it. Lysimachus is converted by her eloquent plea, and gives her gold, asking her that she think well of him, and says that if she ever hears from him in the future it shall be for her good. Bolt enters and asks for money but Lysimachus scolds him and tells him that without the virtuous Marina to "prop" their bawdy house, it would "sink and overwhelm" him.

Lines 113–186: With Lysimachus gone, Bolt resolves to rape Marina so that they can start to make some money with her. The Bawd enters and Bolt tells her Marina has driven away Lysimachus. Bawd tells Bolt to do as he had intended and have his way with Marina. Left alone with Marina, Bolt tries to force her to yield to him, but again she pleads passionately and eloquently and Bolt is eventually moved by her words. She gives him the gold that Lysimachus gave her and tells him that she can sing, dance, and sew, and will do any of these things, but will not prostitute herself. Bolt agrees to help her out of their brothel and into the company of "honest women."

ACT 5 CHORUS

Gower tells us of Marina's escape from the brothel and of the much-admired gifts of song, dance, and needlework at which she excels in her new life in "an honest house." He moves our imaginative attentions back toward Pericles, who, having escaped the storm, is anchored off the coast of Mytilene. Lysimachus, honoring the feast of Neptune at the seafront, spots the mysterious sail of Pericles' ship and sails out in his barge to meet its crew.

ACT 5 SCENE 1

Lines 1–77: On board Pericles' ship, Lysimachus is introduced to Helicanus by a Sailor, and the two men greet each other warmly. Helicanus explains to Lysimachus who they are and why they are there, telling him that Pericles, the King of Tyre, is on board, and that he has not spoken to anyone for three months, eating only enough to keep him alive that he may "prorogue his grief." He tells also of the reason for Pericles' silence: the loss of his wife and child. Lysimachus asks to see Pericles, and tries to get him to speak, but in vain. A Lord notes that there is "a maid in Mytilene" who might "win some words of him," and Lysimachus agrees, thinking her "sweet harmony" could move him where others have failed. They bring

Marina to Pericles, and Lysimachus comments on her beauty and her goodness.

Lines 78–200: She asks the others to stand aside while she sings to Pericles, but he is unmoved by her song. She speaks, saying she has "a grief / Might equal yours" and that her ancestors were "equivalent with mighty kings" but that "time hath rooted out [her] parentage." Pericles stirs, moved by her words, and looks at her, and is at once amazed by her resemblance to his "dearest wife," contending that "such a one / My daughter might have been." He asks her where she comes from and who she is, but she tells him that if she were to do so, "it would seem / Like lies disdained in the reporting." He tells her to speak freely, and that he will believe her "To points that seem impossible," telling her she looks "Like one I loved indeed." Marina tells Pericles her name, and misinterprets his shock for incredulity, but he pleads with her to go on. She tells him her father was a king, that she was born at sea, that her mother died in childbirth, and that her nurse was called Lychorida, each time urged on by Pericles in the face of her suspicion that he does not believe her. She finally tells him that King Pericles was her father, and he calls to Helicanus.

Lines 201–288: Pericles asks Helicanus if he knows who this maid is that has "made me weep," but he does not. Lysimachus tells him that she would never tell who her parents were when asked, but would "sit still and weep." Pericles sinks to his knees and tells Helicanus that she is his daughter, Marina, asking her to name her mother for final assurance: she correctly names Thaisa, and Pericles embraces her, knowing at last that he has found his lost daughter. He hears music that no one else hears, and says it is the "music of the spheres." All the others, believing him overwrought with emotion, leave him to rest awhile, and in his sleep he sees the goddess Diana, who tells him to go to her temple in Ephesus and tell the assembled people the story of his wife's loss. He awakes and sets about fulfilling Diana's command, summoning all to go with him. Lysimachus tells Pericles he has a "suit" to him, and Pericles guesses that it concerns Marina, saying that he would gladly consent to their betrothal as he perceives Lysimachus has "been noble towards her."

ACT 5 SECOND CHORUS

Gower tells us that the play is almost finished, and of the joyful festivities Lysimachus held for Pericles and Marina in Mytilene. He tells also of Lysimachus' betrothal to Marina, which may not be finalized in marriage until Diana's will has been performed. He tells us that the entire party has arrived in Ephesus to help fulfil Pericles' promise.

ACT 5 SCENE 2

In Ephesus, Pericles tells his story to the assembled crowd, and Thaisa, a nun at Diana's temple since her resuscitation by Cerimon fourteen years earlier, recognizes her long-lost husband and faints. Cerimon tells Pericles that she is his wife, and of the circumstances of how he found and revived her. Thaisa wakes and asks Pericles if he is really her husband. He recognizes her voice at once, and she also tells him that the ring he wears was given to him by her father, confirming her identity. They lovingly embrace, and Pericles reunites her with Marina. He introduces her to Helicanus, whom she has never met, asking if she remembers the name of the counselor of whom he had spoken to her many times: she does, which acts as further confirmation of who she is. Cerimon invites them all to his house to show Pericles the letter and jewels found in Thaisa's coffin and to tell the whole story of her recovery. Pericles offers to do oblations to Diana, and tells Thaisa that Marina and Lysimachus are to be married, and that he will at last "clip to form" his hair and beard for their wedding. Thaisa tells Pericles that her father, Simonides, is dead, and Pericles wishes that the "Heavens make a star of him." He resolves that he and Thaisa will spend the rest of their days in Pentapolis, leaving Tyre to be ruled by Marina and Lysimachus.

EPILOGUE

Gower recapitulates much of the play's action and its moral lessons: he tells of Antiochus and his daughter's divine punishment for their "monstrous lust"; of Pericles, Thaisa, and Marina's tribulations, finally ended with joy and reunification; of Helicanus' goodness; of Cerimon's charity. He also tells us that Cleon and Dionyza, when the story of their attempted murder of Marina had broken out, were burned alive in their palace by the angry people of Tarsus. He wishes that "New joy wait on" the audience, and signals the ending of the play.

PERICLES
IN PERFORMANCE:
THE RSC AND BEYOND

The best way to understand a Shakespeare play is to see it or ideally to participate in it. By examining a range of productions, we may gain a sense of the extraordinary variety of approaches and interpretations that are possible—a variety that gives Shakespeare his unique capacity to be reinvented and made "our contemporary" four centuries after his death.

We begin with a brief overview of the play's theatrical and cinematic life, offering historical perspectives on how it has been performed. We then analyze in more detail a series of productions staged over the last half-century by the Royal Shakespeare Company. The sense of dialogue between productions that can occur only when a company is dedicated to the revival and investigation of the Shakespeare canon over a long period, together with the uniquely comprehensive archival resource of promptbooks, program notes, reviews, and interviews held on behalf of the RSC at the Shakespeare Birthplace Trust in Stratford-upon-Avon, allows an "RSC stage history" to become a crucible in which the chemistry of the play can be explored.

Finally, we go to the horse's mouth. Modern theater is dominated by the figure of the director, who must hold together the whole play, whereas the actor must concentrate on his or her part. The director's viewpoint is therefore especially valuable. Shakespeare's plasticity is wonderfully revealed when we hear directors of highly successful productions answering the same questions in very different ways. We are also including an actor's viewpoint here, that of Laura Rees, who played Marina to great acclaim in the 2005 production at Shakespeare's Globe.

FOUR CENTURIES OF *PERICLES*: AN OVERVIEW

The stage history of *Pericles* closely reflects academic debates over the play's authorship and canonicity. Rarely performed before the twentieth century, the play has more recently become a regular and popular part of the modern repertoire. Yet it has retained a marginal position that has allowed it to particularly appeal to itinerant and minority groups, appropriating the play's discourses of migration and dislocation to find striking contemporary resonances in Pericles' painful adventures.

The play was witnessed by Zorzi Guistinian, the Venetian ambassador, resident in London between 1606 and 1608: a dating that matches the play's title page claims for performance at the Globe prior to 1609. A play of the same name, which may have been Shakespeare's, was in the repertory of a traveling company in York in 1609. Later documented appearances include performances at Whitehall in 1619 and the Globe again in 1631. When we consider the multitude of references to the play, including Ben Jonson's 1629 condemnation of it as "some mouldy tale,"[28] the picture appears to be one of continuous revival during the early modern period, appealing to both courtly and popular tastes.

Despite its omission from the First Folio of 1623, *Pericles* was the first of Shakespeare's plays to be revived after the Restoration. John Rhodes staged it at the Cockpit Theatre in 1660, with Thomas Betterton as Pericles. The plot of a lost king restored to power no doubt appealed to supporters of Charles II. Although the play was included in all collected editions of Shakespeare between 1664 and 1724, Rhodes' production was not revived, and it would be nearly two centuries before a play close to the Quarto text returned to the London stage.

The most important performances in the eighteenth century came in the form of George Lillo's adaptation *Marina*, staged in 1735 at Covent Garden. The Prologue tells its audience:

> With humour mix'd in your fore-fathers way,
> We've to a single tale reduc'd our play.

Charming Marina's wrongs begin the scene;
Pericles finding her with his lost Queen,
Concludes the pleasing task. Shou'd as the soul,
The fire of Shakespear animate the whole,
Shou'd heights which none but he cou'd reach, appear,
To little errors do not prove severe.[29]

This melodrama begins with Philoten, daughter of the deceased Cleon and Dionyza, instructing Leonine to kill the pious Marina, a plot thwarted by the pirates. Pericles' return to Tarsus is fully dramatized, at the end of which Leonine and Philoten kill each other. The brothel scenes are played with relative fidelity to the original text and the action builds toward the climactic recognition scene. It was relatively unsuccessful however, and revived only twice.[30]

After a century's absence from the stage, the play was rescued from obscurity by Samuel Phelps, who produced it in an uncharacteristically spectacular version at Sadler's Wells in 1854.[31] The production was the biggest commercial success of Phelps' theater, running for fifty-five performances. Phelps' performance text (based partially on Lillo) dealt severely with three aspects that would long trouble the sensibilities of audiences and directors: the deliberately old-fashioned Gower Choruses, the incest of Antiochus and his daughter, and the "inappropriate" brothel sequence. Gower was cut entirely and replaced by new expository passages distributed among various characters, and the brothel scenes were combined and heavily cut:

> The scene was a marvel of delicate innuendo, with lots of verbal fencing about "honour" standing in for the droolingly lascivious wordplay of Pandar and Boult and the wolfish propositions of Lysimachus.[32]

The cutting of the Antioch scene to avoid all references to incest, however, rendered the action unintelligible. In line with the age's fear of female sexuality, more blame was placed on the lavish beauty of Antiochus' daughter, on whom the curtain rose, than on the almost-sympathetic Antiochus. Critics agreed, however, on the power of the lead role in Phelps' hands. Combining dignity and emotion, the reunion scene immediately became the play's key draw:

> Grief has rendered [Pericles] almost incapable of hope, and, unwilling to believe the unaccustomed approach of joy, he looks at his child with fixed eye and haggard cheek, gasping with anxiety, till doubt at last gives way to certainty, and he falls weeping on the neck of Marina.[33]

A critical and commercial success, Phelps' production defined the play for the remainder of the century.

Its Stratford fortunes began with three performances in April 1900 under the direction of John Coleman, who also played Pericles. Critical hindsight has not been kind to the production, which was received favorably by many critics, despite the ongoing uncertainty over the question of authorship. Coleman cut the "irrelevant" Gower and the first act entirely, instead devoting his first two acts to the meeting of Pericles and Thaisa. Concern for Victorian decorum was particularly felt in the rewriting of the Marina episodes. In the words of the *Chronicle*:

> The difficulty as regards the share of Marina in the story is got over rather lamely by the girl, after capture by the pirates, being taken to the market-place at Mytilene, where she is sold as a slave to the governor, Lysimachus, who, in the Coleman version, does not show in such a favourable light as in that of Shakespeare. He brings Marina with a party of dancing women to one of his bacchanalian revels, and attempts to clasp her in his arms, whereupon she rushes to the balcony of the palace and threatens to throw herself into the sea beneath if he come a step nearer. The act ends with the body of the supposed Marina being placed on a funeral pyre, which is lighted just as the wretched Pericles rushes in to learn the fate of his daughter.[34]

While the textual edits were derided, the production's sets and decorum were praised. Coleman himself was felt to be excessive by some reviewers, but others felt he demonstrated the best of the "old school," particularly in his passionate appeal to Diana. T. B. Thalberg's Lysimachus was heavily criticized:

> Lysimachus, for instance, is in this version, but a meaningless stage-type, sobered from a bout of drunkenness by a sudden attempt at suicide on the part of Marina. How great a fall from the firm study of character represented by the quiet, gentlemanly Lysimachus of Shakespeare.[35]

The appeal for many, though, was in seeing those characters with Shakespearean resonances. Miss Wetherall's Dionyza was singled out for praise, the actress channeling aspects of Lady Macbeth into the malicious queen, and Marina was seen to be closely related to Miranda and Perdita.

Two world wars had passed before the play returned to Stratford, this time under the direction of Nugent Monck and with the still-young Paul Scofield in the lead role. Monck continued the tradition of cutting the Antioch scenes, to the disappointment of many critics, but restored Gower, establishing the convention of having the character sing many of his choric speeches. Monck's priority was to insist on the play's coherence as a narrative whole, and Scofield was central to this:

> Paul Scolfield's [sic] approach to Pericles is quiet and restrained. Always he gives the impression of emotion very present but well in hand. In the recognition scene this discipline has a rich effect, for Mr. Scolfield's suggestion of trembling affection is much more moving than would be any dramatic outburst.[36]

The restored brothel scenes were a resounding success, with John Blatchley's Bolt "a nice smear of oily insolence . . . the period version of a 'spiv.' "[37] Against this seedy backdrop, Daphne Slater was an outstanding Marina, displaying an innocence and pathos that were particularly powerful as she knelt before her father in the recognition scene.

1. Shakespeare Memorial Theatre 1947, directed by Nugent Monck, with Paul Scofield as Pericles, Irene Sutcliffe (second left) as Thaisa, and Daphne Slater (kneeling) as Marina. Scofield's Pericles was "quiet and restrained": in the recognition scene his "suggestion of trembling affection is much more moving than . . . any dramatic outburst."

Tony Richardson's 1958 production was the third and final at the Stratford Memorial Theatre before the inception of the modern RSC. Gower was central to this production, which adopted a framing device featuring a group of sailors listening rapt to his story and responding appropriately, hissing Dionyza for example. The part of Gower was originally offered to Paul Robeson, who was unable to get a visa, so it was then offered to the West Indian actor Edric Connor, who became the first black actor to perform on the Stratford stage. Claiming that "I am going to kill the 'Jim Crow' idea of the Negro on the stage,"[38] Connor half-spoke, half-sang his lines in a calypso style, emphasizing throughout that *Pericles* was a story being told. As a result, the action was heightened, as if taking place in the overactive imaginations of the sailors. The conceit was not to the taste of all reviewers, many of whom complained of Connor's inaudibility, but the device was to prove lastingly influential.

A hollow ship provided the base of the set, which rocked and swayed during a spectacular storm sequence: "Rigging and trees toss about. Huge areas of the stage rise solidly into the air, stews appear up out of the ground. Troops of stars speed across the sky."[39] This was the first Stratford production to include the Antioch scenes, decorated with skulls mounted on processional poles and Paul Hardwick playing Antiochus as a majestic monster. Lysimachus, too, was redeemed as "a thoughtless but generous-hearted playboy."[40] Richard Johnson played Pericles with conviction, and the production found heart under the stage trickery, particularly in Cerimon's mystical revival of Thaisa.

Beyond Stratford, the play's early-twentieth-century fortunes were not widely spread. The infrequency of its early performances has had lasting effects, including a failure to establish itself in the regular repertory of non-English-speaking countries or on the silver screen. Jacques Rivette's 1961 film *Paris nous appartient* (*Paris Belongs to Us*) is a rare exception to both, a French-language backstage drama centered around a group rehearsing *Pericles*. A straight screen production would wait until the BBC's 1984 version, one of the better entries in its complete series of films. Taking advantage of the possibilities of television, Edward Petherbridge's Gower wanders through the action, narrating over dissolves between scenes and

2. Shakespeare Memorial Theatre 1958, directed by Tony Richardson, with Edric Connor as Gower. The first black actor to perform on the Stratford stage, he claimed he was "going to kill the 'Jim Crow' idea of the Negro on the stage." The Sailors, from left to right, include Roy Dotrice (to the immediate left of Gower), Thane Battany (in shadow), and Edward de Souza (far right).

addressing the camera directly. The production's melancholic tone is set by Mike Gwilym's solemn Pericles, whose embattled endurance is exaggerated by camera close-ups. The banquet and extended dance at Tarsus are played at a leisurely pace, giving Pericles and Thaisa time to build on their initial glances, and the recognition scene—played in a small cabin with Gwilym muttering his lines under his breath in a dreamlike denial—effectively captures Pericles' struggle to accept good fortune.

Tony Robertson directed the first of his three productions for Prospect Theatre in Edinburgh and London, 1973–74, with Derek Jacobi as Pericles. Set in an eastern Mediterranean brothel, the production attempted to contrast the purity of its central characters with the "iridescent purulence" of the brothel and its "inspired grotesques."[41] In 1980 Robertson returned to the play in New York with the Jean Cocteau Repertory Company. Here, "male and female prostitutes solicit their clientele, and old Gower . . . is turned into a sardonic master of ceremonies."[42] Pericles was a Madison Avenue businessman, handed a copy of the play by Gower, who began acting it out with the help of the locals. Deborah Wright Houston doubled Thaisa and Marina, removing her prostitute costume as she became the latter. Robertson continued to push the conceit to extremes in his 1983 version for the Acting Company, to the point of having two imaginary infants drop-kicked across the stage at the close of Act 1, to the disgust of reviewers.

Following Richardson and Robertson, more directors were choosing to place the play within a meta-theatrical storytelling framework. At the 1974 New York Shakespeare Festival, Edward Berkeley began with a troupe of actors entering in two covered wagons and performing circus entertainments, then presented *Pericles* in a spirit of partial parody, the actors presenting their characters throughout rather than becoming them. While drawing attention to the play's humor and folktale aspects, it denied any psychological or emotional investment. The 1979 production for the Berkeley Shakespeare Festival split the role of Pericles among three actors, breaking the character into three distinct eras, the oldest of which wore Gower's costume, taking on that character's wisdom and gravity. The following year, Edward J. Feidner's production at Champlain created scenery such as the foamy sea from the bodies of actors and had Vincent Rossano's Gower present throughout to narrate events.

Peter Sellars directed the play in Boston in 1983, recreating the spirit of Richardson's production by casting a local street jive artist, Brother Blue, to play the part of Gower, singing and rapping in complex rhythms. The African American actor Ben Halley Jr. "looks like a young Paul Robeson and plays Pericles in the grand manner of the 19th-century field marshals of the stage."[43] In the same year, David Ultz's company blended music hall and pantomime in London that placed Gerard Murphy's Pericles against a backdrop of hinged boxes from which the characters at the various ports of call were repeatedly revealed. Doubling was again used to provide unity:

> The kings in Pericles's various ports of call are all played by Brian Protheroe, who draws a nice distinction between the lusts of Antioch and Cleon's passion for model building—whenever Pericles arrives there is always some new monument to show off.[44]

In 1985, Declan Donnellan directed a seminal production for Cheek by Jowl with only seven actors. Amanda Harris doubled as Antiochus' daughter and Marina, emphasizing a duality in the two characters, and simple visual images were used to tie together the emotional nuances of the plot: "the sheet that serves as Pericles's and Thaisa's bed becomes the bundle that is the infant Marina, and the same sheet grows into the shroud in which Thaisa is buried, drowned."[45] With the only pieces of set two long wooden casks which served as beds, ships, and coffins, the emphasis was placed on the family relationships rather than spectacle.

The 1987 Hartford Stage Company, reviving Wilkins' title *The Painful Adventures of Pericles, Prince of Tyre*, created "a modern Mediterranean never-never land where Pericles mingles with glitterati, Arab terrorists, street punks, cruise-ship tourists, prostitutes, vestal virgins, blue collar fishermen and an Elizabethan narrator who tells our hero's story," yet found moments of pathos and quiet amid the chaos.[46] This mixture of styles and periods had by now become a hallmark of productions, as in Paul Barry's 1989 New Jersey production, which imagined a tacky cruise party encountering Caribbean folklore as told by local storytellers.

From the 1990s, *Pericles* took on more serious inflections. Simon Usher's production at Leicester Haymarket in 1990 drew on the topicality of child abuse scandals to turn Antiochus' daughter into a "pitiable, anorexic victim," although the *Independent* reviewer felt this strained the text.[47] Joe Banno's 1998 production for the Washington Theater Company took a more political state-of-the-nation focus, with Antioch as a U.S. military base, Tarsus a hippie commune, and Tyre a rural plantation. The National Theatre's 1994 production in London (featuring the chameleonic Kathryn Hunter doubling a variety of roles including Antiochus, Cerimon, and the Bawd) was more playful, with "all the grandiosity and verse of the best musical or dance productions" and the Olivier's revolving stage pressed into judicious service.[48] Henry Goodman's commanding Gower was unanimously praised, while Douglas Hodge offered a moving lament for Thaisa during the storm scene.

In the new millennium, productions have proliferated in the light of growing investment in the play's central concerns. 2003 saw three major productions in London alone. Yukio Ninagawa's Japanese-language version, hosted by the National Theatre, located the play within a framework of war refugees, shuffling onstage and drawing comfort from the story told by a husband-and-wife pair. The production was described by reviewers as heart-wrenching, as "the victims of a fearful disaster enact a needed fable about the continuity of human existence," emblemized in the reunion of father and daughter.[49] Meanwhile, in a Southwark warehouse, Cardboard Citizens (a professional company who work with refugees and homeless people) turned its audience into itinerant wanderers like Pericles. Audience members were given tags and subjected to immigration questionnaires before being escorted from one loading bay to another as Pericles called at different ports. Here, the play itself remained fragmented in keeping with the audience/refugee experience, the wandering audience itself becoming the production's unifying feature—co-produced with the RSC, it is discussed in more detail below with the RSC productions and by director Adrian Jackson in "The Director's Cut."

Neil Bartlett's version at the Lyric Hammersmith recast Pericles' tribulations as a psychodrama set in an implied hospital ward, with Pericles attempting to atone for leaving the daughter of Antiochus to her fate. This was echoed in Andrew Hilton's 2005 production at Bristol's Tobacco Factory, where Antiochus' daughter "hands [Pericles] the written riddle with such eloquent, dignified pleading in her eyes, albeit offset by a royal reserve, that you wonder why the absconding hero thinks only of himself."[50] Also in 2005, Kathryn Hunter directed the play for Shakespeare's Globe. Pericles was here played by two actors, with the older Corin Redgrave watching Robert Luckay as his younger self abandoning his daughter and crying "I could have saved her!" Gower (Patrice Naiambana) was an African storyteller who doubled as Cerimon to bring Thaisa back to life in a tribal ritual. The production employed a group of aerialists, swinging from the eaves of the theater, who illustrated the action throughout, turning "the tournament at Pentapolis into a spectacular modern Olympics as they hang upside down from ropes or dangle dangerously from circus hoops."[51]

As the play grows in familiarity and critical esteem, so too is it being staged more frequently around the world. Although it was neglected for many years, the spiritual, political, and sociological questions raised by the play have rendered it increasingly relevant to a globalized and dislocated society, as evidenced by the growing number of productions in recent years. Paradoxically, it is this very marginality of *Pericles* that has brought it back to the center of the performed canon.

AT THE RSC

Pericles was not included in the 1623 First Folio of Shakespeare's plays, probably because Heminges and Condell, who put the Folio together, knew that it was not the work of Shakespeare alone. Modern word analysis techniques have shown that the first nine scenes (the first two acts) are not by Shakespeare, but that the rest of the play is. The author of the early scenes is thought to be George Wilkins, a minor playwright, one of whose plays was performed by Shakespeare's company, the King's Men, in 1608. The first two acts are weak, the action jerkily episodic, and the language often simplistic and banal. In addition, the 1609 Quarto edition of the play is full of errors and omissions, so that performance texts depend on reconstructions by modern editors and vary widely. A director taking on the play has not only to find an approach but to choose a text. With all these disadvantages, it is one of Shakespeare's least performed plays, but the "mouldy tale," as Ben Jonson called it, the rambling and at times ill-written chronicle of Pericles' travels and sufferings that appears, on the page, strange and intractable, has, like *Cymbeline* (written two years later), a way of working magically on the stage.

The play seems to relate rather particularly to a turning point in Shakespeare's own life at the time: during 1607–8, when he must have been working on the play (it was first performed in 1608), his elder daughter, Susanna, married and gave birth to a daughter; three years later, Shakespeare would return to live in Stratford, to be reunited with the wife and daughters from whom he had been separated during his working life in London. The themes of the play, death and birth, loss and restoration—in particular the reunion of father and daughter—seem to have obsessed him: they are worked over again in the other late plays, *The Winter's Tale* and *Cymbeline* (written between 1609 and 1611). In fact, on all five occasions that *Pericles* has been produced at Stratford since 1961 it has been paired with one of these other, more popular, plays: with *The Winter's Tale* in 1969, 2002, and 2006, and with *Cymbeline* in 1979 and 1989. One might think that it was felt to lack validity on its own.

Telling the Tale

1969, 1979, 1989—Gower's invention

When Terry Hands directed the play at the RST in 1969, it had not been seen at Stratford for eleven years. Richard Johnson had played Pericles in 1958 and Paul Scofield in 1947; before that, a production in 1900 is the only one on record. Hands gave cohesion and drive to the play by making the narrator, Gower, the linchpin of his production: the play was Gower's tale and the characters and events were his invention and under his control. Emrys James, as a Welsh, bardic

Gower, remained onstage throughout, watching, managing, and explaining. The critic of the *Financial Times* grumbled,

> Terry Hands has gone all out for the symbolism, so much so that there is little left of the fairytale quality of the play as it appears on the stage. From beginning to end he has given us a ritual, performed not by men and women but by puppets conjured up from Gower's brain as he tells the story.[52]

Other critics embraced the approach:

> All this serves to hold naturalism at bay, and keep the storytelling flexible and relaxed. Flexibility is one of the play's merits. The play itself matches improbable incidents with extreme changes between tragic passions, magic and low comedy, and Mr. Hands is equal to them all.[53]

Hands' inspiration in celebrating, rather than attempting to disguise, the folktale aspects of the play was reflected in two subsequent productions.

In 1979, Ron Daniels, in his first Shakespeare production for the RSC, again placed Gower's narrative at the center of the play. He directed a bare-bones, lucid, gently allegorical version at the Other Place, a theater more accustomed to the new and experimental. Exploiting the starkness of the venue, he placed the action on a bare wooden circle and employed a minimum of emblematic props, summoned by Griffith Jones as a sonorous and commanding Gower. Embracing the simplicities of the play's moral framework, he costumed the actors symbolically—white for the good, black for the bad. Disguising the weakness of the first two acts, he arrived, as critic Michael Billington commented, at "an extraordinarily tactful"[54] solution, filling out the deficiencies in the verse of the early scenes with percussive music (composed by Stephen Oliver), which gradually gave way as Shakespeare's verse took over with its own vocal music. Like the best productions of *Cymbeline*, it had "the spellbinding charm of a Shakespearean fairytale."[55]

Peter Holland wrote of David Thacker's 1989 production at the

3. The Other Place 1979, directed by Ron Daniels: embracing the simplicities of the play's moral framework, he costumed the actors symbolically—
white for the good, black for the bad. With Julie Peasgood as Marina and
Peter Clough as Lysimachus.

Swan Theatre, "What the production exuded through every pore
was sheer delight in the possibilities of telling a story in the theater."[56] Again the production depended on the strong presence of
Gower to knit the story together, particularly in the shaky first two
acts, and to guide the audience on its tour of Greece and Asia Minor:

> [Rudolph] Walker's Gower was a genial author-narrator, read-
> ing from a book, watching the action from a comfortable arm-
> chair, a figure closer perhaps to the traditions of television
> storytelling, as if the stage of the Swan were no different from

the set for BBC's *Jackanory* and the audience an avid group of children, eager to know what happened next.[57]

Thacker exploited the theatrical potential of the Swan Theatre, making use of the galleries to present emblematic tableaux and to frame Nigel Terry's Pericles, at each stage of his journey, at the top of the central stairs that ran from stage to gallery. He filled the stage with color and movement for the pentathlon at Simonides' court and created a delicate stage magic in the scene where Cerimon restored Thaisa to life. By recasting the Lord Cerimon as a female healer-priestess, surrounded by female attendants, he gave the scene a hushed gentleness that contrasted beautifully with the noise and movement of the preceding storm scene and carried echoes of Paulina's restoration of Hermione at the end of *The Winter's Tale*.

2002—a spectacular masque

This production started life, together with the other late plays, *The Winter's Tale* and *The Tempest*, in London's Roundhouse, moving to the RST a month later. The Roundhouse is a huge, echoing venue which is not easy to fill. Adrian Noble, who directed the trio, had just stepped down as artistic director of the RSC, following a troubled time in which he had made some unpopular decisions, including giving up the Barbican Theatre as the RSC's London home. It was crucial that these plays should succeed in this venue, and *Pericles*, in a boldly reconstructed text, was certainly received with rapture by audiences. The critics, however, were more divided. Benedict Nightingale shared the rapture:

> Noble's revival has the pace and intensity, the sense of wonder and, yes, the magic to bounce us into believing pretty much anything . . . It is full of exotic moments . . . yet the décor never distracts or overwhelms.[58]

Other critics differed, feeling that the play was not allowed to speak for itself or weave its own magic, drawing attention to Noble's recent work directing a musical: Michael Billington suggested "Noble treats this wonderful neglected play as if it were a spectacular masque or Jacobean musical,"[59] while Paul Taylor of the *Independent* called it "a *Pericles* that keeps threatening to turn into a feel-good family musical."[60]

Taylor acknowledged that the production had "a powerfully involving atmosphere, a genuine sense of wonder and a strongly bonded company"[61] but agreed with Billington that "the language was buried under effects."[62] These effects were powerfully theatrical: in the first scene, as Pericles entered Antioch to woo Antiochus' daughter, severed heads dropped on him from above—the unsuccessful wooers who had preceded him; in Ephesus, the goddess Diana plunged from the heavens and the reunited family was showered from above with rose petals.

There was also continuous background music, composed by Shaun Davey: turbaned musicians, playing instruments that included Greek clarinet and bouzouki, were onstage throughout, and the storm scene was accompanied by furious drumming. Some found the score over-sentimental and "Lloyd-Webberish,"[63] but audiences, for the most part, appeared to differ.

2003—real-life stories

In a disused London warehouse, Adrian Jackson directed a production in collaboration with Cardboard Citizens, a theater company formed by homeless people. The production took the play's themes of wandering and loss, and linked them very directly to the experience of twenty-first-century asylum seekers. For the audience, the theatrical experience was made physically and emotionally uncomfortable: the venue was set up as a refugee holding station, and audience members were "processed" on arrival—issued with numbers and instructions on how to behave. They were then taken into an "Education Room," where they listened to the personal testimonies of asylum seekers before taking part in a promenade performance of the play, which involved trekking considerable distances around the chilly, echoing warehouse. Critics found it a difficult evening and complained not only of the physical discomfort but of the serious audibility problems caused by the combination of an echoing acoustic and largely inexperienced actors, but they were all won over to some extent by the emotional intensity of the performance. Sam Marlowe spoke for many: "This is an imperfect evening, and at times a crude and infuriating one. But it has the buzz of a true theatrical event—and its passion cannot be doubted."[64]

Some of the personal testimonies were poignantly apposite: an Indonesian woman described how the boat that was carrying her and four hundred others capsized and three of the pregnant women on board went into labor; in the ensuing chaos, as she clung to the upturned boat, she saw a dead woman float by with her baby floating beside her, still attached by its umbilical cord. Kate Bassett commented that "Jackson never quite captures the transcendent poignancy of those scenes where broken lives seem suddenly mercifully blessed,"[65] but perhaps that was Jackson's intention. He intercut the family's final reunion with a filmed scene in which a therapist talked to a silent refugee, too traumatized to speak—no easy resolution here. The late romances make sense of grief and dislocation by offering the magical possibility of restoration, and we weep tears of relief, but set against the unreconciled losses of real-life narratives they may test our credulity too far.

2006—as though it was new

When Dominic Cooke directed *Pericles* and *The Winter's Tale* with the same company, at the Swan for the Complete Works season in late 2006, he was about to take over as artistic director at the Royal Court. Paul Taylor, reviewing the plays in the *Independent*, reminded us that "the rubric of The Royal Court is to direct new plays as though they were classics and classic plays as though they were new."[66] Cooke fulfilled this aim in his direction of both the plays, which emerged new-minted, contemporary, and engrossing. They were performed in a transformed Swan: all the seats had been taken out of the stalls and the theater turned into "a ramshackle adventure playground."[67] Mike Britton designed a wide, curving ramp reaching from ground to Gallery One level, with elevated walkways and a raised, enclosed acting area for intimate scenes. While seats were still available in the galleries, the rest of the audience stood in the stalls area, where they were closely involved in the action. In fact, among the contemporary costumes, there was no clear distinction between cast and audience. The promenaders were corralled at gunpoint in the military dictatorship of Antioch; they danced and feasted in Pentapolis and sat on the floor and wept at the reunion of Pericles and Marina. They, and the rest of the audience, were guided and reassured by Joseph Mydell as a commanding but playful Gower, moving among the audience, driving the action along.

The Mediterranean World

One might think that one of the challenges for director and designer would be to let the audience know where they are in a play that makes a two-decade tour of the Mediterranean, taking in Antioch, Tyre and Tarsus, Pentapolis, Mytilene, and Ephesus, but most, in fact, establish an overall mood and atmosphere, allowing events and places to flow freely one to another.

1969—"a country where a marvel is an acceptable commonplace"[68]

David Nathan so described the world that Terry Hands, Timothy O'Brien (designer), and Guy Wolfenden (composer) created in the first RSC production. In Hands' version, the individual cities were not differentiated, and the audience located itself through Gower's narration and direction. The action took place on a bare, white-walled stage, onto which Gower summoned his characters, who moved with classical economy and in formal groupings. Above the stage hung a hollow gold dodecahedron, which evoked Platonic philosophy, a belief in order and form, underpinning the play's non-Christian world.

1979—an allegorical world

At the Other Place, Ron Daniels too let the narrative speak for itself. At Gower's command, skulls on poles took us to Antioch; the tournament at Pentapolis was suggested by the clashing of staves; a pole and a rope was enough for a storm: "A slanting rope is stretched across the stage and as the characters cling precariously to it in lightning flashes the sense of being in tempest is instantly conveyed."[69] While no attempt was made at geographical realism, the black and white costumes told the audience the moral worth of each city: they knew that Pentapolis, under white-clad "good Simonides" was a genuine safe haven, but feared for the safety of baby Marina, left in the care of black-turbaned Queen Dionyza.

1989—the Grand Tour

For David Thacker's production at the Swan, Fran Thompson took the audience into a loosely eighteenth-century world (though the tourney at Pentapolis for the hand of Thaisa was medieval): Nigel Terry, as Pericles, wore a tattered frock coat, like a gentleman on the Grand Tour who has run into difficulties on his travels, and the scenes in the brothel in Mytilene were vivid evocations of Hogarth cartoons. Again the audience knew where it was by relying on Gower's lucid narrative.

2002—Levantine splendor

For Adrian Noble's production, which started at the Roundhouse and transferred to the Royal Shakespeare Theatre, Peter McKintosh designed an impressive peninsular stage, richly carpeted and bordered by walkways, hung with a myriad oriental lamps and opening into a bulb-shaped inner stage, where the jousting at Pentapolis was played, as well as the brothel scenes and the reunion of Pericles and Marina.

2003—the holding center

In the warehouse venue of the production with Cardboard Citizens, the "set" was inventive and even witty. It included large shipping containers, strings of children's clothes, and industrial washing machines, which churned and spewed during the storm scene. The attempted rape of Marina was filmed with brutal realism and shown on a large screen, while Diana's temple was a huge picture of Diana, Princess of Wales, complete with a sea of floral tributes. It had the additional advantage, not available in more conventional venues, of a clammy coolness that chilled the audience to the bone.

2006—Africa

In Dominic Cooke's promenade performance at the Swan, the cities of Asia Minor became unequivocally African. The black actors who, for the most part, took minor roles in *The Winter's Tale*, took center stage: King Antiochus became an African dictator—a Mugabe or Amin—surrounded by genuinely frightening, trigger-happy soldiers, and the exhausted white-swathed citizens of Tarsus evoked television images of famine. Pentapolis, under the good Simonides, was strikingly contrasted, a world of feasting and laughter; this is the only opportunity for laughter that the play offers (apart from a grim smile in the brothel scenes) and Cooke exploited it to the full: the jousting became a comic pentathlon that included a spoof steeplechase and an inspired parody of Olympic swimming. The curtained inner stage enabled a naturalistic set to be revealed for the Mytilene brothel; in its cramped seediness, Marina appeared truly trapped, fluttering in her white dress like a moth inside a grubby lamp shade.

Deliberate Doubling

The episodic nature of this play makes the doubling of roles eminently practical, and most productions have used it to some extent, but, practicality aside, there is an enormous amount to be gained from doubling in such a way as to highlight the mirroring of events and characters that patterns the play. Paul Taylor, regretting the absence of doubling in Adrian Noble's 2002 production, wrote,

> There have been productions that have highlighted (through doubling and visual echoes) the eerie psychological continuity of a play where the sin of incest, discovered at Antioch, seems to resurface in a minatory coded form at all of the hero's subsequent ports of call, until the threat is finally confronted and redeemed by reunion with his daughter.[70]

1969 was a year of "deliberate doubling": in Trevor Nunn's production of *The Winter's Tale*, Judi Dench doubled the mother and daughter roles of Hermione and Perdita, while Susan Fleetwood doubled Thaisa and Marina in *Pericles*. Such doubling is not easy to manage, since doubles have to be brought on at the end of the plays for the final reunions, but much is gained dramatically by these daughters' literally embodying the virtues of their apparently dead mothers. In the 1969 production, there was further deliberate doubling: Morgan Shepard doubled the incestuous and brutal King Antiochus with Bolt, the whoremaster in the Mytilene brothel, while Brenda Bruce doubled the murderous Queen Dionyza with the Bawd. High and low, tragic and blackly comic, these characters who beset Pericles and Marina were mirrored in the same actors.

In 1979, in Ron Daniels' simple emblematic production, a cast of fourteen played thirty-eight roles, so doublings, treblings, and quadruplings were to be found, not all of them significant. Some of the doublings were telling, however, not in their mirroring but in their reversing: Julie Peasgood played first—in black—Antiochus' incestuous daughter, and then—in white—Pericles' virtuous, and properly loved, Marina; Suzanne Bertish doubled the destructive Dionyza with the restorative goddess Diana; Heather Canning played the nurse, Lychorida, who brought Marina into the world, and the Bawd in Mytilene who would have destroyed her. The 2003 Warehouse production was played with a cast of twelve and again produced some telling doubling: Leonine and Cerimon were doubled—murderer and healer—and David Mara doubled Cleon and Lysimachus—two flawed rulers; the one damned, the other saved.

In 1989, Russell Dixon doubled the wily and benevolent King Simonides with a coarsely threatening performance as Bolt, the whoremaster, and Helen Blatch moved from the tranquil healer, Cerimon, restoring Thaisa to life, to a raging Bawd in the brothel, so that the two protectors of Thaisa, her father and her rescuer, became the persecutors of her beleaguered daughter. In 2006, three doublings were exploited: Ony Uhiara, appearing first as pure jailbait in school-girl white ankle socks in the role of Antiochus' silent daughter, returned as a fiercely eloquent, virginal Marina, while Richard Moore doubled a jovial Simonides with a malevolent Pander, and

Linda Bassett followed up a life-enhancing scene as Cerimon with a devastatingly coldhearted performance as the Bawd. In this production, though, there were further echoes, since the same company played *Pericles* and *The Winter's Tale*: those who saw both plays saw the affecting Kate Fleetwood restored to life both as Thaisa and as Hermione, and saw Linda Bassett as her tender restorer, both as Cerimon and as Paulina.

The Prince of Tyre

The character of Pericles is, in some ways, a blank. Each actor makes of the character what he finds there. It is a role that is slow to build, partly because the non-Shakespearean language of the first two acts gives an actor limited scope; it is interesting how often critics quote Pericles' lines,

> The god of this great vast, rebuke these surges
> Which wash both heaven and hell

at the beginning of Act 3, as the point at which Shakespeare takes over and the actor comes into his own. His final test is the scene of reunion with his daughter, a scene to rival the end of *The Winter's Tale*, or even the reconciliation of Cordelia and Lear. It rarely fails.

In 1969, "Ian Richardson was a sad, patient prince": "Richardson, his face the bearded face of a grandee from an El Greco canvas, his voice a silver bugle, makes an imposing figure despite his slight build."[71] Peter McEnery, ten years later, also sent the critics reaching for musical metaphors: "Peter McEnery's noble voice rings like a trumpet for the young Pericles, tolls like a funeral bell for the bowed heartbroken Pericles of Acts 4 and 5, whose fingernails have grown like vulture's talons in his self-neglect."[72] In the intimate space of the Other Place, McEnery's reunion with his daughter produced an extraordinary breathless hush. In 1989, Nigel Terry was an aristocratic, powerful Pericles, convincing in the early scenes as his intelligence, his integrity, and his physical prowess are tested, and moving in the reunion scene with Suzan Sylvester as Marina, who made a "stunning"[73] Stratford debut, compellingly convincing in her unaffected virtue.

4. RST 1969, directed by Terry Hands, with Ian Richardson as Pericles and Susan Fleetwood as Thaisa, Simonides (Derek Smith, background left), Gower (Emrys James, background right): "Richardson, his face the bearded face of a grandee from an El Greco canvas, his voice a silver bugle, makes an imposing figure despite his slight build."

In 2002, Ray Fearon was a "strong, virile presence"[74] and "so wonderfully warm a man as well as so intensely chivalric a prince, that his grief meant more than usual."[75] So wrote Benedict Nightingale, who admitted, hard-boiled critic though he was, to being moved to tears by Fearon's father–daughter reunion with Kananu Kirimi. In the 2003 production, the role was split, with Christopher Simpson as the younger Pericles and Kevork Malikyan as the older, giving "a magnificent portrayal of quiet desolation."[76] In 2006, Lucian Msamati, though physically not altogether convincing as the Olympic champion, started as sturdy and stoical and rose to vocal and emotional power. The reunion scenes, first with Ony Uhiara as Marina, and then with Kate Fleetwood as Thaisa, were extraordinarily moving, played in and among the audience.

THE DIRECTOR'S CUT: INTERVIEWS WITH ADRIAN NOBLE, ADRIAN JACKSON, AND DOMINIC COOKE

Adrian Noble, born in 1950, arrived at the RSC from the Bristol Old Vic, where he had directed several future stars in productions of classic plays. His first production on the main stage of the Royal Shakespeare Theatre in Stratford was an acclaimed 1982 *King Lear*, with Michael Gambon as the king and Antony Sher as an extraordinarily powerful Fool. Two years later his *Henry V* sowed the seed for Kenneth Branagh's film. Among his other major productions during his two decades at the RSC were *Hamlet*, again with Branagh in the title role, *The Plantagenets*, based on the *Henry VI/Richard III* tetralogy, and the two parts of *Henry IV*, with Robert Stephens as Falstaff. Noble's 1994 *A Midsummer Night's Dream* was made into a film. He was artistic director of the RSC from 1991 to 2003, since when he has worked as a freelance director. His production style is characterized by strong use of colors and objects (such as umbrellas), and fluid scenic structure. He is here discussing his 2002 production, which started at the Roundhouse before moving to the RST in Stratford.

Adrian Jackson is the founder-director and chief executive of Cardboard Citizens, a theater company he conceived in 1991 in which the performers and many administrative employees are homeless and ex-homeless people, refugees, or asylum seekers. The company has held charitable status since 1994, and tours theater productions, especially interactive Forum Theatre—a technique developed by the late Augusto Boal, the influential Brazilian writer-director, four of whose books Jackson has translated—to many kinds of venues, including hostels, day centers, schools, and theaters. Jackson has also mounted a number of larger-scale productions with the company, including *The Beggar's Opera* (with ENO), *The Lower Depths* (with London Bubble), and *Mincemeat*. In 2003 he directed a coproduction of *Pericles* for Cardboard Citizens with the RSC, which he discusses here. In 2006 he returned to Stratford with his company with a boardroom-themed *Timon of Athens* for the RSC's Complete Works festival, which was performed at the Shakespeare Birthplace Trust. He is a strong advocate and practitioner of Boal's Theatre of the Oppressed work, which he has taught in many contexts throughout Europe, as well as in Asia, Africa and Latin America, as well as working on theater projects with other marginalized groups, including Irish Travellers, deaf people, and adults with learning difficulties.

Dominic Cooke was born in London in 1966, and studied at Warwick University, taking up his first job in television as a runner shortly after graduating. He founded his own theater company, Pan Optic, which he ran for two years before starting work as an assistant director for the RSC, as well as freelance director, in the early 1990s. In 1996 he joined the Royal Court as an assistant director under Stephen Daldry, returning to the RSC in 2003 to direct a production of *Cymbeline*. Other successes with the company include *Macbeth* (2004), *As You Like It* (2005), and promenade productions of *The Winter's Tale* and *Pericles*—which he discusses here—for the RSC's Complete Works season in 2006. That same year he helmed a production of *The Crucible*, also for the RSC, for which he won the Olivier Award for Best Director. He has been the artistic director of the Royal Court theater since 2006.

This question might seem pointless, but what is the play broadly "about" in your view (if, say, *Macbeth* is "about" murder and its consequences, or *Othello* is "about" jealousy and deception)? Or can we not answer the question in this way?

AN: It's a useful question to try to answer because a lot of people when they approach this play can find that its meaning can slip like sand through their fingers. I think it is about the pursuit of grace. Pericles undertakes a spiritual journey. That journey is embodied by a literal journey around the eastern Mediterranean but it's also a metaphor for a spiritual journey toward a state of grace.

AJ: The aspects of *Pericles* which drew me to make this particular production of the play were related to the main characters' experiences of loss and separation, coupled with their fairy-tale reconvergence in the final scenes of the play. With my company Cardboard Citizens, which works particularly with homeless people and refugees, I have had much experience making theater for and with displaced people over the past twenty years, and I was interested to test a hypothesis that *Pericles* would speak very directly to them. To this end, I made a very cut-down storytelling version of the play with five performers, three from Cardboard Citizens, who had had first-hand experience of refugeedom, and two who had worked with the RSC. This version was rapidly rehearsed and then toured for two weeks to places where newly arrived refugees and asylum seekers were gathered. Each night we played to a different cultural group— one night it would be people from the Horn of Africa; the next, people from the Balkans; the next, people from Iraq or Iran, the Turkish Kurds, and so on. The groups tended to be quite ethnically homogeneous, and many of them had little English. It was remarkable how much they were able to follow and engage with the play, and for sure they did connect their own experiences with those of the play's characters. After the performances each night we would sit down with the people and hear and record their stories reciprocally— sometimes this would be the beginning of a longer relationship.

Following on from this "mini-*Pericles*," we then mounted a full-scale site-specific promenade production of the play, staged as if in a refugee processing center, of the kind much in the news at the time, both in actuality in Sangatte and in proposal form by various European governments, including our own. In this version a number of the testimonies we had recorded were intertwined with the Shakespearean text, in such a way that each text complemented the other.

DC: I think it's about the possibility of life after death; that it's only through an acceptance and an experience of loss that we learn to value life. That's a journey that Shakespeare explores repeatedly in the late plays. The play has several images of people being brought back to life, both literally as in the case of Thaisa, and metaphorically in the case of Pericles at the end of the play.

It's now largely believed that George Wilkins wrote the first two acts of the play, with Shakespeare taking over for the final three. Were you aware of the join, or does the play work as a coherent whole?

AN: I was certainly conscious of at least two hands in the authorship, for the following reasons: the actors found it much easier to learn certain parts of the text, and those parts of the text had been identified by scholars as being by Shakespeare; and those parts of the text lent themselves to a larger degree of psychological examination than the earlier parts of the text. As to whether that affects the coherence of the play as a whole: no, not in the slightest. That depends on how you direct. I took certain views not just on that play but on the whole of the season in which it was presented. My production of *Pericles* was part of a whole season I set up at the Roundhouse [alongside productions of *The Tempest* directed by Michael Boyd and *The Winter's Tale* directed by Matthew Warchus]. It's important to contextualize what I have to say about *Pericles* within that particular experiment. All of the late plays to some degree tell the story of a spiritual journey and a search for a state of grace. Shakespeare uses very similar dramatic techniques in those last four plays. There are very strong links in particular between *Pericles*, *Cymbeline*, and *The Winter's Tale*. There are very powerful similarities of dramaturgy between those late plays, and I wanted to expose those and reveal them to the audience during that Roundhouse season.

AJ: We were very aware of the joint authorship of the play, and this is one of the reasons that we felt fully licensed to interfere with the text—baldly speaking, much of it is clearly by a lesser hand, and one felt no compunction at cutting vast swaths of text and replacing them with interpolated testimony, which spoke more eloquently to our modern audiences. If more text is to be inserted, and if it is to be more than a token presence, the obvious danger is about the overall length of the production—so again, the substandard stuff from the first two acts in particular was a godsend.

DC: It's an undeniable fault line. The difference in the quality of the writing is very marked. If you have any knowledge of Shakespeare, of his persona as a writer, when you get to the storm scene at the beginning of Act 3 the voice is unmistakable. The beauty of the language, a depth of understanding, and a shading that just isn't present beforehand. The writing up to this point has a functional quality, a flatness. The narrative is strong but it is rendered in a slightly workmanlike style. The writing really lifts off as soon as Shakespeare takes over and I felt that in performance this is where the play takes off.

What kind of worlds did you create for your production? What was the story you wanted to tell?

AN: I designed a theater at the Roundhouse with the audience on a rake for 300 out of the 360 degrees. I then countersunk the stage and put carpets down around it; I created a walkway around at the juncture, so there were seats and standing space, divided by a narrow walkway for the performers, thus making a semi-promenade environment. The audience could either sit down or stand up depending on how they felt. I was seeking to create an environment in which the stories of those three plays could be told in an informal, highly atmospheric, almost festival atmosphere. I wanted going to the Roundhouse to feel like the best party you've ever been invited to. There would be music and dance and food and singing and festivities from the moment you arrived to the moment you left, and part of that experience was the telling of the story. With *Pericles*, we were looking to create an experience for the audience that was replicated in space.

AJ: As I have noted earlier, our setting for the production was very specific. A number of vast, soulless modern warehouse spaces, used previously amongst other things as the setting for the annual vast Crisis At Christmas temporary homeless hostel, became for us a version of a refugee processing center. At the time, the media were full of images and stories from Sangatte, the huge equivalent shelter outside Calais, from which groups of asylum seekers would launch nightly forays into the Channel Tunnel seeking access to the UK. The images of fences bedecked with drying clothes spoke volumes for

5. A 2003 collaboration between the RSC and Cardboard Citizens directed by Adrian Jackson: "At the time, the media were full of images and stories from Sangatte, the huge equivalent shelter outside Calais, from which groups of asylum seekers would launch nightly forays into the Channel Tunnel seeking access to the UK. The images of fences bedecked with drying clothes spoke volumes for us—all these clothes were lives. We echoed this in many spaces; there was a room in which we played some of the storm scenes, full of washing machines running at full blast." With Adna Sabljic as the Bawd.

us—all these clothes were lives. We echoed this in many spaces; there was a room in which we played some of the storm scenes, full of washing machines running at full blast, then opened to let water lap at the audience's feet; another room contained nothing other than some fifty or so camp beds, with a forlorn Pericles sitting in the middle of them.

Each room was different, and offered the possibility of subworlds within this larger world. One of the most shocking spaces was dominated by a single container such as might travel on the back of a lorry—another recent story was the tragedy of some thirty Chinese migrants found suffocated in just such a container. During one of the storm scenes, women in the company became waves throwing themselves against the outside of this container, in a poignant evocation both of the storm and the shocking experiences of people seeking asylum and being met with steely indifference. There is an epic quality to *Pericles*, and the promenade form lent itself well to this.

6. Swan Theatre 2006–07: Dominic Cooke's "production played on the very contemporary idea of human trafficking and sex trafficking. The pirates were Somalis. It was a journey round the Horn of Africa and we chose Somalia as it didn't have any rulers and was very dangerous, as it remains."

DC: We set our production against a contemporary background of sex trafficking. Antioch was based on Somalia. We chose Somalia as it is a very unstable country, run by feudal warlords, which felt right for the ruthless unpredictability of Antiochus and his court. Then we made a journey north, through North Africa, across the Mediterranean to Greece. Mytilene was like present-day London, a seedy Soho or King's Cross. The world of the brothel is very detailed in the play. It's a failing business that needs pepping up and Marina is seen as their solution. The detail of the brothel as a business suited a realistic setting, which is what we gave it.

Pericles is very episodic, which makes it quite unusual within the Shakespeare canon. Does this narrative structure create problems in the theater or lend the play a unique effect?

AN: It certainly lends the play a unique effect. It means you've got to direct it, act it, and set it in a certain way. That's not a problem though: it's like saying, Are the songs in a musical a problem? Sure—but they're also the great glory of it, and the episodic nature of *Pericles* is one of its great glories. We made it into part of the meaning of the play. It is episodic and we matched the production to the style of writing.

AJ: It's a play about journeys, and our production was a promenade, moving from space to space for each new world; in each vast room of a warehouse complex we were able to install a different environment.

The episodic nature of the play was another reason why it was a good candidate for this radical treatment—it breaks easily down into chunks, which can easily take the insertion of other text, which becomes a kind of commentary on the real text. The important thing of course is to keep the flow of the narrative and the drama. Testimony on its own can be a bit dry, a bit worthy—after all, it's best delivered clean and unadorned, the fact of its authenticity demands an honorable and unmessy treatment. So we chose some five or so stories to focus on, of which we delivered relevant fragments around each of the episodes of Pericles' adventures.

DC: A bit of both. It doesn't have the self-analysis that, for example, *Macbeth* or *Hamlet* have. In those plays much of the drama happens in soliloquy, in self-exploration. But in *Pericles* it's action, action, action all the way. The meaning is revealed through the choices and actions of the characters rather than through reflection or self-analysis. That's very particular to this play above other Shakespeare plays and it does make for a very entertaining experience. The travelogue aspect gives variety to the play that's refreshing and audience-friendly.

Many audiences have found *Pericles* utterly charming, having a strong capacity to move. Could you perhaps share your views on the nature of the play's emotional power? How did your audiences react?

AN: They shed a tear and gave a standing ovation for about fifteen minutes. In terms of audience reaction it was one of the most successful productions I have ever done in my life. The response was overwhelming. People were crying and shouting: it was quite extraordinary. The play has that same power to move, to stir emotions in the audience, as *The Winter's Tale*. The story is very emotional because it's about finding that which is lost. Shakespeare uses the same button that he uses in different ways in *The Winter's Tale* and *Cymbeline*. It's a powerful button: the horror that most parents have at the prospect of losing their children.

I wanted to use the opportunity Shakespeare gave me for ceremony, for music, which heavily underscored the text in my production. I used a friend of mine, Shaun Davey, an Irish composer who writes most emotional music. We told the story and then, when Shakespeare kicks in in the latter parts of the play, the audience were absolutely ready to engage in a full-blown, psychologically realized situation, particularly the reunion between father and daughter.

AJ: Surely the recognition scene near the end of the play is Shakespeare's best in that genre, and our audiences were as moved as any. Our general audiences, for the full-scale production, were also greatly affected by the extraordinary contemporary stories of flight we told—and our refugee audiences during our first small tour quite simply identified with the characters and their experiences. It's perhaps worth recounting a story gathered in that research period, dur-

7. Adrian Noble 2002, with Ray Fearon as Pericles and Kananu Kirimi as Marina: "We told the story and then, when Shakespeare kicks in in the latter parts of the play, the audience were absolutely ready to engage in a full-blown, psychologically realized situation, particularly the reunion between father and daughter."

ing the tour of our mini-*Pericles*. One night we performed at a club for Latin American elders in Camberwell, called *Los Años Dorados* ("The Golden Years"), to an audience of perhaps fifteen people. At the end of the show, one woman, the lady who ran the club, was in floods of tears. Gently our conversations started, and of course I asked her why the play had moved her so much. She said: "My mother was born at sea and called Marina." She then unfolded a remarkable story of three generations of refugeedom, crossing from Spain to Chile and then, in flight from Pinochet, first to Argentina, then to the UK. The entire audience for the two weeks of perform-ances of the mini-*Pericles* cannot have been more than three hun-dred people—so what were the chances of this meeting? Of course, the story of Amada Vergara Silva Espinosa became one of the stories we told in the larger production of the play.

DC: Our production played in promenade and we were very keen to involve the audience physically and emotionally as much as possible. There is something powerfully redemptive about Pericles being brought back to life when he finds his daughter at the end of the play. I think that the notion of a second chance in life is universally attrac-tive and the audience responded to it. A sense of geographical dis-placement was clear in our production: the father and daughter are meeting on the other side of the world and their journey has taken them thousands of miles away from home. They meet as displaced foreigners in a strange land. There was a sense of the possibility of grace even in the most unlikely places. As with all Shakespeare reunions, the redemption can't completely compensate for the scars left by the prior separation. Nothing can make up for the suffering of those lost years. This adds to the emotional power of the moment.

It's a very artificial, demonstrative play in some ways, featuring lots of dumb shows. Is that a part of it that you embraced willingly?

DC: I feel that if you're producing any of the late plays you have got to simultaneously take them seriously—emotionally, psychologi-cally, politically—but also allow the playful theatricality of the play's form to emerge. It's important to embrace this theatrical aspect of the plays. Pentapolis was a Greek island in our production and the tournament scene was an Olympic pentathlon. We did it in a very playful, theatrical way. There are some other bravura theatrical moments written into the play, like the storm and the wedding sequence. It would be a shame not to honor them in production.

AJ: The variety of theatrical modes is another of the gifts the play offers a modern director—audiences now are used to many different ways of telling stories, so dumb shows and choric narrative sit easily alongside all the other devices. Our production also made use of video as a shorthand way of dealing with exposition. As for artificiality—well, theater is artificial, so this is no problem. We also played with notions of the "dumb" show—the idea of some people never being allowed to tell their story, the idea of being struck dumb in trauma.

What kind of role is Pericles for an actor to play? What do you think are its major challenges?

AN: It's a wonderful part but as an actor you have to be quite generous with it, because you have to wait quite a long time before you get your big scene. The play swirls and swirls around you and you have to accept that the dramatic language of the early part of the play is written in a particular way. It's not written as mature middle Shakespeare whereby every turn of the character is explored through the text, as is the case with Hamlet or Richard of Gloucester, for example. Every turn of Pericles is not explored through the text. It becomes that later, but not early on and you have to accept that. The early parts of the play are not psychological and there's nothing you can do about that. But they're fantastically exciting to play if the production around you is cooking. Then you get the most wonderful things to play in the latter part of the play.

AJ: We had two Pericles, young and old. This makes some aspects of the transition easier, and makes it easier to cast and play; to my mind the second Pericles, the old man, is almost Howard Hughes-like, and, short of ridiculous stage beards, a difficult transformation to effect. I suppose the challenge for a younger actor is to find the experience of loss that anybody over a certain age has easily at their grasp. The recognition scene is so beautifully written, so carefully constructed and paced, that I actually think it's a gift to an actor—though I would not want to play down the challenge of playing out the journey from deep trauma to almost ecstatic bliss; this is a Lear who lives.

DC: It's a tricky part. There's not much self-analysis or self-reflection with which to reveal character. Therefore, as an actor you've got to fill the gaps, find how each event contributes to the spiritual evolution of the character. It's an extreme journey but up to the director and actor to join the dots. The extremity is exciting though and we went for it. In the first scene Pericles is politically naive—dangerously so— and he brings about a very risky and dangerous situation as a result of not being as tactical as he could. Later he has a complete breakdown. He's crippled with grief and unable to function. We went for those extremes at the beginning and the end and worked out how they joined together through the action of the play.

And Marina?

AN: Kananu Kirimi (KK), who played Marina in our production, was sublime. She had a very particular quality. I think because she came from the Isle of Skye she had a strange, very light Scottish accent. There was always a remoteness about her, which is perfect for that role. Marina is this very special child, a rather unusual creature born with a very strong sense of morality. Some children are born with an innate sense of good and bad and she captured that completely. It's a little bit difficult to cast, to find in an actor if they haven't got that. Not all actors can play it. You have got to have it for that part. KK had this wonderful gift of an inner stillness, this beautiful voice, and gave a real moral sense to the choices the character made.

AJ: Marina is perhaps more difficult: to bring her back to earth, to avoid her becoming too saintly. Of course the device of her overcoming rape with mere eloquence is difficult in a modern production. The concept of sexual slavery is after all only too familiar now, and we doubt that the hardhearted dealers in flesh we read about would pay too much heed to such a plea. That's if we take it literally—for most productions it's presumably about the power of eloquence, the way women in Shakespeare often rise above their given status by means of the power of speech. I preferred to think of it as a species of wish fulfillment on Marina's part—she rises above the incident by the power of her mind, as one hears tell that the only way to deal with such a horror in reality is to turn off part of consciousness and rise above it. We tried, unsuccessfully I think, to convey this idea by having the scene break down for a moment at this point. The attempted rape took place in a nasty builders' cabin in the corner of one of the spaces—the audience could either watch it through peep-holes cut in the paper covering the windows, or on a projected CCTV version. At the moment when, to my mind, this psychological feat took place, there was a sound, the image froze for a while, and then resumed, as if in some other register. The rape is no one's business—in a kind of way, it's irrelevant if she's raped; what is remarkable is that she survives it and remains strong.

DC: I think Marina is an even harder part to play than Pericles because she is one of those characters that's in danger of being too good to be true. Her presence in the play denotes innocence and purity—qualities that are hard to act and can easily feel cloying for an audience. Casting that part was hard. We must have seen thirty very strong actresses for it. When Ony Uhiara came in she wasn't acting: she has an integrity that doesn't need to be acted or played. It's just who she is. What's interesting about Marina is that people see their own potential for goodness in her. So she has to be played to have a quiet neutrality that the other characters can project onto.

How much importance did you attach to the role of magic in the play and how did you realize it onstage in your productions?

AJ: The most literally magical moment is the emergence of Thaisa recovered, after the ministrations of the healer. This was played in a combination of video projected onto the open side of the container, and the emergence of the living actress through this video. For me, magic per se is not interesting—I want to know how a trick is done; I want to understand how something that seems like magic is in fact real. Reality is often magical. The regathering of Pericles' family at the end of the play was mirrored by events we hear from an Iranian asylum seeker, who thought his scattered family was dead, only to receive a phone call from Australia some six years after he had last seen them.

The goddess Diana is taken to be magical—but in our production we had the only Diana we could have, the princess who had died a decade earlier. She was an ordinary person of course, but the world elevated her, particularly after death, to a magical and deified status. This is how magic is done, by projection; the magic is in our imaginations. We ended our production with an evocation of the sea of flowers that became the shrine of Princess Di. The tongue was near the cheek . . .

DC: If you deny the presence of magic in the play, you're in danger of reducing the scale of experience that the play charts in order to fit it into an empirical, materialist, twenty-first-century view of the world. Magic in the play is metaphor for many things, mostly the rejuvenative power of nature and the possibility of healing and transformation. Cerimon was played by a woman: the same actor, Linda Bassett, who played the Bawd. She also played Paulina, who brings Hermione back to life in *The Winter's Tale* and is called a "bawd" by Leontes. This created an interesting continuity between both plays. We set the revival of Thaisa in a New Age community: somewhere where pagan magic would be believed and practiced. Cerimon was an elder within that community. We created a world outside mainstream society, a hidden world of unconventional values. When Cerimon brought Thaisa back to life it was powerful and moving in performance. Of course, we were helped by having two exceptionally committed and talented actresses in the roles in Linda Bassett and Kate Fleetwood as Thaisa.

One of the unique things about *Pericles* within the late plays is its use of Gower as a Chorus (only *The Winter's Tale* does something similar, featuring one speech by the figure of Time). What effect does Gower's presence have on the experience of the play, and how did you depict him?

AN: There is a kind of framing device in both *Cymbeline* and *The Winter's Tale*. They both start with two gentlemen talking and giving you the story up to that point. This is formalized in *Pericles* through the character of Gower, but its function is no different. Somebody tells a story and that story is enacted and brought to life. At a stroke, that embraces the episodic nature of *Pericles* and makes it a virtue. You have to go down that line. The actors and the audience are gathered in by Gower and it becomes an informal, exotic experience. Gower repeats, comes back and forth during the whole piece and ties everything up at the end. He is the glue, he is the narrator, he is the person who is the direct contact between the audience and the characters.

AJ: Gower just became a shared chorus for us. He was not one person, just the voice of the narrative. Sometimes Pericles younger or older spoke his lines, sometimes others. For us the idea of Gower was not important, only the choric function. The idea of an older man speaking to a younger self is powerful too.

The whole play offers any director a huge freedom, and lends itself well to contemporary illustration or reference. For me, the keynote of a production partly performed and heavily informed by refugees and outcasts is the glorious metaphor offered early in the play, as a warning: "The blind mole casts / Copped hills towards heaven, to tell the earth is thronged / By man's oppression, and the poor worm doth die for't."

DC: What's interesting is that Gower's version of events isn't quite borne out by the scenes. He's a propagandist, putting forward a particular and partial reading of the story and guiding the audience to make moral judgments on the characters. Shakespeare frequently explores, to quote from *All's Well That Ends Well*, how "The web of our life is of a mingled yarn, good and ill together." If what Shakespeare is interested in exploring are those gray areas, then Gower is a hard-line medieval moralist. Because our production had started in Africa, Gower was the village storyteller, telling the story retrospectively. It really worked well, with Joseph Mydell as a hard-line, didactic, possibly quite Christian, African man to whom the notions of good and bad are very clear and distinct. He was clearly disapproving of some of the characters, and that gave the play an interesting texture, inviting the audience to make a choice about who to believe.

PLAYING MARINA: LAURA REES

Laura Rees trained at the Academy Drama School and the Royal Welsh College of Music and Drama, where she was the recipient of the Prudence Emilyn-Jones Prize for Movement, Dance and Ballet along with multiple student acting awards. She graduated in 2001, and subsequent stage roles have included Gerd in Adrian Noble's 2003 production of Ibsen's *Brand* for the RSC, alongside Ralph Fiennes in the lead role; Ophelia in Yukio Ninagawa's 2004 production of *Hamlet*; and Viola in Philip Franks' production of *Twelfth Night* at the Chichester Festival Theatre in 2007. She worked at the Globe Theatre in 2005 playing Marina in Kathryn Hunter's production of *Pericles*, which she discusses here, returning the following year to play Lavinia in Lucy Bailey's *Titus Andronicus* (for which she was nominated for the Ian Charleson Award) and Luciana in Christopher Luscombe's production of *The Comedy of Errors*. She has worked extensively in television and radio, and has appeared in several films, including Richard Curtis' *Love Actually* (2003). She is also currently an active member of the London artistic collective the Factory Theatre Company.

Clearly this question might seem pointlessly reductive, but what is the play broadly "about" in your view (if, say, *Macbeth* is "about" murder and its consequences, or *Othello* is "about" jealousy and deception)? Or can we not answer the question in this way?

LR: I find it difficult to pinpoint a central theme in *Pericles*. It seems to be about a man's journey through life and its unpredictable twists and turns. The triumph of good over evil: virtue versus vice: loss, reunion.

It's now largely believed that George Wilkins wrote the first two acts of the play, with Shakespeare taking over for the final three. Were you aware of the join, or does the play work as a coherent whole?

LR: I remember people talking a lot about this. As far as playing Marina was concerned, the character is not born in the first half of the play so I was lucky and only had the really great stuff to say! There does seem to be a change in style from Act 2 to 3; but I still think the play works in its entirety. What starts as a kind of fable— "To sing a song that old was sung"—shifts into a much more emotional level in Act 3 with the great storm, the birth of Marina and supposed death of Thaisa; and the language matches this.

Many audiences have found *Pericles* utterly charming, with a strong capacity to move. Could you perhaps share your views on the nature of the play's emotional power? How did your audiences react?

LR: The audience has the chance to go with a man on his journey through life. They meet him when he is young. They relive extraordinary events with him. They see him find happiness only to have it snatched almost immediately away. They meet his daughter, who in turn faces tremendous suffering through no fault of her own. She eventually finds her way to him when he needs her most and they are reunited in arguably the most beautiful scene ever! It's a rollercoaster ride with a very happy ending. I remember wonder and joy radiating around the Globe every time we performed those final scenes of the play.

What was Marina like as a character to you? How did you go about playing her?

LR: Marina has many talents. She sings, dances, sews, and weaves. She is a "goodly creature": an innocent. It was important to me that I didn't get caught in the trap of "playing" goodly or innocent so I worked hard at extracting her other qualities. In the first week of rehearsals our director, Kathryn Hunter, initiated a series of improvisations for us to better get to know our characters and the various worlds they inhabit. One was of Marina's tenth birthday party (she is fourteen when we first meet her in the play) and we discovered what her relationships were like with her guardians Cleon and Dionyza and their daughter Philoten, and the reasons behind their growing resentment toward Marina. Another improvisation gave me my rela-

8. Globe 2005, directed by Kathryn Hunter, with Laura Rees as Marina and Patrice Naiambana as Gower: "Marina has many talents. She sings, dances, sews, and weaves. She is a 'goodly creature'; an innocent."

tionship with the nurse, Lychorida, over whose grave Marina weeps when we first meet her in the play.

I did a lot of research into prostitution and abduction, which included reading *I Choose to Live* by Sabinne Dardeene. Sabinne was kidnapped in Belgium aged twelve and spent three months in captivity with a pedophile. I wanted to understand as best I could what it might feel like to be snatched and sold into prostitution, as Marina is in the play. Despite the terrifying situations she finds herself in, Marina is able to see the best in people. To the man who is sent to kill her—"You have a gentle heart"—and to the man about to rape her she asks, "If you were born to honour, show it now." She shows people a mirror and demands that they do not ignore their own image. My job as an actor, through rehearsal and right until the last performance, is to develop how this person moves, thinks, and speaks; and how that changes through the course of the play.

How does she fare against some of the other more famous heroines in Shakespeare? Is it an undervalued role?

LR: My concerns about playing a sweet, innocent, two-dimensional role were unfounded. Marina experiences grief, her attempted murder, kidnapping, abuse, freedom, and a reunion with both her parents from whom she was separated at birth. Throughout this trajectory she remains completely unselfish, continues to look outward and enable those who come into contact with her to heal themselves. I cannot think of another Shakespearean heroine who is able to do this. She is completely unique. Undervalued? Perhaps. Possibly because this play is not as widely known as, for example, *Macbeth* or *Romeo and Juliet*.

How old is Marina supposed to be? Pericles says that Cleon tried to murder her at "fourteen years." Did you see much more time as having elapsed between that and the Mytilene scenes? Did you try to convey a childlike quality in your body language, for example?

LR: Marina is fourteen when Leonine is hired to kill her. I think everything happens pretty quickly after that and if there is a significant passage of time it takes place once Marina has escaped the dangers of the brothel and gained employment "amongst honest women." I wanted to avoid worrying about playing "age" too much, and although Marina seems very wise at times in what she says, she also retains the inquisitiveness of a child in asking "why?" so often. Kathryn and I worked on Marina's physicality with an improvisation where I took myself physically through the stages of the story. It began with all the freedom of play, expansiveness, without inhibition. As Marina was faced with more grief and trauma she slowly closed off her body until she was finally curled up into a tight ball. Continuing through the story into the reunion scene, Marina returns to her expansiveness but with the added burden of her experiences, more stature, and probably more age.

Her two big set pieces are the brothel scene with Lysimachus and the reunion scene. What were they like to play, and what were their principal challenges, starting with the brothel scene?

LR: Up until her meeting with Lysimachus, Marina has somehow managed to cling on to her chastity. Men that arrive to take it from her leave soon after vowing to "hear the vestals sing" or "do anything . . . that is virtuous." What could she possibly be doing or saying to achieve this? For me, the principal challenge of this scene in the brothel was managing a balance between fear and control. Marina turns each of Lysimachus' questions round on him, as if she has no idea what it is he could be after; but below the surface she sees the horror descending all around her and she is very frightened and very alone. It was an emotional scene to play and had to remain completely real in order for it to work. I remember one performance pleading to the gods to "set me free from this unhallowed place, / Though they did change me to the meanest bird / That flies i'th'purer air!" at which moment an extremely scruffy pigeon that had been wandering about on the corner of the stage took flight and circled once around the auditorium of the Globe until escaping into the night sky. About 1,500 people gasped as one.

And the reunion? It's proved time and again to be an extremely moving moment for audiences. What were your experiences of playing it?

LR: I found the less "baggage" I brought to the reunion scene with Pericles the better. It plays as a perfectly formed piece of music, and as long as the notes were sung one by one, without strain or overindulgence, the audience is effortlessly carried along to its miraculous climax. Of course, it takes a great deal for Marina to talk to this stranger of her past; she has not confided in anyone until this point, and the scene has a subtle incestuous undertone where Pericles is attracted to a young girl that so closely resembles his wife; but ultimately I found the playing of it extremely pure, with a feeling of astonishing inevitability without my character having an inkling of what was coming.

What about the reunion scene with Thaisa—another emotionally draining moment?

LR: Shakespeare gives Marina only one line when she is reunited with her mother. It is impossible to contain her joy and there is nothing left but to return to her mother's arms. It is not an accident that she otherwise remains silent and I remember feeling like Marina was able to float through the final scene, experiencing a mixture of infinite awe and undeniable ecstasy. Not a bad feeling to take home!

SHAKESPEARE'S CAREER
IN THE THEATER

BEGINNINGS

William Shakespeare was an extraordinarily intelligent man who was born and died in an ordinary market town in the English Midlands. He lived an uneventful life in an eventful age. Born in April 1564, he was the eldest son of John Shakespeare, a glove maker who was prominent on the town council until he fell into financial difficulties. Young William was educated at the local grammar in Stratford-upon-Avon, Warwickshire, where he gained a thorough grounding in the Latin language, the art of rhetoric, and classical poetry. He married Ann Hathaway and had three children (Susanna, then the twins Hamnet and Judith) before his twenty-first birthday: an exceptionally young age for the period. We do not know how he supported his family in the mid-1580s.

Like many clever country boys, he moved to the city in order to make his way in the world. Like many creative people, he found a career in the entertainment business. Public playhouses and professional full-time acting companies reliant on the market for their income were born in Shakespeare's childhood. When he arrived in London as a man, sometime in the late 1580s, a new phenomenon was in the making: the actor who is so successful that he becomes a "star." The word did not exist in its modern sense, but the pattern is recognizable: audiences went to the theater not so much to see a particular show as to witness the comedian Richard Tarlton or the dramatic actor Edward Alleyn.

Shakespeare was an actor before he was a writer. It appears not to have been long before he realized that he was never going to grow into a great comedian like Tarlton or a great tragedian like Alleyn. Instead, he found a role within his company as the man who patched up old plays, breathing new life, new dramatic twists, into tired repertory pieces. He paid close attention to the work of the university-educated dramatists who were writing history plays and tragedies for the public stage in a style more ambitious, sweeping, and poetically grand than anything which had been seen before. But he may also have noted that what his friend and rival Ben Jonson would call "Marlowe's mighty line" sometimes faltered in the mode of comedy. Going to university, as Christopher Marlowe did, was all well and good for honing the arts of rhetorical elaboration and classical allusion, but it could lead to a loss of the common touch. To stay close to a large segment of the potential audience for public theater, it was necessary to write for clowns as well as kings and to intersperse the flights of poetry with the humor of the tavern, the privy, and the brothel: Shakespeare was the first to establish himself early in his career as an equal master of tragedy, comedy, and history. He realized that theater could be the medium to make the national past available to a wider audience than the elite who could afford to read large history books: his signature early works include not only the classical tragedy *Titus Andronicus* but also the sequence of English historical plays on the Wars of the Roses.

He also invented a new role for himself, that of in-house company dramatist. Where his peers and predecessors had to sell their plays to the theater managers on a poorly paid piecework basis, Shakespeare took a percentage of the box-office income. The Lord Chamberlain's Men constituted themselves in 1594 as a joint stock company, with the profits being distributed among the core actors who had invested as sharers. Shakespeare acted himself—he appears in the cast lists of some of Ben Jonson's plays as well as the list of actors' names at the beginning of his own collected works—but his principal duty was to write two or three plays a year for the company. By holding shares, he was effectively earning himself a royalty on his work, something no author had ever done before in England. When the Lord Chamberlain's Men collected their fee for performance at court in the Christmas season of 1594, three of them went along to the Treasurer of the Chamber: not just Richard Burbage the tragedian and Will Kempe the clown, but also Shakespeare the scriptwriter. That was something new.

The next four years were the golden period in Shakespeare's

career, though overshadowed by the death of his only son, Hamnet, aged eleven, in 1596. In his early thirties and in full command of both his poetic and his theatrical medium, he perfected his art of comedy, while also developing his tragic and historical writing in new ways. In 1598, Francis Meres, a Cambridge University graduate with his finger on the pulse of the London literary world, praised Shakespeare for his excellence across the genres:

> As Plautus and Seneca are accounted the best for comedy and tragedy among the Latins, so Shakespeare among the English is the most excellent in both kinds for the stage; for comedy, witness his *Gentlemen of Verona*, his *Errors*, his *Love Labours Lost*, his *Love Labours Won*, his *Midsummer Night Dream* and his *Merchant of Venice*: for tragedy his *Richard the 2*, *Richard the 3*, *Henry the 4*, *King John*, *Titus Andronicus* and his *Romeo and Juliet*.

For Meres, as for the many writers who praised the "honey-flowing vein" of *Venus and Adonis* and *Lucrece*, narrative poems written when the theaters were closed due to plague in 1593–94, Shakespeare was marked above all by his linguistic skill, by the gift of turning elegant poetic phrases.

PLAYHOUSES

Elizabethan playhouses were "thrust" or "one-room" theaters. To understand Shakespeare's original theatrical life, we have to forget about the indoor theater of later times, with its proscenium arch and curtain that would be opened at the beginning and closed at the end of each act. In the proscenium arch theater, stage and auditorium are effectively two separate rooms: the audience looks from one world into another as if through the imaginary "fourth wall" framed by the proscenium. The picture-frame stage, together with the elaborate scenic effects and backdrops beyond it, created the illusion of a self-contained world—especially once nineteenth-century developments in the control of artificial lighting meant that the auditorium could be darkened and the spectators made to focus on the lighted stage. Shakespeare, by contrast, wrote for a bare platform stage with a standing audience gathered around it in a courtyard in full daylight. The audience were always conscious of themselves and their fellow spectators, and they shared the same "room" as the actors. A sense of immediate presence and the creation of rapport with the audience were all-important. The actor could not afford to imagine he was in a closed world, with silent witnesses dutifully observing him from the darkness.

Shakespeare's theatrical career began at the Rose Theatre in Southwark. The stage was wide and shallow, trapezoid in shape, like a lozenge. This design had a great deal of potential for the theatrical equivalent of cinematic split-screen effects, whereby one group of characters would enter at the door at one end of the tiring-house wall at the back of the stage and another group through the door at the other end, thus creating two rival tableaux. Many of the battle-heavy and faction-filled plays that premiered at the Rose have scenes of just this sort.

At the rear of the Rose stage, there were three capacious exits, each over ten feet wide. Unfortunately, the very limited excavation of a fragmentary portion of the original Globe site, in 1989, revealed nothing about the stage. The first Globe was built in 1599 with similar proportions to those of another theater, the Fortune, albeit that the former was polygonal and looked circular, whereas the latter was rectangular. The building contract for the Fortune survives and allows us to infer that the stage of the Globe was probably substantially wider than it was deep (perhaps forty-three feet wide and twenty-seven feet deep). It may well have been tapered at the front, like that of the Rose.

The capacity of the Globe was said to have been enormous, perhaps in excess of three thousand. It has been conjectured that about eight hundred people may have stood in the yard, with two thousand or more in the three layers of covered galleries. The other "public" playhouses were also of large capacity, whereas the indoor Blackfriars theater that Shakespeare's company began using in 1608—the former refectory of a monastery—had overall internal dimensions of a mere forty-six by sixty feet. It would have made for a much more intimate theatrical experience and had a much smaller capacity, probably of about six hundred people. Since they paid at least six-pence a head, the Blackfriars attracted a more select or "private" audience. The atmosphere would have been closer to that of an indoor performance before the court in the Whitehall Palace or at Richmond. That Shakespeare always wrote for indoor production at court as well as outdoor performance in the public theater should make us cautious about inferring, as some scholars have, that the opportunity provided by the intimacy of the Blackfriars led to a significant change toward a "chamber" style in his last plays—which, besides, were performed at both the Globe and the Blackfriars. After the occupation of the Blackfriars a five-act structure seems to have become more important to Shakespeare. That was because of artificial lighting: there were musical interludes between the acts, while the candles were trimmed and replaced. Again, though, something similar must have been necessary for indoor court performances throughout his career.

Front of house there were the "gatherers" who collected the money from audience members: a penny to stand in the open-air yard, another penny for a place in the covered galleries, sixpence for the prominent "lord's rooms" to the side of the stage. In the indoor "private" theaters, gallants from the audience who fancied making themselves part of the spectacle sat on stools on the edge of the stage itself. Scholars debate as to how widespread this practice was in the public theaters such as the Globe. Once the audience were in place and the money counted, the gatherers were available to be extras on-stage. That is one reason why battles and crowd scenes often come later rather than early in Shakespeare's plays. There was no formal prohibition upon performance by women, and there certainly were women among the gatherers, so it is not beyond the bounds of possibility that female crowd members were played by females.

The play began at two o'clock in the afternoon and the theater had to be cleared by five. After the main show, there would be a jig—which consisted not only of dancing, but also of knockabout comedy (it is the origin of the farcical "afterpiece" in the eighteenth-century theater). So the time available for a Shakespeare play was about two and a half hours, somewhere between the "two hours' traffic" mentioned in the prologue to *Romeo and Juliet* and the "three hours' spectacle" referred to in the preface to the 1647 Folio of Beaumont and Fletcher's plays. The prologue to a play by Thomas Middleton refers to a thousand lines as "one hour's words," so the likelihood is that about two and a half thousand, or a maximum of three thousand lines made up the performed text. This is indeed the length of most of Shakespeare's comedies, whereas many of his tragedies and histories are much longer, raising the possibility that he wrote full scripts, possibly with eventual publication in mind, in the full knowledge that the stage version would be heavily cut. The short Quarto texts published in his lifetime—they used to be called "Bad" Quartos—provide fascinating evidence as to the kind of cutting that probably took place. So, for instance, the First Quarto of *Hamlet* neatly merges two occasions when Hamlet is overheard, the "Fishmonger" and the "nunnery" scenes.

The social composition of the audience was mixed. The poet Sir John Davies wrote of "A thousand townsmen, gentlemen and whores, / Porters and servingmen" who would "together throng" at the public playhouses. Though moralists associated female play-going with adultery and the sex trade, many perfectly respectable citizens' wives were regular attendees. Some, no doubt, resembled the modern groupie: a story attested in two different sources has one citizen's wife making a post-show assignation with Richard Burbage and ending up in bed with Shakespeare—supposedly eliciting from the latter the quip that William the Conqueror was before Richard III. Defenders of theater liked to say that by witnessing the comeuppance of villains on the stage, audience members would repent of their own wrongdoings, but the reality is that most people went to the theater then, as they do now, for entertainment more than moral edification. Besides, it would be foolish to suppose that audiences behaved in a homogeneous way: a pamphlet of the 1630s tells of how two men went to see *Pericles* and one of them laughed while the other wept. Bishop John Hall complained that people went to church for the same reasons that they went to the theater: "for company, for custom, for recreation . . . to feed his eyes or his ears . . . or perhaps for sleep."

Men-about-town and clever young lawyers went to be seen as much as to see. In the modern popular imagination, shaped not least by *Shakespeare in Love* and the opening sequence of Laurence Olivier's *Henry V* film, the penny-paying groundlings stand in the yard hurling abuse or encouragement and hazelnuts or orange peel at the actors, while the sophisticates in the covered galleries appreciate Shakespeare's soaring poetry. The reality was probably the other way around. A "groundling" was a kind of fish, so the nickname suggests the penny audience standing below the level of the stage and gazing in silent openmouthed wonder at the spectacle unfolding above them. The more difficult audience members, who kept up a running commentary of clever remarks on the performance and who occasionally got into quarrels with players, were the gallants. Like Hollywood movies in modern times, Elizabethan and Jacobean plays exercised a powerful influence on the fashion and behavior of the young. John Marston mocks the lawyers who would open their lips, perhaps to court a girl, and out would "flow / Naught but pure Juliet and Romeo."

THE ENSEMBLE AT WORK

In the absence of typewriters and photocopying machines, reading aloud would have been the means by which the company got to know a new play. The tradition of the playwright reading his complete script to the assembled company endured for generations. A copy would then have been taken to the Master of the Revels for licensing. The theater book-holder or prompter would then have copied the parts for distribution to the actors. A partbook consisted of the character's lines, with each speech preceded by the last three or four words of the speech before, the so-called "cue." These would have been taken away and studied or "conned." During this period of learning the parts, an actor might have had some one-to-one instruction, perhaps from the dramatist, perhaps from a senior actor who had played the same part before, and, in the case of an apprentice, from his master. A high percentage of Desdemona's lines occur in dialogue with Othello, of Lady Macbeth's with Macbeth, Cleopatra's with Antony, and Volumnia's with Coriolanus. The roles would almost certainly have been taken by the apprentice of the lead actor, usually Burbage, who delivers the majority of the cues. Given that

9. Hypothetical reconstruction of the interior of an Elizabethan playhouse during a performance.

apprentices lodged with their masters, there would have been ample opportunity for personal instruction, which may be what made it possible for young men to play such demanding parts.

After the parts were learned, there may have been no more than a single rehearsal before the first performance. With six different plays to be put on every week, there was no time for more. Actors, then, would go into a show with a very limited sense of the whole. The notion of a collective rehearsal process that is itself a process of discovery for the actors is wholly modern and would have been incomprehensible to Shakespeare and his original ensemble. Given the number of parts an actor had to hold in his memory, the forgetting of lines was probably more frequent than in the modern theater. The book-holder was on hand to prompt.

Backstage personnel included the property man, the tire-man who oversaw the costumes, call boys, attendants, and the musicians, who might play at various times from the main stage, the rooms above, and within the tiring-house. Scriptwriters sometimes made a nuisance of themselves backstage. There was often tension between the acting companies and the freelance playwrights from whom they purchased scripts: it was a smart move on the part of Shakespeare and the Lord Chamberlain's Men to bring the writing process in-house.

Scenery was limited, though sometimes set pieces were brought on (a bank of flowers, a bed, the mouth of hell). The trapdoor from below, the gallery stage above, and the curtained discovery space at the back allowed for an array of special effects: the rising of ghosts and apparitions, the descent of gods, dialogue between a character at a window and another at ground level, the revelation of a statue or a pair of lovers playing at chess. Ingenious use could be made of props, as with the ass's head in *A Midsummer Night's Dream*. In a theater that does not clutter the stage with the material paraphernalia of everyday life, those objects that are deployed may take on powerful symbolic weight, as when Shylock bears his weighing scales in one hand and knife in the other, thus becoming a parody of the figure of Justice, who traditionally bears a sword and a balance. Among the more significant items in the property cupboard of Shakespeare's company, there would have been a throne (the "chair of state"), joint stools, books, bottles, coins, purses, letters (which are brought onstage, read or referred to on about eighty occasions in the complete works), maps, gloves, a set of stocks (in which Kent is put in *King Lear*), rings, rapiers, daggers, broadswords, staves, pistols, masks and vizards, heads and skulls, torches and tapers and lanterns that served to signal night scenes on the daylit stage, a buck's head, an ass's head, animal costumes. Live animals also put in appearances, most notably the dog Crab in *The Two Gentlemen of Verona* and possibly a young polar bear in *The Winter's Tale*.

The costumes were the most important visual dimension of the play. Playwrights were paid between £2 and £6 per script, whereas Alleyn was not averse to paying £20 for "a black velvet cloak with sleeves embroidered all with silver and gold." No matter the period of the play, actors always wore contemporary costume. The excitement for the audience came not from any impression of historical accuracy, but from the richness of the attire and perhaps the transgressive thrill of the knowledge that here were commoners like themselves strutting in the costumes of courtiers in effective defiance of the strict sumptuary laws whereby in real life people had to wear the clothes that befitted their social station.

To an even greater degree than props, costumes could carry symbolic importance. Racial characteristics could be suggested: a breastplate and helmet for a Roman soldier, a turban for a Turk, long robes for exotic characters such as Moors, a gabardine for a Jew. The figure of Time, as in *The Winter's Tale*, would be equipped with hourglass, scythe, and wings; Rumour, who speaks the prologue of *2 Henry IV*, wore a costume adorned with a thousand tongues. The wardrobe in the tiring-house of the Globe would have contained much of the same stock as that of rival manager Philip Henslowe at the Rose: green gowns for outlaws and foresters, black for melancholy men such as Jaques and people in mourning such as the Countess in *All's Well That Ends Well* (at the beginning of *Hamlet*, the prince is still in mourning black when everyone else is in festive garb for the wedding of the new king), a gown and hood for a friar (or a feigned friar like the duke in *Measure for Measure*), blue coats and tawny to distinguish the followers of rival factions, a leather apron and ruler for a carpenter (as in the opening scene of *Julius Caesar*—and in *A Midsummer Night's Dream*, where this is the only sign that Peter Quince is a carpenter), a cockle hat with staff and a pair of sandals for a pilgrim or palmer (the disguise assumed by Helen in *All's Well*), bodices and kirtles with farthingales beneath for the boys who are to be dressed as girls. A gender switch such as that of Rosalind or Jessica seems to have taken between fifty and eighty lines of dialogue—Viola does not resume her "maiden weeds" but remains in her boy's costume to the end of *Twelfth Night* because a change would have slowed down the action at just the moment it was speeding to a climax. Henslowe's inventory also included "a robe for to go invisible": Oberon, Puck, and Ariel must have had something similar.

As the costumes appealed to the eyes, so there was music for the ears. Comedies included many songs. Desdemona's willow song, perhaps a late addition to the text, is a rare and thus exceptionally poignant example from tragedy. Trumpets and tuckets sounded for ceremonial entrances, drums denoted an army on the march. Background music could create atmosphere, as at the beginning of *Twelfth Night*, during the lovers' dialogue near the end of *The Mer-*

chant of Venice, when the statue seemingly comes to life in *The Winter's Tale*, and for the revival of Pericles and of Lear (in the Quarto text, but not the Folio). The haunting sound of the hautboy suggested a realm beyond the human, as when the god Hercules is imagined deserting Mark Antony. Dances symbolized the harmony of the end of a comedy—though in Shakespeare's world of mingled joy and sorrow, someone is usually left out of the circle.

The most important resource was, of course, the actors themselves. They needed many skills: in the words of one contemporary commentator, "dancing, activity, music, song, elocution, ability of body, memory, skill of weapon, pregnancy of wit." Their bodies were as significant as their voices. Hamlet tells the player to "suit the action to the word, the word to the action": moments of strong emotion, known as "passions," relied on a repertoire of dramatic gestures as well as a modulation of the voice. When Titus Andronicus has had his hand chopped off, he asks "How can I grace my talk, / Wanting a hand to give it action?" A pen portrait of "The Character of an Excellent Actor" by the dramatist John Webster is almost certainly based on his impression of Shakespeare's leading man, Richard Burbage: "By a full and significant action of body, he charms our attention: sit in a full theater, and you will think you see so many lines drawn from the circumference of so many ears, whiles the actor is the centre."

Though Burbage was admired above all others, praise was also heaped upon the apprentice players whose alto voices fitted them for the parts of women. A spectator at Oxford in 1610 records how the audience were reduced to tears by the pathos of Desdemona's death. The Puritans who fumed about the biblical prohibition upon cross-dressing and the encouragement to sodomy constituted by the sight of an adult male kissing a teenage boy onstage were a small minority. Little is known, however, about the characteristics of the leading apprentices in Shakespeare's company. It may perhaps be inferred that one was a lot taller than the other, since Shakespeare often wrote for a pair of female friends, one tall and fair, the other short and dark (Helena and Hermia, Rosalind and Celia, Beatrice and Hero).

We know little about Shakespeare's own acting roles—an early allusion indicates that he often took royal parts, and a venerable tradition gives him old Adam in *As You Like It* and the ghost of old King

Hamlet. Save for Burbage's lead roles and the generic part of the clown, all such castings are mere speculation. We do not even know for sure whether the original Falstaff was Will Kempe or another actor who specialized in comic roles, Thomas Pope.

Kempe left the company in early 1599. Tradition has it that he fell out with Shakespeare over the matter of excessive improvisation. He was replaced by Robert Armin, who was less of a clown and more of a cerebral wit: this explains the difference between such parts as Lancelet Gobbo and Dogberry, which were written for Kempe, and the more verbally sophisticated Feste and Lear's Fool, which were written for Armin.

One thing that is clear from surviving "plots" or storyboards of plays from the period is that a degree of doubling was necessary. *2 Henry VI* has over sixty speaking parts, but more than half of the characters appear in only a single scene and most scenes have only six to eight speakers. At a stretch, the play could be performed by thirteen actors. When Thomas Platter saw *Julius Caesar* at the Globe in 1599, he noted that there were about fifteen. Why doesn't Paris go to the Capulet ball in *Romeo and Juliet?* Perhaps because he was doubled with Mercutio, who does. In *The Winter's Tale*, Mamillius might have come back as Perdita and Antigonus been doubled by Camillo, making the partnership with Paulina at the end a very neat touch. Titania and Oberon are often played by the same pair as Hippolyta and Theseus, suggesting a symbolic matching of the rulers of the worlds of night and day, but it is questionable whether there would have been time for the necessary costume changes. As so often, one is left in a realm of tantalizing speculation.

THE KING'S MAN

On Queen Elizabeth's death in 1603, the new king, James I, who had held the Scottish throne as James VI since he was an infant, immediately took the Lord Chamberlain's Men under his direct patronage. Henceforth they would be the King's Men, and for the rest of Shakespeare's career they were favored with far more court performances than any of their rivals. There even seem to have been rumors early in the reign that Shakespeare and Burbage were being considered for knighthoods, an unprecedented honor for mere actors—and one that in the event was not accorded to a member of the profession for nearly three hundred years, when the title was bestowed upon Henry Irving, the leading Shakespearean actor of Queen Victoria's reign.

Shakespeare's productivity rate slowed in the Jacobean years, not because of age or some personal trauma, but because there were frequent outbreaks of plague, causing the theaters to be closed for long periods. The King's Men were forced to spend many months on the road. Between November 1603 and 1608, they were to be found at various towns in the south and Midlands, though Shakespeare probably did not tour with them by this time. He had bought a large house back home in Stratford and was accumulating other property. He may indeed have stopped acting soon after the new king took the throne. With the London theaters closed so much of the time and a large repertoire on the stocks, Shakespeare seems to have focused his energies on writing a few long and complex tragedies that could have been played on demand at court: *Othello*, *King Lear*, *Antony and Cleopatra*, *Coriolanus*, and *Cymbeline* are among his longest and poetically grandest plays. *Macbeth* survives only in a shorter text, which shows signs of adaptation after Shakespeare's death. The bitterly satirical *Timon of Athens*, apparently a collaboration with Thomas Middleton that may have failed on the stage, also belongs to this period. In comedy, too, he wrote longer and morally darker works than in the Elizabethan period, pushing at the very bounds of the form in *Measure for Measure* and *All's Well That Ends Well*.

From 1608 onward, when the King's Men began occupying the indoor Blackfriars playhouse (as a winter house, meaning that they used the outdoor Globe only in summer?), Shakespeare turned to a more romantic style. His company had a great success with a revived and altered version of an old pastoral play called *Mucedorus*. It even featured a bear. The younger dramatist John Fletcher, meanwhile, sometimes working in collaboration with Francis Beaumont, was pioneering a new style of tragicomedy, a mix of romance and royalism laced with intrigue and pastoral excursions. Shakespeare experimented with this idiom in *Cymbeline*, and it was presumably with his blessing that Fletcher eventually took over as the King's Men's company dramatist. The two writers apparently collaborated on three plays in the years 1612–14: a lost romance called *Cardenio* (based on the love-madness of a character in Cervantes' *Don Quixote*), *Henry VIII* (originally staged with the title "All Is True"), and *The Two Noble Kinsmen*, a dramatization of Chaucer's "Knight's Tale." These were written after Shakespeare's two final solo-authored plays, *The Winter's Tale*, a self-consciously old-fashioned work dramatizing the pastoral romance of his old enemy Robert Greene, and *The Tempest*, which at one and the same time drew together multiple theatrical traditions, diverse reading, and contemporary interest in the fate of a ship that had been wrecked on the way to the New World.

The collaborations with Fletcher suggest that Shakespeare's career ended with a slow fade rather than the sudden retirement supposed by the nineteenth-century Romantic critics who read Prospero's epilogue to *The Tempest* as Shakespeare's personal farewell to his art. In the last few years of his life Shakespeare certainly spent more of his time in Stratford-upon-Avon, where he became further involved in property dealing and litigation. But his London life also continued. In 1613 he made his first major London property purchase: a freehold house in the Blackfriars district, close to his company's indoor theater. *The Two Noble Kinsmen* may have been written as late as 1614, and Shakespeare was in London on business a little over a year before he died of an unknown cause at home in Stratford-upon-Avon in 1616, probably on his fifty-second birthday.

About half the sum of his works were published in his lifetime, in texts of variable quality. A few years after his death, his fellow actors began putting together an authorized edition of his complete *Comedies, Histories and Tragedies*. It appeared in 1623, in large "Folio" format. This collection of thirty-six plays gave Shakespeare his immortality. In the words of his fellow dramatist Ben Jonson, who contributed two poems of praise at the start of the Folio, the body of his work made him "a monument without a tomb":

> And art alive still while thy book doth live
> And we have wits to read and praise to give . . .
> He was not of an age, but for all time!

SHAKESPEARE'S WORKS:
A CHRONOLOGY

1595–97	*Love's Labour's Won* (a lost play, unless the original title for another comedy)
1595–96	*A Midsummer Night's Dream*
1595–96	*The Tragedy of Romeo and Juliet*
1595–96	*King Richard the Second*
1595–97	*The Life and Death of King John* (possibly earlier)
1596–97	*The Merchant of Venice*
1596–97	*The First Part of Henry the Fourth*
1597–98	*The Second Part of Henry the Fourth*
1598	*Much Ado About Nothing*
1598–99	*The Passionate Pilgrim* (20 poems, some not by Shakespeare)
1599	*The Life of Henry the Fifth*
1599	"To the Queen" (epilogue for a court performance)
1599	*As You Like It*
1599	*The Tragedy of Julius Caesar*
1600–01	*The Tragedy of Hamlet, Prince of Denmark* (perhaps revising an earlier version)
1600–01	*The Merry Wives of Windsor* (perhaps revising version of 1597–99)
1601	"Let the Bird of Loudest Lay" (poem, known since 1807 as "The Phoenix and Turtle" [turtledove])
1601	*Twelfth Night, or What You Will*
1601–02	*The Tragedy of Troilus and Cressida*
1604	*The Tragedy of Othello, the Moor of Venice*
1604	*Measure for Measure*
1605	*All's Well That Ends Well*
1605	*The Life of Timon of Athens*, with Thomas Middleton
1605–06	*The Tragedy of King Lear*
1605–08	? contribution to *The Four Plays in One* (lost, except for *A Yorkshire Tragedy*, mostly by Thomas Middleton)

1606	*The Tragedy of Macbeth* (surviving text has additional scenes by Thomas Middleton)
1606–07	*The Tragedy of Antony and Cleopatra*
1608	*The Tragedy of Coriolanus*
1608	*Pericles, Prince of Tyre*, with George Wilkins
1610	*The Tragedy of Cymbeline*
1611	*The Winter's Tale*
1611	*The Tempest*
1612–13	*Cardenio*, with John Fletcher (survives only in later adaptation called *Double Falsehood* by Lewis Theobald)
1613	*Henry VIII (All Is True)*, with John Fletcher
1613–14	*The Two Noble Kinsmen*, with John Fletcher

FURTHER READING
AND VIEWING

CRITICAL APPROACHES

Healy, Margaret, "*Pericles* and the Pox," in *Shakespeare's Romances: New Casebooks* (2003), ed. Alison Thorne. Intriguing reading of the "medico-moral politics" of the play through its frequently overlooked representations of syphilis.

Jackson, MacDonald P., *Defining Shakespeare—Pericles as Test Case* (2003). Full and excellent account of the collaboration between Shakespeare and Wilkins on the play.

McDonald, Russ, *Shakespeare's Late Style* (2006). Invaluable close study of Shakespeare's somewhat strange and experimental language use throughout the late plays in general.

Mullaney, Stephen, "All That Monarchs Do: The Obscured Stages of Authority in *Pericles*," in *Shakespeare: The Last Plays* (1999), ed. Kiernan Ryan. Argues for *Pericles* as a work that reflects Shakespeare's changing attitude toward his role as a commercial playwright.

Nevo, Ruth, "The Perils of Pericles," in *Shakespeare: The Last Plays* (1999), ed. Kiernan Ryan. Psychoanalytic reading that attempts to reveal the play as a profound tale of forbidden desire and oedipal guilt.

Relihan, Constance C., "Liminal Geography: *Pericles* and the Politics of Place," in *Shakespeare's Romances: New Casebooks* (2003), ed. Alison Thorne. Looks at how the play's non-European setting complicates the traditional perceived generic characteristics of romance plays.

Skeele, David (ed.), *Pericles: Critical Essays* (2000). Compendious selection of critical material on the play, with the volume divided equally between the play's literary and performance heritages.

Skeele, David, *Thwarting the Wayward Seas* (1998). Book-length study that serves as a very good introduction to the play's critical and theatrical fortunes in the nineteenth and twentieth centuries.

Traversi, Derek, *Shakespeare: The Last Phase* (1954). Examines the poetic and formal characteristics of Shakespeare's later work. Chapter 2 deals with *Pericles*.

Wilson Knight, G., *The Crown of Life* (1947). Classic study of Shakespeare's late plays: chapter 2 deals with *Pericles*.

THE PLAY IN PERFORMANCE

Holland, Peter, *English Shakespeares: Shakespeare on the English Stage in the 1990s* (1997). Features superb analysis of productions by Phyllida Lloyd, John Peter, and David Thacker.

Skeele, David (ed.), *Pericles: Critical Essays* (2000). Compendious selection of critical material on the play's stage history, from the mid-nineteenth century onward.

Warren, Roger, *Staging Shakespeare's Late Plays* (1990). Excellent analysis of the staging considerations of Shakespeare's late plays, with a chapter devoted to *Pericles*, using the 1986 Stratford, Ontario, and 1989 RSC productions as case studies.

AVAILABLE ON DVD

Pericles, directed by David Hugh Jones for the BBC Shakespeare series (1984, DVD 2005). One of the better entries in the BBC series, Mike Gwilym as Pericles, Amanda Redman as Marina, Juliet Stevenson as Thaisa, and Edward Petherbridge as Gower.

REFERENCES

1. Quoted in John Munro, ed., *The Shakspere Allusion-Book*, 2 vols. (1909), vol. 1, p. 209. The spelling and punctuation of quotations from this book have been modernized.

2. Quoted in Munro, *The Shakspere Allusion-Book*, vol. 1, p. 248.

3. Ben Jonson, "Ode to Himself" (c. 1629), quoted in Munro, *The Shakspere Allusion-Book*, vol. 1, p. 341.

4. John Dryden, *A Defence of the Epilogue, Or, An Essay on the Dramatique Poetry of the Last Age* (1672), quoted in Munro, *The Shakspere Allusion-Book*, vol. 2, p. 174.

5. John Dryden, "A Parallel Betwixt Painting and Poetry," in C. A. Du Fresnoy, *De Arte Graphica. The Art of Painting* (1695), quoted in Munro, *The Shakspere Allusion-Book*, vol. 2, p. 403.

6. John Dryden, "An Epilogue," in *Miscellany Poems* (1684), quoted in Munro, *The Shakspere Allusion-Book*, vol. 2, p. 303.

7. MacDonald P. Jackson, *Defining Shakespeare: Pericles as Test Case* (2003), p. 166.

8. Nicholas Rowe, *Some Account of the Life, &c of Mr. William Shakespeare*, in *The Works of Shakespeare* (1709), quoted in *William Shakespeare: The Critical Heritage, vol. 2, 1693–1733*, ed. Brian Vickers (1974), p. 192.

9. Lewis Theobald, *The Works of Shakespeare* (1733), quoted in Vickers, *William Shakespeare: The Critical Heritage*, p. 500.

10. Henry Tyrell, *The Doubtful Plays of Shakespere* (1860), quoted in *Pericles: Critical Essays*, ed. David Skeele (2000), p. 58.

11. F. G. Fleay, *Shakespeare Manual* (1876), p. 211.

12. The most detailed summary of the authorship debate, the various candidates, and the methodologies employed can be found in Jackson, *Defining Shakespeare*; Doreen DelVecchio and Antony Hammond mount a strident argument for Shakespeare's sole authorship in their Cambridge University Press edition (1998).

13. Edward Dowden, *Shakspere*, Literature Primers (1877), pp. 60, 55–6.

14. David Skeele, *Thwarting the Wayward Seas: A Critical and Theatrical History of Pericles* (1998), pp. 33–4.

15. G. Wilson Knight, *The Crown of Life: Essays in the Interpretation of Shakespeare's Late Plays* (1947), pp. 70, 73.

16. Lytton Strachey, "Shakespeare's Final Period," *Independent Review* 3 (August 1904), pp. 114–15 (p. 415).

17. Suzanne Gossett, ed., *Pericles* (2004), p. 54.

18. William Watkiss Lloyd, *Essays on the Life and Plays of Shakespeare* (1858), quoted in Skeele, *Pericles: Critical Essays*, p. 55.

19. C. L. Barber, "'Thou That Beget'st Him That Did Thee Beget': Transformation in *Pericles* and *The Winter's Tale*," *Shakespeare Survey* 22 (1969), pp. 111–30 (p. 61).

20. Coppélia Kahn, *Man's Estate: Masculine Identity in Shakespeare* (1981), pp. 194, 196–7, 213, 214.

21. Janet Adelman, *Suffocating Mothers: Fantasies of Material Origin in Shakespeare's Plays, Hamlet to The Tempest* (1992), p. 196.

22. Ruth Nevo, *Shakespeare's Other Language* (1987), pp. 59, 60.

23. Margaret Healy, "*Pericles* and the Pox," in *Shakespeare's Late Plays: New Readings*, ed. Jennifer Richards and James Knowles (1999), pp. 92–107 (pp. 101, 104).

24. Steven Mullaney, *The Place of the Stage: License, Play, and Power in Renaissance England* (1995), p. 147.

25. Amelia Zurcher, "Untimely Monuments: Stoicism, History, and the Problem of Utility in *The Winter's Tale* and *Pericles*," *ELH* 70 (2003), pp. 903–27 (pp. 904, 921, 922).

26. Constance C. Relihan, "Liminal Geography: *Pericles* and the Politics of Place," *Philological Quarterly* 71 (1992), pp. 281–99 (pp. 281, 291–2).

27. Stuart M. Kurland, "'The Care . . . of Subjects' Good': *Pericles*, James I, and the Neglect of Government," *Comparative Drama* 30 (1996), pp. 220–44 (p. 220).

28. Ben Jonson, "Ode (To Himself)," *Ben Jonson*, ed. C. H. Herford and Percy and Evelyn Simpson (1925–32), vol. 6, pp. 492–3.

29. George Lillo, *Marina: A Play of Three Acts* (1738), p. 7.

30. See Sonia Massai, "From *Pericles* to *Marina*: 'While Women Are to Be Had for Money, Love, or Importunity,'" *Shakespeare Survey* 51 (1998), pp. 67–77.

31. For detailed information on this production, see Skeele, *Thwarting the Wayward Seas*.

32. Ibid., p. 41.

33. *The Times* (London), 16 October 1854.

34. *Chronicle*, 25 April 1900.

35. *Morning Leader*, 26 April 1900.

36. *Birmingham Post*, 16 August 1947.

37. *Observer*, 17 August 1947.

38. *Daily Herald*, 9 July 1958.
39. *Liverpool Daily Post*, 9 July 1958.
40. Ibid.
41. *Plays and Players*, October 1973.
42. *New York Times*, 15 December 1980.
43. *Boston Globe*, 13 October 1983.
44. *The Times* (London), 2 November 1983.
45. *Punch*, 23 January 1985.
46. *Philadelphia Inquirer*, 12 March 1987.
47. *Independent*, 15 March 1990.
48. *Mail on Sunday*, 29 May 1994.
49. *Guardian*, 31 March 2003.
50. *Independent*, 22 February 2005.
51. *Guardian*, 6 June 2005.
52. B. A. Young, *Financial Times*, 3 April 1969.
53. Irving Wardle, *The Times* (London), 3 April 1969.
54. Michael Billington, *Guardian*, 5 April 1979.
55. Ibid.
56. Peter Holland, *English Shakespeares* (1997), p. 64.
57. Ibid., p. 65.
58. Benedict Nightingale, *The Times* (London), 8 July 2002.
59. Billington, *Guardian*, 8 July 2002.
60. Paul Taylor, *Independent*, 10 July 2002.
61. Ibid.
62. Billington, *Guardian*, 8 July 2002.
63. Taylor, *Independent*, 10 July 2002.
64. Sam Marlowe, *The Times* (London), 26 July 2003.
65. Kate Bassett, *Independent on Sunday*, 3 August 2003.
66. Taylor, *Independent*, 17 November 2006.
67. Charles Spencer, *Telegraph*, 17 November 2006.
68. David Nathan, *Sun*, 3 April 1969.
69. Billington, *Guardian*, 5 April 1979.
70. Taylor, *Independent*, 10 July 2002.
71. Young, *Financial Times*, 30 July 1969.
72. Young, *Financial Times*, 5 April 1979.
73. Billington, *Guardian*, 14 September 1989.
74. Billington, *Guardian*, 8 July 2002.
75. Nightingale, *The Times*, 8 July 2002.
76. Ian Shuttleworth, *Financial Times*, 30 July 2003.

ACKNOWLEDGMENTS
AND PICTURE CREDITS

Preparation of *"Pericles* in Performance" was assisted by a generous grant from the CAPITAL Centre (Creativity and Performance in Teaching and Learning) of the University of Warwick for research in the RSC archive at the Shakespeare Birthplace Trust.

Thanks as always to our indefatigable and eagle-eyed copy editor Tracey Dando and to Ray Addicott for overseeing the production process with rigor and calmness.

Picture research by Michelle Morton. Grateful acknowledgment is made to the Shakespeare Birthplace Trust for assistance with picture research (special thanks to Helen Hargest) and reproduction fees.

Images of RSC productions are supplied by the Shakespeare Centre Library and Archive, Stratford-upon-Avon. This library, maintained by the Shakespeare Birthplace Trust, holds the most important collection of Shakespeare material in the UK, including the Royal Shakespeare Company's official archive. It is open to the public free of charge.

For more information see www.shakespeare.org.uk.

1. Directed by Nugent Monck (1947) Angus McBean © Royal Shakespeare Company
2. Directed by Tony Richardson (1958) Angus McBean © Royal Shakespeare Company
3. Directed by Ron Daniels (1979) Joe Cocks Studio Collection © Shakespeare Birthplace Trust
4. Directed by Terry Hands (1969) Reg Wilson © Royal Shakespeare Company
5. Directed by Adrian Jackson (2003) Robert Day © Royal Shakespeare Company

6. Directed by Dominic Cooke (2006) Keith Pattison © Royal Shakespeare Company

7. Directed by Adrian Noble (2002) Manuel Harlan © Royal Shakespeare Company

8. Directed by Kathryn Hunter (2005) Donald Cooper © photostage.co.uk

9. Reconstructed Elizabethan Playhouse © Charcoalblue

ABOUT THE TYPE

This book was set in Photina, a typeface designed by José Mendoza in 1971. It is a very elegant design with high legibility, and its close character fit has made it a popular choice for use in quality magazines and art gallery publications.

MODERN LIBRARY IS ONLINE AT
WWW.MODERNLIBRARY.COM

MODERN LIBRARY ONLINE IS YOUR GUIDE
TO CLASSIC LITERATURE ON THE WEB

THE MODERN LIBRARY E-NEWSLETTER

Our free e-mail newsletter is sent to subscribers, and features sample chapters, interviews with and essays by our authors, upcoming books, special promotions, announcements, and news. To subscribe to the Modern Library e-newsletter, visit **www.modernlibrary.com**

THE MODERN LIBRARY WEBSITE

Check out the Modern Library website at
www.modernlibrary.com for:

- The Modern Library e-newsletter
- A list of our current and upcoming titles and series
- Reading Group Guides and exclusive author spotlights
- Special features with information on the classics and
  other paperback series
- Excerpts from new releases and other titles
- A list of our e-books and information on where to buy them
- The Modern Library Editorial Board's 100 Best Novels and
  100 Best Nonfiction Books of the Twentieth Century written in
  the English language
- News and announcements

Questions? E-mail us at **modernlibrary@randomhouse.com**.
For questions about examination or desk copies, please visit
the Random House Academic Resources site at
www.randomhouse.com/academic